LANGUAGE AND LITERACY SERIES

Dorothy S. Strickland and Celia Genishi, SERIES EDITORS

KINGS BRIDGE ROAD RESEARCH TEAM

Benton Elementary School Research Team

Lolita Brown, *Chapter 1*

Lori Davis, *Pre-Kindergarten*

Patty Griffith, *4/5 Resource Room*

Mary Jane Hilley, *Media Specialist*

Patsy Lentz, *Principal*

Cheryl Poponi, *5th Grade*

Dorothy Rice, *3rd Grade*

Jane Rogers, *1/2/3 Resource Room*

Holly Ward, *5th Grade*

Jennifer White, *Kindergarten*

Marilynn Cary, *Speech Therapist, Research Team Coordinator*

South Jackson Elementary Research Team

Gwen Bailey, *Kindergarten*

Carol Carr Kieffer, *4th Grade*

Jan Kimbrell-Lee, *4/5 Resource Room*

Linda Morrison, *2nd Grade*

Ruth Rowland, *4th Grade*

Terry Wood, *5th Grade*

Lisa James Delgado, *Media Specialist, Research Team Coordinator*

University of Georgia Researchers and Facilitators

Janet Benton, Bob Hanley, Terry Warren, and Jane West, *Language Education*

Melvin Bowie, *Instructional Technology*

Frances Hensley, *UGA Initiative Research Coordinator*

Ronald Kieffer, *UGA Initiative Co-Researcher*

Joel Taxel, *UGA Initiative Project Director*

JoBeth Allen, *Research Coordinator*

Exploring
Blue Highways

LITERACY REFORM, SCHOOL CHANGE, AND THE CREATION OF LEARNING COMMUNITIES

JoBeth Allen
Marilynn Cary
Lisa Delgado

COORDINATORS OF THE
Kings Bridge Road Research Team

Teachers College, Columbia University
New York and London

Published by Teachers College Press, 1234 Amsterdam Avenue, New York, NY 10027

Chapter 3 is adapted from "The Inclusive Writing Workshop," by Jan Kimbrell-Lee and Terry Wood, in *Toward Inclusive Classrooms*, Teacher-to-Teacher Books, Washington, D.C.: National Education Association. Copyright © 1994 by NEA Professional Library. Reprinted by permission.

Chapter 7 is adapted from "Changing Portfolio Process: Our Journey Toward Authentic Assessment," by Ronald Kieffer and Linda Morrison, *Language Arts*, vol. 71, pp. 411–418. Reprinted by permission.

Library of Congress Cataloging-in-Publication Data

Allen, JoBeth.
　　Exploring blue highways : literacy reform, school change, and the creation of learning communities / JoBeth Allen, Marilynn Cary, Lisa Delgado.
　　　　p.　cm. — (Language and literacy series)
　　Includes bibliographical references and index.
　　ISBN 0-8077-3474-8 (cloth). — ISBN 0-8077-3473-X (pbk.)
　　1. School improvement programs—United States—Case studies.
　　2. College-school cooperation—United States—Case studies.
　　3. Language arts (Elementary)—United States—Case studies.
　　4. Language experience approach in education—United States—Case studies.　5. Benton Elementary School (Nicholson, Ga.)　6. South Jackson Elementary School (Jackson County, Ga.)　I. Cary, Marilynn.
II. Delgado, Lisa.　III. Title.　IV. Series: Language and literacy series (New York, N.Y.)
LB2822.82.A56　1995
371.2'009758'145—dc20　　　　　　　　　　　　　　　　95-35969

ISBN 0-8077-3473-X (paper)
ISBN 0-8077-3474-8 (cloth)

Printed on acid-free paper
Manufactured in the United States of America

01　00　99　98　97　96　95　　　8　7　6　5　4　3　2　1

Contents

Foreword

"When you read this book it is kind of fun but when you act it out it is more fun."

So spoke Felicia after informal drama in Ms. Kieffer's fourth-grade class. Ms. Kieffer is one of the more than 20 colleagues who researched themselves, their students, their parents, their colleagues, and their own two elementary schools in this book, *Exploring Blue Highways*.

I am rather well acquainted with the teachers, administrators, and university staff who have and are participating in this long-term effort to reform learning, teaching, and schooling. All of them, from public schools and the University of Georgia, are my professional colleagues. Together, we have worked together in a network of schools involved in purposeful, longitudinal, school renewal efforts (The League of Professional Schools). But even with years of familiarity, quite frankly, I was not prepared for the work that I read.

The faculty of these schools work in communities that face most of the great educational and social challenges of today (high poverty, high-risk infant births, undereducated parents and caretakers). These teachers, principals, and specialists don't have the luxury of great time, small classes, or advanced degrees. They are normal educators working daily in highly demanding educational environments. These educators have their prototypes in virtually every nonelite public school in America.

It is revealing that when teachers and administrators began a collaboration with the university, they thought they would be exploited and manipulated to fit some hidden agenda of "higher" education. Eventually they came to believe that this was not the case; instead, they were invited to raise their own questions about educational practices, form their own methods of study, and use their findings to fuel their own school-based decision making. University teachers were engaged in a joint and parallel discovery of new ways of thinking about their practices. When given the opportunity, all of us, children and adults, desire to know and understand. We all learn to understand by inventing what Piaget called our own puzzlements.

It is the inquisitive power of humans to understand and act upon their understandings that makes this book so powerful. Money did provide some release time for professionals, some outside consultatnts did provide requested techniques and resources, and a collaboration with 58 other schools did help in overcoming the norms of classroom and school isolation. But none of these additions would be valuable if (1) humans were not curious and (2) teachers did not care about their students and their craft.

What is remarkable about this book is not so much the studies themselves, although I found exciting the range of studies of students, parents, preschool, classes, schools, media centers, special education, portfolios, and transitions. A critic could point out that there are instances where studies could be more comprehensive, other methods might be more valid, and other ways of involving students and parents could be found. For example, I would like to have seen more students involved in the actual research and more research in the scientific and aesthetic domains of the curriculum. But such criticism misses the point of school renewal. Research by caring participants in schools is ongoing; it never ends. What is learned one year provides directions to what should be studied in future years.

The ponderous *Handbook of Research on Teaching* does not contain a single page by a teacher. Yet every single page in this book is written or influenced by practicing school professionals who *use* their studies to change their practices. In this remarkable book, teachers and administrators have reshaped their literacy practices, restructured their media center services, won a state innovative grant, received waivers from their district to pilot new forms of student assessment, changed labels and placement of students, and worked within the school and district to ensure greater continuity of students as they move on to the next levels of schooling.

These are ordinary people doing what is currently extraordinary work. Action research of ourselves, our students, and our own settings simply becomes the ordinary work of all schools. Hopefully, we will reach the day that there are lessons to be learned by all of us. To paraphrase 10-year-old Felicia, read this book and it will be fun. But if you "act out" this book and study your own questions to improve the education of your students, "it will be funner."

—*Carl Glickman*

Acknowledgments

We are most indebted to the students at Benton and South Jackson Elementary Schools who teach us daily, and to our colleagues at both schools and the University of Georgia (UGA) who informed our teaching and our research. We are grateful for the support, encouragement, and collaboration of principals Pam Johns (South Jackson) and Patsy Lentz and Pat Wells (Benton), and Jackson County curriculum coordinator Mary Leuzinger. We appreciate the interest and support of Superintendent Russell Cook and his successor Andy Byers. We have had strong support and encouragement from both deans of the UGA College of Education, Al Buccino and his successor Russell Yeany. Special thanks also go to Anita Peck, who provided skillful secretarial and editorial assistance, and to Mandy McMichen, who transcribed so many tapes so well.

Funding came from two sources: The National Reading Research Center (administered by the Office of Educational Research and Improvement in the Department of Education) and the Coca-Cola Foundation which has sponsored the UGA Education Initiative, directed by Joel Taxel, a partnership for the coreform of teacher education and public school education. Through the efforts of these agencies and individuals, our partnership will continue to grow in its support of reflective practice and the life-long literacy engagement of all students.

PART I

EVOLVING TEACHING AND RESEARCH COMMUNITIES

CHAPTER 1

Discovering New Routes to Literacy and Learning

JoBeth Allen, Frances Hensley, Terry Wood, and Jane Rogers

On the old highway maps of America, the main routes were red and the back roads blue . . . it's that time when the pull of the blue highway is strongest, when the open road is a beckoning. . . .
(William Least Heat Moon, 1982, p. 1)

This book is about two schools that left the roads most traveled in favor of the less traveled blue highways, to discover for ourselves what no map could show us. Both schools began the journey as teaching faculties, developed into self-directed teaching communities, and are evolving as teaching/researching communities. As faculties, we shared personal joys and sorrows, but little professional inquiry. As individuals, we made important daily decisions about instruction, but our decisions were often individual, not shared with colleagues. We were not encouraged to create our own curriculum. We did not have a voice in school-wide curriculum decisions. We were traveling the interstate highways of packaged curriculum, where one-road-serves-all mandates provided uniform materials, lesson plans, and evaluation. It was the easiest, and safest, way to travel.

We were often reflective about our instruction; we talked in twos and threes among ourselves about teaching and its accompanying pressures, problems, and rewards, without a public forum. Usually, however, that reflection and sharing led to frustration rather than collective action, because we did not feel we had the power, the authority, to make changes. Lewis Allen's (1993) interviews with teachers indicated that to have a real voice—"to have our say"—teachers felt they had to have someone who "really listened" to them, and the listener(s) had to be in a position to effect change. We did not have such a voice.

This is an account of traveling from that tried-but-untrue land to new territory on an uncertain route in both instruction and governance, a journey not without its own frustrations, but one that led to teaching communities. In those teaching communities, we discussed, debated, tried, evaluated, rejected, adopted, adapted, and created new pathways to learning for our students and new roads to decision making. In the teaching communities, reflection led to action. Now we are extending our teaching communities as researchers. Systematic and intentional reflection on many aspects of teaching and learning is taking us off the thoroughfares and onto the blue highways. According to a *New York Times* reviewer, Broyard (1983), Least Heat Moon (1982) "wrote a book about his travels in order to find out where he was trying to arrive." We have done the same, and invite you to travel the blue highways with us, in the hope that our journey might intersect with yours.

TWO TEACHING COMMUNITIES

Both Benton Elementary and South Jackson Elementary are located in Jackson County, Georgia. According to the 1990 census, the population of the county included 26,943 of European descent, 2,904 of African American descent, and 115 of other origins. Two-thirds of the county population live in unincorporated areas. Surveys place high school graduation rates of adults over 25 between 41% and 48% for the county. The county health department identified half of the 4-year-olds in the county as being "at risk" due to poverty, abuse, or other factors.

Benton is located in the rural town of Nicholson, Georgia, population 535. It is a real center of the community, adjacent to the town hall, library, and fire department. Veteran teacher Dorothy Rice reflected:

> The school and community have close ties. The night the old school was set on fire in the early 70s, the whole community of Nicholson came out there at midnight, helplessly watching "their school" burn. We have many children who are second or third generation Benton students. Strong community support makes teaching here more enjoyable; many teachers have been here more than 10 years, and six of us over 15 years.

The school grew rapidly, from about 300 students grades K–8 in 1978 to 750 in 1989; now the school has about 500 students pre-K through fifth grade. Children attending Benton live in small towns or rural areas. Most adults are waged laborers for various industries, including many poultry processing plants, pulp wood plants, and fabric mills. In the past 10 years, a significant number of low-income families have moved into the Benton district; 55% of the children receive school meal assistance.

South Jackson Elementary School is located 12 miles from Benton, via Kings Bridge Road, a county back road. South Jackson is surrounded by farmlands and draws much of its population from unincorporated areas of the county. Begun in 1954 as a two-room, two-teacher school, the school now houses nearly 400 students. The student population is 17% African American, 81% European American, and 1% each Asian and Hispanic. Over half of the students qualify for school meal assistance. Families are primarily farmers and blue collar workers, many working in local businesses such as dairies or electrical cooperatives. South Jackson is a Georgia Public School of Excellence.

OUR TRAVELING COMPANION

There really is a third school involved in the story we are about to tell, the School of Teacher Education (STE) at the University of Georgia (UGA). As you will learn in this chapter, we are part of a *co-reform* effort through which Benton, South Jackson, and the STE examined together the best ways to educate students as well as prospective teachers of those students. While our story focuses on the changes in our two elementary schools, it is important to know something about our traveling companion, UGA. Less than 30 minutes from both South Jackson and Benton, it is the oldest land grant university in the country and, with an enrollment of approximately 28,000 students, is the largest institution of higher education in the state of Georgia. The student body is 87% Caucasian, 6% African American, and the remaining 7% a mixture of Asian American, Native American, Hispanic, and international students. The UGA College of Education is the largest teacher preparation institution in the state. The college has more than 240 faculty in four schools, including Teacher Education, which is organized in the content areas of language arts, mathematics, reading, science, social science, and elementary education.

PREPARING FOR THE JOURNEY

In Chapters 1 and 2, we tell the story of our journey of instructional reform and describe our individual and collective evolution as teachers, facilitators, decision makers, researchers, collaborators, and partners.

These changes in our roles and relationships, although unstated as an initial goal of our work, have emerged as critical to our progress and success.

For the purposes of this account, we separate the discussion of our work into sections related to instruction, governance, and research. This separation, as you will see, is an artificial one, because the different aspects of this work are overlapping, connected, and interdependent.

Groundwork for Change

Our story begins in 1989. For some time the district administration had been promoting school and community involvement to make the climate of the schools more sensitive to the needs of students, teachers, and the community. Newly created local advisory committees included teachers, administrators, and community members in each school community; these groups discussed concerns and issues and worked to promote better communication. A district-level advisory committee included an elected teacher representative from each school and met regularly with the district administration.

At the school level, we elected teachers to school climate committees to promote a positive learning atmosphere for both students and staff. The initial focus of the school climate committees was to improve student attendance. Teachers attended presentations related to developing and implementing schoolwide programs, and the schools initiated several activities. We experienced—many of us for the first time—the work and rewards associated with efforts that cut across the traditional organizational and administrative hierarchy of schools. We were introduced to the world of group dynamics, group planning, communication strategies, team building, and consensus making. About this same time, the principals at both schools became intrigued with the idea of shared decision making, particularly the benefits of teacher ownership of instructional decisions. Before they could move beyond tentative investigation of this approach, both principals accepted jobs in other systems. Several propitious events then occurred.

First, Patsy Lentz and Pam Johns became the new principals at Benton Elementary and South Jackson Elementary, respectively. Both had been in the school district for a number of years; Patsy was the district's director of special education services and Pam was a teacher at South Jackson, but neither had been a principal. They came to their positions eager to involve teachers in decision making. As Dorothy Rice, a teacher at Benton, recalls, ''She [Patsy] came in real excited. She called a little nucleus of us together and said, 'Now I need for you all to help me decide what to do' . . . and asked us immediately to start making decisions.'' At South Jackson teachers had already begun to assume leadership roles. The previous spring, they had voted to join the League of Professional Schools, a network of schools devoted to instructional reform through shared governance. In a public display of their commitment to shared decision making, the faculty wrote a letter to the superintendent in support of Pam as principal and expressed a wish to have a principal who ''is a strong supporter of teacher empowerment and shared governance.''

The second critical event was an invitation from the district office to meet with UGA faculty to talk about a possible instructional partnership; this invitation came about because Mary Leuzinger, the county curriculum coordinator, had invited UGA professor Donna Alvermann to provide an inservice on reading. This opportunity prompted us to begin thinking about what we really wanted for our schools and how the university might help us. The third event was moving the middle school students to their own building; that same fall was the first time both of the schools were only K–5, rather than K–8. This reorganization bought us meeting time. Previously, students had left at 3:15, teachers at 3:30. Now, students left at 2:20, and teachers had time for after-school seminars, planning, and discussion.

Everything seemed to line up at the right time that fall of 1990. We were ready for a change, but inexperienced in making decisions about either governance or instruction. Indeed, we had not been encouraged to make such decisions. As one teacher remembered, ''For the last 4 years we had not been asked one thing about what we thought about anything. We were told. We were dictated to.'' In Apple's (1986) words, we had become ''deskilled.'' Marilynn Cary agreed: '' 'Deskilled' really fit. We wanted a change but we didn't know how to go about it.''

The Role of the University

Just as we were beginning to examine and explore our practice, the nearby University of Georgia was examining its own roles in teaching and learning and its relationships with K–12 schools and educators. A growing number of university educators also were interested in leaving the interstate for the blue highways. Some saw public school education as the most critical place to devote their educational interest. As JoBeth Allen shared,

> We didn't leave public school because we were burnt out, unsuccessful, or intellectual elitists, as the private speculation of-

ten goes. Rightly or wrongly many of us really believed we could have a broader impact on education through teacher education; we have a personal and professional need to connect with schools who want us.

There were also UGA faculty who were frustrated by the isolation in which they prepared preservice teachers and by the lack of rewarding or satisfying field experiences for their students. Isolation is caused in part by the organization of the college by content areas; there is little planning or integration across the departments. Joel Taxel, director of the UGA Initiative, recounted a personal experience: "I am teaching a children's lit class and I know that students are taking other methods classes and I never had a conversation with any other faculty who were teaching those students. There was no dialogue, no conversation."

The traditional model for field experiences at UGA was often a source of tension and frustration for everyone involved. Students were assigned to a supervising teacher, and a university faculty member dictated the requirements of the field experience and evaluated the student's performance. As might be expected in these arbitrary arrangements, there was often little alignment or shared vision of teaching and learning and little opportunity to build one. Teachers viewed university faculty members as arrogant and critical: "These are my requirements, you [student teachers] get out there and . . . just go do them. I want you to do these things. And teachers, you make time." Teachers in turn were sometimes seen as undermining the work of the university.

> [Students] learn while they're here and then they get placed in a school that doesn't share that vision and the cognitive and emotional dissonance that they experience is too much for most of us. And it takes all of the good things that we do and just throws them out the window.

The lack of communication, negotiation, and joint construction of roles led to a great deal of mistrust and hostility between and among UGA and school faculties.

Faculty members began to question and reject their traditional role in working with schools. In particular, the outsider-in, top-down inservice model was found by some faculty members as inappropriate, ineffective, and frustrating. Lee Galda, another of our university colleagues, related her personal decision to reject this model.

> They ask you to go to a school and give the teachers what the administrator has decided the teachers need. And the teachers

don't have a vested interest in it. It's a frustrating experience. And I stopped doing what I would call inservices. I just stopped doing them. . . . I didn't like going in and saying, "This is what you need, folks."

In response to these concerns and issues, UGA faculty members individually and collectively began to take action. For example, faculty members developed collaborative research projects and inservice models with local schools. Individual faculty members jointly began to plan and align their undergraduate teacher education courses. During the summer of 1990, five UGA faculty members from four departments met several times to plan a "literacy initiative" that would establish an Interdisciplinary Literacy Faculty at the university and would work with one or more local public school systems interested in addressing literacy instruction. Carl Glickman, a UGA faculty member, was developing long-term relationships with local schools for the purpose of instructional improvement using a shared decision-making model. Growing out of these individual and group efforts at the university and funded by generous support both inside and out of the university, three major initiatives served as the framework around which we built our new partnerships.

The Initiatives

These initiatives were the UGA Educational Initiative, the Program for School Improvement, and the National Reading Research Center.

The UGA Educational Initiative. Those who study educational change point out that it must occur at all levels simultaneously, and in synchronization, for the effects to be meaningful and lasting (Fullan & Miles, 1992; Goodlad, 1990). The UGA Initiative, funded by a generous grant from the Coca-Cola Foundation, is a 5-year, co-reform effort attempting systemic change by (1) changing two of its teacher education programs to emphasize more holistic, student-centered, experiential learning; (2) supporting school-based change efforts including Foxfire, interdisciplinary teaching, reading and writing workshops, and other whole language approaches; and (3) placing interns who have been prepared in the new teacher education programs in the evolving whole language schools, so that there is a better match of instructional philosophies than often occurs.

As detailed in later sections, together we drew new curriculum maps and forged new roles and relationships. The UGA Initiative provided release time, university personnel, and encouragement for us to learn from each other as well as from UGA faculty. JoBeth Allen and Joel Taxel provided support through their almost daily presence and dedicated persistence, as well as through inservice classes, hundreds of children's books, classroom visits, grade-level planning meetings, and so forth. Other faculty provided specifically requested inservice throughout the years.[1]

Program for School Improvement. Carl Glickman, professor at UGA, founded the Program for School Improvement (PSI) and its League of Professional Schools as a way of supporting school change efforts. After working closely for several years with two schools that had invited his involvement in their governance and change efforts, in 1989–90 Carl issued invitations to every school in the state to develop a league based on three principles. Those principles are that school decisions are made through shared governance, that the focus of decision making is on educational improvement, and that both needs and subsequent curricular changes are studied through action research (Allen & Glickman, 1992). By 1993, the league consisted of 61 elementary, middle, and high schools.

Both South Jackson and Benton schools voted to become members of the League of Professional Schools (an 80% vote is required) and worked hard to establish a shared governance procedure that included making curriculum decisions. For example, teachers at both schools formed communication groups (or "clusters") that meet regularly to raise and address issues ranging from the hiring of new teachers to the development of classroom libraries. Using a shared decision-making process, each school established motivation to read (helping children become engaged readers) as the top priority, with investigation of whole language principles as the primary vehicle.

Affiliation with PSI provided important links to other educators and schools. Through PSI-sponsored activities such as a fall conference, winter and spring meetings, and summer institutes, we have formed partnerships with each other and networked with other schools. A hallmark of all PSI activities is the opportunity to learn from one another; we both have learned from other educators about instruction and governance processes and have shared our experiences and knowledge with others. Other PSI activities that supported and enhanced our work included access to research and other information related to teaching, learning, and governance through an Information Retrieval System and the assistance of an Action Research Consortium (ARC) of experienced teacher researchers who help others get started. Benton teacher Jane Rogers is a member of the ARC. This ongoing networking among school-based professionals is a critical element of school renewal (Allen & Lundsford, 1995).

National Reading Research Center. The University of Georgia, in partnership with the University of Maryland, received funding from the federal government to study literacy development and practices. The National Reading Research Center (NRRC) was funded for 5 years (1992–1997), in part because of its strong commitment to teacher research. JoBeth, a member of the NRRC Executive Committee who submitted the original proposal, described the emergence of their resolution.

> This commitment came from asking ourselves: Who does reading research? Who learns from it? Who asks the questions? Who determines what really matters in reading instruction? Who decides if kids really are becoming readers, how their development is evaluated, and what difference being or not being a reader makes in their lives? We believed that teachers were asking the really important questions, and wrote in our proposal, "NRRC activities will enlist teachers as collaborative researchers and establish permanent research sites where university- and school-based researchers plan, conduct, synthesize, and report research." (Alvermann & Guthrie, 1991, p. 5)

There is extensive support of teacher research in several NRRC projects, including a School Research Consortium; support for the Benton and South Jackson research teams included teacher researcher travel money, a graduate assistant, and JoBeth's time.

Although each of these initiatives had its own set of goals, purposes, activities, funding sources, and personnel, they were alike in critical ways. Their underlying philosophies honored the knowledge and experience of school-based educators. They shared a desire to abandon the traditional model of school–university relationships for a more equitable and collaborative one. A final commonality among the three initiatives was the involvement of the same key university personnel in active roles across the partnerships. In particular, teachers pointed to JoBeth's involvement and leadership in all three of the initiatives as a unifying and significant force.

We were fortunate that these three initiatives occurred simultaneously at UGA and we had the opportunity to participate in them all. The UGA Initiative's partnership invitation came after the district's invitation to conduct inservice; the PSI invitation was issued to every school in the state; and the NRRC grant was awarded because we were already engaged in meaningful literacy reform. The opportunities arose not by chance, but rather as a result of the efforts of a growing community of school and university educators working to change the face of education and their roles in it.

DRAWING NEW MAPS

Our paths intersected and we were poised at the crossroads. We had funding, the blessings of our respective organizations, and people who were interested in this work. We left the well-known and long-traveled interstate highways with high excitement and great anticipation, and with little awareness of the obstacles and difficulties that would await us around every turn.

Instructional Reform

There was a well-mapped but limited relationship between Benton and South Jackson. The two schools were put in the position of competing for recognition within the district and for standardized test scores (as most public schools are when scores are published in local papers by school). They were traditional rivals that did not really know each other in spite of being only 12 "blue highway" miles apart.

One of the most difficult things for all of us was getting rid of the maps that already existed in our heads, written by years of experience, maps that clearly defined the previous relationships between university and schools. There were existing relationships between the two schools and UGA. Teachers worked with student teachers from UGA, at times voicing frustration with the methods student teachers were asked to implement (e.g., writing workshops), which were in opposition to their own teaching (e.g., textbook lessons and exercises), and frustration with the passive role they were forced to play. On the positive side, South Jackson had worked with the UGA Mathematics Education faculty on a multiyear geometry project involving several teachers. At both schools many teachers were graduates of UGA; a very few were in graduate school.

Like a city orchestra, with little funding but great community expectations, education is always trying to improve itself. Countless new programs and practices have been adopted, coopted, or mandated; many of them flashed briefly, then floundered, and eventually failed. When educational change movements are unsuccessful, "postmortems" often reveal that teachers have been consigned to passive, consumer roles rather than being engaged as active, reflective agents of school change (Oakes, Hare, & Sirotnik, 1986). In many such efforts, administrators learn of promising educational innovations and hire university or independent "experts" to "train" teachers. These efforts are characterized by top-down, outsider-in purposes and instruction, and research that is product evaluation rather than genuine inquiry. Often it is the teachers themselves who get evaluated. Myrna Cooper (1988) wrote:

> School people have surely not prospered, or even benefitted from "received" culture and imposed wisdom. Yet school inhabitants have lived as though they were unsophisticated natives ministered to by well-meaning missionaries who exude paternalism. Practitioners have had their shortcomings and inadequacies catalogued and classified and, sadly, have come to accept the blueprint of their deficiencies as though they had drawn it themselves. (p. 45)

Many of us from both the schools and the university wanted to throw away these old maps of university–school association. Ironically, however, the beginning of our partnerships could be characterized in similar ways.

Mary Leuzinger invited several members of the UGA Initiative's Literacy Task Force to conduct two districtwide inservices that August, one for primary teachers and one for intermediate. Donna, Joel, JoBeth, and Steve White addressed how teachers establish communities of readers and writers, improve text understanding and critical thinking, and promote understanding of self and others. We shared a process for formulating classroom and school goals that had been developed by another local school. These workshops, with a definite whole language grounding, gave the teachers and principals from all five elementary schools in the district an idea of the university faculty members' interests and philosophical orientation.

The next meeting was with principals of all five elementary schools, the superintendent, teachers from each school, and a school board member. The bottom line question from several principals and the superintendent was, "Can you help us raise our test scores?" We said we could not. Two schools were still interested in exploring literacy instruction. The best fit at that time seemed to be with Benton Elementary School, which became the first partnership school; South Jackson became the second the following year. We then entered into a lengthy, and sometimes rocky, process of establishing the agenda, priorities, and processes for change.

At both schools, the first step was to explore the needs and interests of both the teachers and the UGA faculty. Joel and JoBeth met with the faculty. Teaching reading and language arts primarily from textbooks was "just not working," they explained. There was homogeneous ability grouping by classroom and again within classrooms. Teachers were frustrated that they did not seem to reach all children, bored with textbooks and workbooks, and dissatisfied that even when they were "successful" in teaching children to read, they were not producing kids who liked to read or write. Teachers reported feeling great pressure to cover the skills in the basal and to produce high test scores on the periodic basal tests as well as on the standardized tests. Their scores were described by one administrator as "mediocre, average for the county but below average for the state."

Both schools were dissatisfied with their current practice in reading and writing, and, after much dialogue, established goals that included

1. Learning about thematic teaching and the integration of the teaching of skills and content.
2. Learning about whole language teaching.
3. Increasing children's interest in reading and motivation to read.

Despite varying degrees of skepticism, teachers moved to address the goals we had established. We asked JoBeth and Joel to (1) teach a staff development course at the schools based on individual needs, (2) conduct demonstration lessons in our classrooms, (3) connect us with other whole language teachers in the area who might serve as mentors, and (4) facilitate grade-level planning. These were familiar roads to new ways of teaching, especially the course and demonstration lesson structures; we still depended on old maps.

The only thing new about our partnership in the beginning was that the university teachers kept asking us to make decisions. We were supposed to decide what we wanted to study, how we learned best, what kinds of readings would be helpful, and so forth. Most of us thought that was their job. But eventually we got the staff development course organized.

The focus of the weekly seminars was on exploring and implementing various whole language instructional strategies, with an emphasis on reading workshops and writing workshops. These daily structures provided students with extended periods of time to select books and writing topics, confer with one another, read and write without interruption, discuss books and drafts of their own writing, respond to literature, and revise and publish their own work. In these workshops we conducted brief whole-class lessons, conducted regular conferences with each child about both reading and writing, modeled our own literacy, and kept extensive documentation about reading and writing development. We read *Transitions* by Regie Routman (1988), a primary grade teacher, and *In the Middle* by Nancie Atwell (1987), a middle school teacher, in addition to various articles on pedagogy and literacy development. Joel and JoBeth also lent teachers many books on requested topics, professional books as well as good children's literature. Class sessions generally consisted of three parts.

1. Discussion of what we learned about teaching reading or writing that week from students, colleagues, and self-reflection.
2. Discussion of what we learned from the shared readings, most of which were by other teachers.
3. Active involvement with some aspect of curriculum planning and/or evaluation, usually in grade-level groups.

It seemed that we were on our way. Teachers voted to enter into a partnership with UGA and established the goals of the endeavor. But a reflection from a Benton teacher belies this simple telling of the story. Following the instructional partnership vote at Benton, which was one vote short of unanimous, Jane Rogers noted in her journal:

> [A colleague] reported that "I heard that we are going to do whole language. That means that we will throw away all the basals. I'm not going to do it. I have taught for 18 years; this too shall pass." . . . I began to see strangers in the school. They were the "experts from UGA, but I bet they have never taught before," my friend confided. . . . I was never sure why they were meeting or who was really in on the meetings. . . . [Soon] there was a faculty meeting. We were going to discuss "whole language" stuff and see what we wanted to do to change to whole language. Before this time no one had ever asked us what we wanted to do without having already made up their mind. . . . As a faculty we started to discuss goals . . . to increase literacy within the school (actually some people discussed, some muttered, and some just stared into space hoping that the meeting would soon be over). . . . Several people at the table said that it wouldn't make a difference what we voted, because the decision had already been made.

These reservations and concerns, based in part on our past experiences with similar efforts, created tension and frustration. Faculty from UGA shared common feelings of ambivalence and skepticism. Joel Taxel later reflected:

> When I began this project, I thought to a significant degree, and I don't think I'm all that different from a lot of university faculty, that if you guys [teachers] would just do what we tell you is the right thing to do then we'll be able to fix this thing.

JoBeth also recalled those first weeks and months.

> Teachers were confused. They met us with a very southern polite silence so as not to hurt our feelings. There was a tension we all felt, teachers and university teachers, between wanting the seminars to be responsive to teacher needs and wanting them to be cohesive and well organized. It was difficult to get a great deal of public input from the group, although a few teachers provided us with valuable private feedback about how they were feeling. Some were stressed by so much change, insecure about their abilities, ambivalent about some of the techniques, and downright angry that we were not providing more concrete answers to their questions. They wanted a well-defined program and set of procedures to replace the security of past programs. In the past, there had always been directives about what to change and specific instructions about how to do it.

One of the principals reflected privately:

> When this project was first initiated, the faculty waited patiently to be told what to do, and I have no doubt that they would have done whatever they were told to do. . . . I saw teachers eager to do something different, but when they weren't told specifically what to do differently, they just became more and more disillusioned. Consequently, many lost faith in Joel and JoBeth, and they felt that they were not giving the staff answers that they really had all along. This disillusionment then led to open resistance, as well as passive resistance. Open resistance was most noted by verbal comments such as, "If they don't know what to do, how can they expect us to know what to do." Staff resisted passively by not attending class or not integrating anything into their daily schedule. Ev-

eryone wanted . . . a recipe. Then I think that they just didn't know how to start. . . . Unfortunately, our teachers have not had to think for so long and then suddenly they're presented with a teaching philosophy that requires them to pull together thoughts, make inferences, compare and contrast, express feelings and emotions. This was foreign territory for [some] teachers and they felt as if they were getting no direction from those who were leading. . . . They didn't want to read to gain information, they wanted to be told.

JoBeth and Joel worried. Joel recalls, "There were times at the beginning of the project . . . when we were absolutely despairing. We never thought that we would ever get this thing going because . . . there was so much tension and resistance." JoBeth, who was leading the seminars, felt especially responsible.

We expected (and probably deserved) a certain amount of skepticism initially. Still, we worried. What were we doing wrong? Should we be more prescriptive, more responsive to teachers' requests? Why wouldn't they talk? Why did they ask for answers, but not read what we provided or suggested? Why did they seem to give us the role in setting the agenda, rather than seize the reins? Some teachers took small, thoughtful steps that year, some took broad, courageous leaps, and some planted their feet firmly in tradition. A lot of people were frustrated.

JoBeth and other UGA faculty recognized that the anxiety we were all experiencing was normal for people making a genuine paradigm shift, but that knowledge did not make the process painless. As Fullan and Miles (1992) point out, for a major change to occur, "individuals must normally confront the loss of the old and commit themselves to the new, unlearn old beliefs and behaviors and learn new ones, and move from anxiousness and uncertainty to stabilization and coherence" (p. 748). We had yet to reach stabilization and coherence. We did realize, however, that our experiences and feelings were similar to those of others and we used this knowledge to soothe ourselves, give ourselves direction, and keep ourselves pointed in the right direction.

For example, Fullan and Miles (1992) reminded us that this type of "intense personal and organizational learning and problem solving" (p. 748) should not be interpreted as resistance, a counterproductive, blame-the-teacher label. Lieberman and Shiman (1973) observed that change efforts of this magnitude often are marked by an initial stage of "tell us what to do" (p. 52), followed by a few people adopting change, followed by questioning of whether the new ways are better than the old ways and general discomfort.

These observations provide some insight and understanding of what we were experiencing, but another important aspect of our resistance, confusion, and requests for more direction related to the fact that many of us at the schools saw this project as another example of the old model of university–school relationship. The UGA Initiative was an external project, not one that we had initiated; we wanted our students to be more motivated readers, but it was the university faculty that believed in the beginning that whole language was the avenue to that motivation. Since not everyone felt initial ownership for the effort, we were not inclined to become active participants in developing it.

Terry Wood explained that she did not like what she saw as another outside effort to get her to change her teaching.

> I disliked you guys [JoBeth, Linda DeGroff, Joel] intensely when you came . . . I felt like you were coming in there trying a new experiment. I felt like you came in there to tell us what to do and then leave us.

She also didn't like being told by the principal that she had to attend the after-school seminars. "If you're going to make me do something or make me change my philosophy," Terry confided later, "I'm not going to do it. But if you give me the option, you know, you'd be surprised. I just might."

JoBeth was aware of this tension. On the one hand, UGA faculty were committed to being facilitators of the change process rather than directors, and to a local reconstruction of literacy instruction rather than the importation of a program. On the other hand, the university was still in the role of teaching the course and modeling strategies. She recalled:

> We hoped that by reading, hearing, and talking about whole language principles and structures, and seeing what other whole language teachers were doing, teachers could begin to clarify their own beliefs and design their own instruction. However, we had come in under the "old model," initially invited by an administrator, early on sharing our own literacy beliefs. Now we were saying, "No, this really isn't the old

model. We are here for the long haul; we want to do what you want us to; we do not have the answers."

This contradiction contributed to our rough start and initially impeded establishing trust and building shared ownership.

Another barrier to developing a trusting partnership in the beginning was the long-standing inequities and implied hierarchies in relationships between schools and universities. As we discussed earlier, universities often use schools for the major responsibility of enculturating student teachers, with little or no recognition or remuneration, and as "subjects" in research experiments. Cheryl Poponi, reflecting on the early days of the partnership, explained:

> I thought this guy [Joel] was coming to tell us about whole language, and he wasn't really telling us about whole language. . . . I think that if you had maybe told us something instead of always saying, "Well, what do you think? Well, it could be whatever you want. Well, you could do this. Well, I can't really tell you that." Then I don't think I would have been quite so upset, but we were doing all the work, but yet he's going to pick our brains, he'll write the paper, and he's getting all this money for it, and he'll get all the recognition. . . . In the beginning people felt they were being used.

Cheryl's assumption that the university partners would "write the paper" was based on a long history of outsider research in schools. "I guess that's just the way things always were," she said of her original suspicions. "No one listened to teachers. Teachers didn't write papers." Terry Wood provided further insights into why initially she and some others rejected both the university and whole language.

> I was a very negative person about the whole situation because I was, I'd never really heard of whole language . . . I didn't want to know. I didn't care. I taught. My kids were going to sit down, they were going to be quiet, and they weren't going to talk and discuss their work and things like that. . . . There were a couple [of teachers] that did whole language, and I thought, "These teachers can't keep control of their class."

Throughout that first year, the forging of a partnership and the refocusing of instructional priorities were slow and often troubled. We did not, however, give up on each other. Instead, we tried to find ways to understand.

Taking Stock Along the Way

At the private advice of one of the teachers, UGA faculty conducted a survey of school faculty at the end of the year to get at some of these feelings and to get a handle on what concerned and interested teachers most. "They won't tell you what they think," she explained, referring to the in-depth interviews UGA faculty conducted annually, "but they might write something anonymously." The survey was a valuable tool in assessing how far we had come during the year and in planning for the next year. Briefly, the majority of the 29 respondents felt they were making progress as whole language teachers and that their students were making progress as readers and writers. In a direct assessment of their third goal, 22 agreed strongly and 9 agreed somewhat that their students had more interest in reading and spent more time reading.

Teachers listed quite an impressive number of changes they had made as a result of participating in the initiative: using a workshop approach to reading and writing, reading aloud more, discussing books, abolishing ability grouping, integrating instruction around a theme, and more choices for students. Different teachers made different changes, but there was widespread infusion of children's literature throughout the day. There were also well-articulated areas of frustration that directly informed instructional planning for 1991–92: integrated skills instruction, authentic evaluation procedures, scheduling to maximize time, and meeting district and state mandates within a whole language philosophy of instruction. Two other areas of great need were familiarity with good children's literature and interdisciplinary or thematic planning. This became our map for inservice in 1992–93.

When asked to reflect on her experiences with the instructional initiative, Terry Wood pinpointed three things that brought her into the whole language teaching community. Individual experiences varied widely, but it seems that these three elements were critical for every teacher. First, school and university faculties developed mutual trust (eventually). Second, teachers influenced and taught each other. Third, and most powerful, children persuaded teachers that they needed time, choices, and interactive communities for learning.

Establishing Trust. Mutual trust was established in part because we made a 5-year commitment to each other. "As time wore on," Terry told JoBeth in a third-year interview, "I noticed that you were here to stay and you weren't going to just leave us, and this was not something that was a fly-by-night kind of idea." Not only did university faculty stay; they asked and "really listened" to what teachers thought, felt, and wanted. Terry reflected:

When we mentioned toward the end of the first year, "What about us? What about the upper grades?" you did something about it. You brought in many people, like [area teachers] and Lee Galda. So you really got me there. I thought, you know, they've stuck with us, they stood by their word and anything we asked them they'd do or help us do.

Learning from Each Other. More important than the outside teachers were colleagues. Teachers learned from other teachers. One of the things we all learned was that the most powerful change agents are teachers themselves. At Benton, Cheryl Poponi, formerly a special education teacher in a self-contained classroom, recalled that her initial disinterest in whole language instruction came from a teacher who was sure such methods had nothing to offer "our kids." Then another special education teacher, Jane Rogers, started talking about the amazing things her kids were writing. "I thought, you've got to be kidding me; you can't be getting those results when those kids were like the students I had," Cheryl remembered. Cheryl began with having her children read predictable storybooks and soon added writing. "[One of the students] really just started reading. I mean, that just kind of amazed me . . . and some of the other students were not only reading much better than they were before, but now their interest was more."

One by one individual teachers shared success stories and strategies with their peers. Some grade levels took the plunge as a whole. Dorothy Rice described the third grade team's early leap, when they put the reading and language textbooks on the shelf and began designing curriculum around children and literature: "We had each other, and it was like we were going into the deep end of the pool, but we held on to each other and jumped together." Cheryl slowly convinced her reluctant friend that whole language might work even with her students. In the spring of 1993, this teacher did several integrated thematic studies. During one, students covered the walls outside their classroom with all they had learned about dinosaurs. As the teacher proudly explained how they had learned so much, she said, "You know, I actually feel like the kids are smarter."

At South Jackson, Terry began to read aloud and have silent reading time as her first steps. Then, she said, "the next year, I wanted to learn more because everybody else was doing it and getting good reviews.'' She began reading articles and then went to a conference where an upper grade teacher talked about her whole language classroom. Terry began to use more trade books for reading.

Teachers visited each other's classrooms in their own school as well as their sister school. We talked, planned, disagreed, and decided. Principals arranged for grade-level planning sessions, sometimes for several hours, and teachers often invited UGA personnel to participate. Kindergarten teachers asked for a special session on emergent literacy; teachers from both schools attended. Teachers from the traditional rival elementary schools started talking. We shared evaluation techniques and frustrations, and eventually proposed a new grading system for the county (it later was outvoted by the three other elementary schools). The two media specialists conducted a joint research project. We attended meetings at each other's schools and visited each other's classrooms. We merged research teams each summer. We were all learning how to communicate and how to create meaningful learning experiences. We were developing not only trust, but genuine friendships.

Learning from Children. But the real turning point for Terry, and for many other teachers, was when she saw her students being successful, engaged, and interested. Terry recalled two specific incidents that changed her literacy teaching. She combined her upper and lower reading groups to do a play, based on *The Wish Giver*. ''The kids loved it. We had parents come out. It was one of the better things that I think I ever did as a teacher. . . . So from then on, I let them choose which books and work together on literary groups and things like that,'' without ability grouping.

The second incident changed the way Terry taught writing. She taught primarily from the language arts textbook and occasionally gave students assignments to write longer pieces. She had just returned the first of these assigned papers.

> I was talking to kids about, you know, you need to work on this and this and this. . . . A child said, ''Well, Ms. Wood, if you'd give us a chance to write, and write what we'd like to write about, we could do it.'' [Others said] ''Yeah, we want to write!'' They were telling me, ''Well, give us practice, let us practice it.'' They wanted more time. I was like, ''Yeah, right, you just want to get down there and talk and play around.'' I remember Matthew said, ''Ms. Wood, we'll do it. I promise,

we'll do it." So we made a deal, and they kept their end of the bargain.

The next year, it happened again. Terry planned to start a writing workshop, but first she wanted to "bombard them with skills." After the second week, a child asked, "Ms. Wood, when are we going to get to write?" They began immediately. To her surprise, three children brought in pieces they had worked on in fourth grade, where they had writing workshops regularly. One said, "I was working on this in Mrs. Rowland's room and I wanted to finish it." Again, the children convinced her that time to write, choice in what they wrote about, and interaction with other writers was the best way for them to become writers.

Terry parlayed her lingering concerns into a research project. She conducted a 2-year examination of her students' transition to middle school. Terry had been a middle school English teacher herself; was she "putting these babies out into the woods with wolves" by not teaching from the textbook, as she was sure the middle school teachers did? Her research included interviews with middle school teachers, her previous students, and their parents. What she learned surprised her.

> [Sixth grade teachers] were frustrated and disheartened the first year of my research because of the problems that they were consistently seeing with the entering sixth graders' writing and reading skills. This changed to excitement and enjoyment of teaching when the reading and writing skills began to transfer to the sixth grade from the elementary grades. One sixth grade teacher said it best. "We're finally seeing some positive results from students familiar with whole language starting in the early grades. . . . It is no longer inconceivable to spend the very first days of school actually writing!"

Parents and students had similar observations. Terry listened to students, not only when she taught them but even after they left.

Instructional change came slowly and steadily, teachers teaching teachers, showing each other specific ways in which they taught, giving testimony about personal successes. For 1993–94, we planned our own inservice, asking each other to present techniques and content such as multicultural literature. But it was really the children who cemented our beliefs, who began to read and write with pleasure, who "got smarter."

Not everyone at South Jackson or Benton (or UGA, for that matter) has a whole language philosophy of teaching. Choice is just as important for teachers as it is for students, and choosing materials, structures, and methods is every teacher's individual responsibility. Now every teacher has an open forum for examining her beliefs and practices, for reaffirming or restructuring. For Terry, as for many other teachers, colleagues, students, and her own inquiry were pathways to responsive, student-centered teaching, and she doesn't think things can ever be the way they were, back before students had choices. ''I don't think we're going to be able to change these children, even if a new superintendent does come in.'' Terry had experienced student empowerment firsthand, and knew that the students of Benton and South Jackson would speak out to keep the curriculum elements they valued, like time, choice, and community.

William Least Heat Moon (1982) traveled the back roads of America to learn about his country and himself. The journey was not easy.

> But without the errors, wrong turns, and blind alleys, without the doubling back and misdirection and fumbling and chance discoveries, there was not one bit of joy in walking the labyrinth. And worse: knowing the way made traveling it perfectly meaningless. (p. 426)

We too constructed meaningful curriculum from errors, wrong turns, and chance discoveries, rejecting what we thought we wanted in the beginning: a prepackaged guide to literacy instruction. Similarly, we restructured our professional lives by stepping off the direct principal-to-teacher route and creating multiple, shared paths to decision making.

The Governance Process

In order for there to be lasting change in schools, Carl Glickman (1992) argues that school faculties first must restructure their vision and decision-making processes. Otherwise, ''the current innovations of whole language, interdisciplinary curriculum, cooperative learning, . . . [and] authentic assessments are doomed to burn bright for a few years, then fade away'' (p. 27). Developing a shared governance system was critical to the instructional evolution of Benton and South Jackson.

Just as literacy instruction, teacher education, and the school–university relationship initially were based on a traditional model, our governance and decision-making relationships within our schools initially reflected traditional roles and relationships. A teacher from South Jackson described the governance of the school prior to 1990.

> Our [previous] principal was pretty much in control. She
> wanted to know what we were doing at all times and would
> sometimes police the area just to make sure we were teaching
> certain things. She didn't like a lot of noise and she liked for
> the children to be very quiet and calm. When she came in the
> door, we kind of got nervous if the children were talking. . . .
> We had to teach from the basals. It had to be in the lesson plans
> perfectly, just like the basal would write it.

During that same time period, teachers at Benton described communication as poor, tension as high, and morale as low. There were
substantive disagreements over issues of curriculum and discipline. The
previous leadership model had been heavily top-down; directives came
from the principal or central administration, and teachers were expected
to comply. "It reached a point where everybody was unhappy," recalled Dorothy Rice. "I would cry every morning before I came to school
because I just didn't want to go. . . . We had a big turnover in those
days. . . . Teachers were leaving because they didn't like it here anymore."

Both of the previous principals, also frustrated with the climate of
the school, tried to initiate shared governance through joining the
League of Professional Schools. Benton was just short of the 80% vote it
needed to join, but South Jackson voted to join during the spring of
1990. In the fall of 1990, however, both schools had new principals and
a new optimism that things could be different. Each initiated shared
governance, South Jackson through its formal affiliation with the
League of Professional Schools and Benton via a less formal avenue
facilitated by Joel and connected to the UGA–Benton partnership.

The change in governance was also rocky. By the second year at
South Jackson, there was even talk of not joining the League again.
There were multiple reasons for these difficult beginnings. Some of the
adjustment related to Pam Johns (the principal), and some to the teachers. As one teacher put it, "They were so used to being told what to do
from previous times that they didn't like not being told what to do."
Some people thought Pam was letting students and teachers "get
away" with things. Many were exhausted from the work of simultaneously changing the structure of school governance and of their classrooms; as several noted, "Whole language is a lot of work, a lot more
work than teaching from a basal." Some teachers did not really understand the big concepts of shared governance, or the specifics of League
membership. Teachers argued, withdrew, became disgruntled.

At Benton, the establishment of trust continued to be a critical issue associated with the establishment of shared decision making, as Jane Rogers pointed out.

> The "experts" came back and discussed the need for a UGA–Benton steering committee to be formed. . . . I still felt that the faculty was being manipulated by the UGA personnel pretending that they wanted to know our opinion and do what we wanted to do. In my journal that night I reflected . . . , "I can't believe that these people thought that we could be gullible enough to believe that they did not have a plan already developed."

Jane noted that those first meetings were "often led by Patsy [Lentz, principal] and Joel, who polled us on what we thought and what the other members of our cluster group thought. We answered the questions and smiled a lot."

For both schools, two elements seemed critical to the subsequent success of the shared governance process. First, teachers developed their own understandings of shared governance and, hence, ownership and responsibility for it. Lisa Delgado, Linda Morrison, and Nancy Maddox, members of South Jackson's elected governance council, attended a PSI meeting where they talked with personnel from other schools and developed a better understanding of what shared governance could be. On their return, they shared this vision with council-member Terry Wood and began addressing the frustration and difficulty they were experiencing. Terry recalled that they said to themselves, "Wait a minute. This is ridiculous. We need to be educated first before we even go any further." They read PSI material, including case studies from other schools (Allen, 1992) and articles by Carl Glickman. One day they stayed several hours after school and created an inservice for the rest of the school. They each took a turn explaining the whys and hows of shared governance, especially as it related to their own school. Terry recalled:

> That's when things changed, because people understood it. . . . We were more organized, we gave every teacher a notebook . . . for League information. . . . We started taking notes [at council meetings]. We said, "Look, we're going to have ballots. We're not going to sit and argue. . . . We'll have a forum the week before, let you think about it, and the next week vote."

Another decision the teachers made was to have no meetings on Thursdays, "so that teachers who are pregnant (there were several!) could go to the doctor." They asked for an official variance from the district for teachers to leave early on Fridays, since they stayed late on Wednesdays for meetings that often extended an hour past their official workday.

The second critical element associated with the establishment of shared governance at the schools was the development of trust and belief in the process. It was important that teachers at both schools believed in the integrity of the governance process. Following attendance at a PSI workshop where Benton teachers listened to teachers from other schools talk about their shared governance processes, as well as instructional changes, Jane Rogers noted in her journal:

> I saw that the partnership was for real, we were really going to participate fully in school governance. The university members truly wanted to know our thoughts and assist us in changing our school. They did not have a prewritten plan that we would follow blindly.

Whereas in the beginning teachers looked to their principal or to university faculty for direction, soon teachers found their voices and grew into new roles. "By the end of the year Joel and Patsy were requested to submit agenda items for the weekly meetings to us in advance," Jane remembered; significantly, faculty now controlled the agenda-setting process as well as ran the meetings. Joel mused, "During this [May 30] discussion it occurred to me that I'm not really needed here. . . . This group has become remarkably self-directed and self-sufficient."

Radical change in governance at both schools was not smooth. It took time for new principals, university faculty, and school faculty to construct local and personal understandings of shared governance and to establish trust in the process and in one another. Since that was accomplished the schools have developed strong, elected leadership teams each year, operated cross-grade communication groups to discuss curriculum and governance decisions, and presented to other teachers within the League. We have replaced district plan books that did not fit whole language planning, requested a district variance to use workbook money for classroom library books, realigned assessment with instruction, and interviewed and hired several new teachers. When Patsy Lentz moved to a new school in 1994, the Benton Steering Committee requested and received central office support for choosing their own principal, an unprecedented process for the district. The South Jackson Council held a day-long planning retreat before the 1994–95 school year, and included parents as equal decision-making partners. We have new voices, and would never, as many avowed, "go back to a dictatorial system."

It is a critical point that both schools put a great deal of time and effort into the establishment of a shared governance process before and during the major instructional change efforts. Many of the problems inherent not only in schoolwide change but also in a university–school partnership were addressed and worked out through this process. Each teacher had a voice in a small-group setting, where we felt most comfortable expressing ideas and reactions.

Linda McNeil's (1988) case studies of schools showed intricate connections among school structures, curricular policies, and the quality of students' educational experiences. Teachers treated students the way administrators treated teachers, too often within a control-oriented system that demanded passive acquiescence. Shedd and Bacharach (1991), who studied schools from the perspectives of organizational management, call these connections "tangled hierarchies." They concluded emphatically:

> If schools are to *teach* creativity and problem solving and cooperation and involvement, they must *practice* them, not just in the classroom but at all levels of the system. . . . Systems where all adults are encouraged to learn and lead, and where children are allowed to teach, can meet demands that no one has yet imagined. (pp. 194–195)

We have become learners as well as teachers, and one of the ways we are learning is through action research. The evolution of our research community, the third leg of our governance/instruction/research triangle, is the focus of the next chapter.

NOTE

1. Donna Alvermann (Reading Education) coordinated the research effort the first year. Tom Valentine (Adult Education), Liz Black (graduate assistant), and Pat Miller (assistant principal, Benton), began a parent discussion group (PLACES) the first year. Martha Allexsaht-Snyder (Elementary Education) and Mary Carter Whitten (graduate assistant) worked with teachers and parents the next year. Steve White (Elementary Education) coordinated the alternative teacher education effort. JoBeth Allen, Linda DeGroff, and Lee Galda (Language Education) led regular inservice sessions on children's literature and whole language instruction. Penny Oldfather (Elementary Education) worked with us on interdisciplinary planning.

CHAPTER 2

Evolving Research Communities

JoBeth Allen, Marilynn Cary, and Frances Hensley

Our beginnings were tentative and often our journey took us to places where travel guides had yet to be written. As Jan Kimbrell-Lee, a teacher researcher at South Jackson, recalls:

> I know whenever I started the research last summer it was like, "Okay, where do we start and what do we do?" . . . And when I started it I had no idea of what I wanted to do and I would go to the meetings and I would be lost. . . . Now I have an idea of where I am going.

Jan does indeed know where she is going; one of her research projects (see Chapter 3) has been published by the National Education Association (Kimbrell-Lee & Wood, 1994), and she has continued to study inclusion issues in a second study. Many of us who were novice researchers 2 years ago are now helping new teacher researchers. The following is an account of our journey as a research community.

STARTING FROM THE OUTSIDE

Research the first year of the partnership was primarily from the outside. University graduate students conducted interviews with all school faculty, student teachers, and school administrators in January and May. Teachers responded to a questionnaire that led to further staff development planning. Two graduate student/classroom teacher teams developed case studies of teacher change processes and how change affected their students (Black & Peters, 1991; West & Rice, 1991). The focus of most participants was on instruction; the purpose of the research was to make better informed decisions about designing learning experiences.

In the second year, Jane West (a graduate assistant) issued an invitation to anyone at Benton who was interested in conducting research. Two Benton teachers, Kelli Potts and Jane Rogers, collaborated with Jane to study children's perceptions about reading, writing, and themselves as learners. They interviewed children who found school easy as well as those who struggled. Together, the researchers analyzed the information, created profiles of three students, and presented what they learned at the UGA Children's Literature Conference.

Several teachers and the principal at Benton told JoBeth in a daylong series of interviews (February 1992) that action research was the aspect of their PSI commitment that they felt least satisfied with. Teachers were saving student work, administrators were filing information, and people had many questions. However, these were not yet research questions, and most teachers did not yet see themselves as researchers.

At South Jackson Elementary School (SJES), there was a combination of outsider and insider research during the first year of the partnership. Graduate students from UGA conducted interviews at the beginning and end of the year. The interviews at SJES revealed that a few teachers felt "forced to participate" in implementing a whole language curriculum and felt pressure from both peers and the principal. More widespread concerns were inappropriate assessment mandates, lack of books, and time issues affecting both planning and delivery of instruction. Two SJES teacher/graduate student teams conducted case studies. One (Treadway & Bailey, 1992) focused on the teacher change process; the second (Dunston & Morrison, 1992) documented the tension many of the teachers felt when school systems embrace literature-based reading instruction, yet adhere to traditional assessment methods.

Teachers at SJES initiated an extended study of assessment, their number one concern (see Chapter 6). They formed a task force to develop more authentic assessment procedures, ones that matched the evolving whole language instruction. Granted a waiver for one year, teachers piloted new techniques, studied their impact, modified procedures and checklists, and applied for a permanent waiver. This action research had a direct impact on the lives of students and teachers.

These first research endeavors were initiated with anxiety and concern on the part of the university. In their desire to study the curricular changes taking place in the schools, the university once more turned back to the traditional and well-known model of outsiders researching schools. As Jane West recalls:

We were so careful that first year to make sure that we didn't do anything that would make teachers not want to work with us because we really wanted to do this to work. . . . I think we were really aware that . . . this could fall apart at any time if we go in and ruffle a bunch of feathers and make people uncomfortable.

MOVING TO THE INSIDE

In May 1992, JoBeth invited interested teachers from both schools to work together that summer to analyze data (both insider and outsider), and to think about forming their own research teams the following fall. Although the university determined both the purpose and process for our work that first summer, JoBeth was determined to move away from this old model. She began by asking what questions we might be interested in investigating. Our responses focused on problematic areas of instruction, such as how to conduct more effective conferences, create better schedules, and get more books. This parallels the findings of Hubbard and Power (1993), facilitators in numerous teacher research communities, who learned that research questions usually started with tensions about teaching. They found that

> As these teacher-researchers thought about these tensions, they began to focus on larger issues of culture, learning, and school structures. The questions they asked were not aimed at quick-fix solutions to errors in classroom techniques . . . [but] involve understanding students and teaching in much deeper ways. (Hubbard & Power, 1993, p. 4)

During that summer, a group of six teachers from Benton and South Jackson met with five UGA faculty and graduate students for 3 weeks; several other teachers, the two principals, and the district curriculum coordinator worked with the group for 2 or 3 days. Our primary purpose was to decide what we should study about the educational initiative we had been involved with. The first 2 days we focused on generating a research focus and guiding questions, reviewing available data sources, exploring specific audiences and purposes for our inquiry, and familiarizing ourselves with various methods of data collection and analysis.

We wrote our reflections on six questions individually, before the meeting. Then we discussed responses in small groups and generated summaries as a whole group. The first question was, *What are the most important developments that have occurred in the past 2 years?* We decided that these were

1. Teachers had a more professional point of view, made more decisions about both governance and instruction, and were more willing to take risks. Teachers described themselves as learners. There was more communication and cohesion among teachers. As one teacher put it, "We are looking more to ourselves and other teachers, less to 'outside authorities.'"

2. Teachers and students were more excited about reading and were reading more for pleasure. There was time to read every day in most classrooms.

3. Nearly every teacher had moved to some degree from textbook-driven to whole language instruction. This move was described as less drill and more discussion, integration of curriculum, students learning from each other, and going from teacher-centered to student-centered classrooms. Teachers had a better understanding of the literacy development of children and based instructional decisions on whole language principles. The schools looked different: There was much more "writing on the walls," and many classrooms had replaced individual desks with group tables.

4. Children were writing more and getting better at it because of time, choice, and instruction on writing.

5. There was a developing sense of trust and open communication between faculty and administration, and between school faculty and UGA faculty. "Change takes time" was more than a slogan for both insiders and outsiders who originally expected more change, more quickly, from more people. Old chasms between university and school were beginning to narrow.

From these responses, we moved to the second question, *What do we as a partnership want to know about the past 2 years?* The questions that we generated here became the working questions for analysis and writing for the remainder of the 3 weeks. Many of them also became research questions for designing new studies.

1. How do we know if we are accomplishing our goals? Did a change really take place? Did teachers change their instruction or does it just look different—is it the basal repackaged? If a change did take place, what was the basic change?

2. Did the change make a difference to the students? What can we learn about students' use of time, test scores, reading with understanding, reading/writing connections, preparation for the next grade, attitudes, critical thinking, and making decisions about their own learning? How do students perceive themselves now as readers, writers, and learners? Have the changes been beneficial for *all* children (gifted, LD, slow learners, average)?

3. Did the change make a difference for teachers? How were attitudes, teaching practices, planning, evaluation, reading, and writing affected, if at all?

4. How do parents view their children's literacy? What are they seeing in home reading, writing, discussions, attitudes, grades, feedback from teachers?

5. How do student teachers view the project? What do they think of the match between UGA courses and Jackson County classrooms?

Third, we discussed *key issues*, most of which were evolving and unresolved. The most pressing were (1) evaluation and assessment and their alignment with new instructional practices; (2) the struggle between individual teachers' freedom to choose instructional practices and the desire of others "to be a whole language school," with consistent philosophy and practices; and (3) issues of the most effective ways of creating systemic change, including transitions to middle and high school, district politics and policies, and the development of a new preschool program. We were also interested in what had been, or could be, effective ways of knowing as we discussed continuing education. Other issues that were important to teachers were getting more books in the classrooms, release time for planning and research, and parental support and involvement.

We generated a list of *information sources* for learning about these issues (Question 4), and then discussed Question 5, *Who might be interested in knowing about what we are learning?* (see Figure 2.1). Sources included teachers' journals, interviews, surveys, classroom research projects, studying students across time (especially as they go to middle

Figure 2.1. Audience, evidence, and products.

Audience	Content/Evidence	Product
Students (Ss)	Findings from classroom studies; direct involvement with future studies as co-investigators of questions important to them; school atmosphere; what is _____ grade like?	Class meetings to share research findings and seek Ss' perspectives; grade-level video tapes narrated by Ss showing what next grade is like (from student research); Ss' writing and projects published in school yearbook
Parents	What does my child look like as a reader (R)? A writer (W)? Where does s/he "fit" with other Rs and Ws? How can we help at home? Are Ss reading and writing more? Enjoying those activities? Capable Rs and Ws? What's going on at the school that's creating this?	Library figures; individual student checklists, portfolios, work samples, reading tapes, videos, conferences; county writing assessment, school newsletter with suggestions for parents
Community, including Parent–Teacher Organization (PTO), Local Advisory Council, school board, business partners	How will the project help the community? 1) engaging Ss in "school" 2) seeing selves as Rs, Ws, and learners belonging and staying in school 3) contributing to work force by a) working collaboratively b) solving problems	Local newspapers; panel presentation of students and teachers; videos and demonstrations at PTO meetings; "Partnership Story" booklet
Teachers	Impact of changes on planning, curriculum, instruction, evaluation, climate, and relationships. Effect on teachers' lives: time, professionalism. Process: getting started, resources, evaluation, stating objectives. Effect on students—Do _all_ benefit? How? Behavior, attitudes, reading and writing	Teacher to teacher: narratives of journeys, articles in journals like _The Reading Teacher;_ talking with other teachers, classroom visits; handbook, including sample lesson plans, Ss' work, people resources, philosophy, and bibliography

Figure 2.1. Audience, evidence, and products (continued).

Audience	Content/Evidence	Product
County teachers, including special education and Chapter 1	How does whole language (WL) affect "our" kids? What does WL look like in resource room? How do our kids perform when fully included?	District, Chapter 1, and special education newsletters; invite to visit, share handbook; meet with middle school teachers, show Ss' work folders
Principals	Patsy's and Pam's first person accounts	Present at state organization conferences
Central office	Levels of teacher involvement; hours of teacher involvement related to student learning (number of books, pieces of writing, projects); UGA dollars invested	One-page executive summary; full annual reports made available; "Partnership Story"; presentation and handout of policy brief
State department	Policy analysis, what assisted, what hindered, needed exemptions from state mandates	Policy brief
Private and government funding agencies	Progress report, all aspects	Quarterly progress reports, research reports, policy brief, book
UGA faculty in teacher education	Overview of project; match between teacher education program and school beliefs and practices (co-reform); student teacher pre–post interview data, comparisons across sites	Distribute conference papers to interested faculty; "Partnership Story"; symposium on establishing collaborative relationships
Other university–school partnerships	Process: what worked, what didn't, what we'd do differently, what we learned, who benefited	Book that includes our collective story, individual stories (case studies, personal journeys), policy brief, focus on *systemic change*; impact on key players
Other researchers	School reform, restructuring, whole language, collaborative research, teacher research	Presentations at local, state, and national conferences

school), student work, analyzing test scores, and using outside observers. Finally, we shared narrative responses to Question 6, *What has your personal journey been like, and where do you see it going?*

Toward the end of our 3 weeks together, we invited Andrew Gitlin to provide feedback on what we were doing and to share with us what the educative research team (Gitlin et al., 1992) had experienced. One of the most important aspects of educative research is that teachers use their written personal and school histories, along with peer evaluation, to generate meaningful research. Our group was already very committed to and involved with its research questions and did not enter into the educative research model per se. However, our visit with Andrew did spark several people to write personal histories and school histories which enriched our inquiry and have contributed to this and the previous chapter of the book.

The summer of 1992 was really the beginning of a combined Kings Bridge Road research community. Together we reflected, analyzed, wrote/read/revised, and learned from each other. We chose to map our own research journey rather than follow an outsider's model (e.g., "program evaluation" or university researcher questions). These common experiences served as a turning point and as the foundation for our future work.

Informational meetings were held at both schools early in the fall. Those of us who had participated in the summer research made presentations to our colleagues describing our experiences and research interests. At the conclusion of the meetings, another invitation was extended to participate in school-based research teams that would meet during the coming school year. Teachers responded to these invitations with some hesitancy but cautious enthusiasm. Linda Morrison recalls her initial response:

> JoBeth invited me to participate and I thought, "Hmm, I don't really have anything to contribute. Gee, I wonder why she wants me to come to this meeting." I had worked on a case study with a graduate student, and really I mean, it was her project, she did the vast majority of the work, I just basically lent her my classroom and did a few things. But I didn't really see myself as somebody who was able to be involved in anything like research. Like a lot of people, I suspect, I looked at it with skepticism. "Ah, this is just some doctoral student who needs to complete her program and needs a classroom and needs some sucker who's willing to do some stuff." So, I didn't really see myself as having much to contribute. But I

went to the meeting and I remember being a little bit hesitant about it and thinking, "Well, I won't say anything, I'll just sit here." And after the first day, I remember thinking, "This is really exciting, there's a lot of stuff going on here." And there were so many ideas, and so much enthusiasm.

Needless to say, Linda did not "just sit there"; she became an active researcher. Why?

REASONS FOR BECOMING RESEARCHERS

Why did we become involved in these research teams? As literacy educators, we had been reflective in the past, with early reflection leading to dissatisfaction with the status quo, and more recent reflection leading us to teaching action. We had been engaged in what Richardson (1994) called "practical inquiry," which is "conducted in one's everyday work life for purposes of improvement" (p. 7). While we valued, and continue to value, that mode of inquiry, we had not formalized the process with the intent to "contribute to a larger community's knowledge" (Richardson, 1994, p. 7). Why did reflection, for many of us, become the "systematic, intentional inquiry by teachers about their own school and classroom work" that Cochran-Smith and Lytle (1992, p. 320) defined as teacher research?

For their 1993–94 research project, Marilynn and Frances asked members of the research teams to reflect on the reasons for their involvement. They talked about the multiple reasons they became involved, including collegiality, the interrelated nature of their work, their desire for professional growth, the recognition and rewards that accompanied the endeavor, and various support systems and people.

Collegiality

Most people who joined the research teams did so because of personal invitations, initially from JoBeth, and increasingly from other teacher researchers. One of the main reasons seemed to be the opportunity to get together as professionals and to be part of a group that seemed to be having a good time as well as contributing to the schools' knowledge base. Special education teacher Patti Griffith remarked, "It's fun to be in a group of people who really care about their profession, you know, enough to change it." Breaking the isolation of the classrooms, getting to know colleagues across grades levels and specialty areas, and sharing

professional talk are examples of collegiality engendered by being engaged in the research team. Gayle Berryman, who joined the research
team the second year, recalls her personal experience.

> We get in a routine and if we don't belong to something . . .
> we're kind of forgotten about. I've gotten to talk to a lot of
> other teachers, and find out a lot of what they're researching
> and what we had in common I never thought about. And, just
> being part of a group [was important].

Gayle's comments are illustrative of what Cochran-Smith and Lytle
(1992) describe as the overall isolation of teachers. In the past, we had
few opportunities for joint discussion and dialogue, and even fewer
where we had in-depth discussions about how our practice was affecting children.

We have seen a strong desire on the part of almost all of us to work
with someone else. Some teachers who dropped out or didn't write
about their experiences stressed that the following year they wanted to
do research *with* someone else. Researchers who worked together valued collaboration. Lori particularly valued the ongoing collaboration of
her partner, Marilynn, who "kind of pulled me through" the rough
times. But she also valued the research team as a whole.

> I don't know if I would be willing to strike out on my own
> completely if no one else was doing research in the school. . . .
> I like collaboration . . . there's a bond between the teachers
> who research with you and kind of understand what the other
> teachers are going through . . . it's made me more aware of
> things that I could do to help other teachers in their research
> and helping out with other people's projects.

Integrated Professional Lives

Just as the initiatives were interrelated and overlapping in purpose, so
they were in practice. Cheryl Poponi talked about the interconnected-
ness of schoolwide task forces and teacher research.

> Being involved with PSI I think that's helped because I've got-
> ten more involved with what goes on within the school now.
> Whereas before I think I would just go to school, teach my
> class, and go home, and now I take a bigger interest in what
> goes on in the school. I think that's part of the reason why you

become more involved is because you do have connections with the other teachers. And things come up through teachers' research that you look into, for like different task forces maybe. Something that might happen in another task force, you might start thinking about a research question.

Teaching and research became interrelated for many of us. Jan explained that research has "made me really look at what the kids are doing more closely than I did before" and document what she was seeing. But the fit was not always an easy one; many times we struggled to balance teaching and researching, and to find ways of recording information that were systematic as well as immediately useful. Patty felt that while reflection was now a "daily occurrence," other aspects of research (especially her journal) had not "become a part of my habit yet."

Professional Growth

Regardless of other motivations, teachers came to the teacher research teams because they had questions related to their practice that they were eager to explore. Dorothy Rice, who studied student perspectives both in her own room, with collaborator Jane West, and across the school with the video interview team, emphasized that her research "makes me think [differently] about relationships with children and their relationships with each other." Holly also pointed to the increased professionalism of the school as teachers collectively ask, "What's going on here in this school? Is it working? Are we truly giving [students] what we need to [in order to] prepare them?" Holly explained the role action research plays in answering such questions: "If what I'm doing is not working, then I have a real direct way of changing it, that says I'm evaluating, you know, my professionalism."

Lisa Delgado also took a whole-school view, but from the perspective of a media specialist. She explained:

I started having questions when all the teachers were making all these [whole language] changes and improving their instruction. I thought, "Well how can I change and improve the instruction in the media center to best fit what they're doing?" And so I had these questions and . . . when we were invited to form a group and to do research, I thought, "Well, I'd give it a shot."

Rewards and Recognition

Being a member of the teacher research teams came with rewards and recognitions as well. Teachers pointed to the value of earning extra money for summer research work; attending and presenting at local, state, and national meetings and conferences; consulting with and assisting other teachers and schools; and publishing articles in local, state, and national outlets. One teacher honestly described her initial involvement during the second year of the research team.

> The first year that they had it [the research team] I didn't want to get involved with it because it sounded like a lot of work. When I found how much [a colleague] got paid for doing it, I said, "I'm going to do that next summer and that's going to be Christmas spending money." And so that's exactly the first thing that really got me, that I would have to say was really the big thing, was the money. But I did come with a legitimate question.

Perhaps related to recognition was professional identity. Over half of the teachers we talked with mentioned an increased sense of pride in their profession. Interestingly, several pointed to husbands and other family members who were university or laboratory researchers, and said that teaching had not always had the status within the family that these other researcher jobs had. Now they "talked the talk" alongside researching relatives. Several teachers liked the new dimension to teaching that research offered. Lori Davis, whose husband is doing doctoral research, told us:

> I have a family at home, I have two little ones, and so I kind of feel guilty sometimes when I start in with my research, but then I'll say, I know that I need an outlet too, need a way to express myself . . . I feel like with [research], I am something besides "Mom."

Lori continued by explaining that aside from the rewards and recognition, it was really the importance of the research itself to her practice that drove her. "Probably the main reason I got involved with the research is I thought, 'We're right on the cutting edge of this pre-K program and they're going to need some research in the area.'" Lori, like all of us, became and remains a researcher for a complex variety of reasons.

Support Systems and People

There were converging forces that supported our development and participation in research teams. First, all of the initiatives with the university supported and encouraged teacher research. Teachers pointed to the freedom and encouragement from their principals, Pam Johns and Patsy Lentz, to make decisions about teaching as leading eventually to researching that teaching. A teacher researcher recently wrote that what supports her research is "the freedom I have to design the curriculum for my classroom. Since I'm free from 'getting through' a science text, or giving basal tests, I have time to make changes based on what I observe my children doing."

Membership in the PSI League of Professional Schools came with PSI's expectation that schools study and report on changes they are making, although both our schools were slow to implement this component. The PSI "Information Retrieval System" was very valuable in allowing us to read what other people had written about topics we were investigating; we could request information on any educational topic and receive several articles within weeks. A major focus of NRRC was teacher research and the development of a school research community. Teacher research was a natural next step in the instructional improvement work supported by the UGA Education Initiative; funds for substitutes, summer stipends, conference travel, and university people were invaluable. We were becoming more comfortable with our newly created literacy curriculum, comfortable enough to take a step back from it to contemplate how it was affecting students, where we wanted to improve it, and what we might teach others about it.

Teachers reported that JoBeth's support was a key element for their involvement. She was actively involved in and served as the school's primary contact for all of the initiatives. She previously had been a member of several teams of outstanding teacher researchers (Allen, Combs, Hendricks, Nash, & Wilson, 1988; Allen, Michalove, & Shockley, 1993; Carr & Allen, 1989; Shockley, Michalove, & Allen, 1995) and often shared with us what she had learned from teacher inquiry. Collaboration with teacher researchers has characterized her work for the past 12 years and she championed the approach. She shared with us a strong belief that the questions that are going to impact classrooms come from those classrooms, not from the university.

It was at this point of readiness and support that JoBeth told a teacher who interviewed her:

> We really started looking at what impact the curricular changes were having. And I think that also came from the university in the way of thinking about it as action research, although the need and interest in finding out the impact I think was there at the school level. So, my role there was to issue an invitation to see who was interested in looking at that [impact of curricular change] in a more systematic way and in starting up a research team.

But her role was greater than inviting us to participate. JoBeth played a critical role in our development as researchers and research communities. She not only invited us, she supported, encouraged, nurtured, and facilitated our interests and efforts. As Jan Kimbrell-Lee told us:

> When we'd come up with an idea, you know, she [JoBeth] would just kind of run with it and say, "That's a great idea." . . . but she was very honest about it. She would tell us whether or not she thought that would be easy to do or pretty difficult to do.

The powerful and necessary combination of these internal and external factors supported our growth as researchers. Cochran-Smith and Lytle (1992) argued that to build and sustain teacher research communities, we must rethink the ways in which we organize time, talk about what we observe, read and jointly construct meanings for our own texts and those of others, and interpret what teachers and students do. In the Conclusion to the book, we will analyze our research community according to this framework. In the following section, we lay out the barriers we have encountered in creating that kind of community.

OVERCOMING OBSTACLES TO TEACHER RESEARCH

Although as research teams we developed over time our own sense of competence, confidence, and direction, during the journey we also encountered obstacles. Cochran-Smith and Lytle (1992) identified "the serious obstacles caused by teacher isolation, a school culture that works against raising questions, a technical view of knowledge for teaching, and the negative reputation of educational research" (pp. 304–305). Through our involvement with shared governance and university partnerships, we had already moved a long way in overcoming the first three barriers. Rather, Kings Bridge Road team members identified definitions of research and university/school roles, lack of confidence and expertise, time constraints, and personality conflicts as sometime barriers.

Redefining Research and Roles

Along with literacy and governance evolution, there was a redefining of the traditional roles for both the university and the school. In the context of the research teams, the issues to be negotiated were: Who asks the questions, who does the research, and who will write and report the research? In the past, that had been seen by all of us as a university role. Patty Griffith spoke for many of us when she said, "The very thought that a teacher could be a researcher was sort of foreign to me. . . . A researcher was in an ivory tower, and you read articles when you had time, and when you were real sleepy because it put you to sleep!"

Many teachers have been "put to sleep" by academic research. And many university researchers have faulted teachers "for not reading or not implementing the findings of such research" (Cochran-Smith & Lytle, 1992, p. 300). We are part of a growing concern in the broad educational community that encompasses both schools and universities. Richardson (1994), a university researcher, wrote:

> Research on the practice of teaching is undergoing significant change: change that reflects considerations of power and voice, the nature of knowledge, and research methods. . . . The scholarly community soon realized that research on teaching should not be conducted in the absence of considerations of two questions: Who owns the knowledge on teaching practice, and who benefits from the research . . . (see Apple, 1993, Ladwig, 1991)? (p. 5)

Within the partnership, both university and school researchers talked about ways in which they had changed over the course of our partnership. None of the university partners except JoBeth had previously conducted collaborative research, nor had they worked closely with teacher researchers. All developed genuine respect for members of the Kings Bridge Road team. Jane West, a doctoral student, was not encouraged to collaborate with teachers in her research methods courses, but through the partnership she and teacher Dorothy Rice worked together in various ways for 3 years. Some of the research was conducted jointly; some Jane conducted with Dorothy "right there in the middle of it, helping me make research decisions and, you know, telling me if I'm getting it right or not, and if I'm misunderstanding, and helping me interpret the data," Jane explained. And it has shaped the way Jane will conduct research for the rest of her career. "I can't imagine myself ever doing research that doesn't involve the teacher."

Researchers learned new roles in collaborative relationships. JoBeth knew very little about school media centers, but learned not only new research techniques (e.g., a method for thematic unit analysis), but also the questions, issues, needs, and functions of media specialists and the role they played in supporting whole language teachers (see Chapter 8). All the university partners worried initially that teachers would not become actively engaged as researchers if they were not reading research of others. The university researchers learned that their thinking was backward, that as people became involved in researching their own questions, they started reading what other researchers (especially teacher researchers) had learned.

Teacher researcher Linda Morrison and Ron Kieffer, a university researcher, had to learn how to collaborate effectively, especially when it came time to write. At first Linda kept trying to write what she thought Ron wanted her to write. Linda recalled:

> When the school year started I thought, "I can't do research. You have to have a Ph.D. to do research." . . . When Ron and I were working on this [Chapter 7 of this book], that was such a frustrating experience. . . . I remember an evening where I had been sitting at the computer writing, still thinking, "I can't do research" and, you know, "It's not going to be right," still looking for this outside standard that I was going to be judged against. . . . Well, I wrote and I wrote and I wrote, and . . . I began to think, "Well maybe I can do this." And it was like the standards began to change, and I didn't think so much about "Is it right? Am I giving them what they want?" . . . This is what's important to me.

One area where many of us changed was in our definitions of what counted as research and ways it might be conducted. One of our colleagues described her initial reaction to an invitation to conduct action research: "I just thought, 'Ugh!' [Research] was that class at the university I was in—just for a few days." A year later, she presented her research at a conference. "I realized that *this* research was not the same as [the research] I reacted to in a negative way. To me, action research is a self-improvement plan." Most of us thought of research only in terms of statistics and experimental designs, as something "distant, uninteresting, and impenetrable" (Cochran-Smith & Lytle, 1992). Patty said she hadn't thought of research as particularly understandable or valuable.

> It used to be so separate and so, oh, there were just so many figures and statistics to get through, you couldn't possibly see how you could apply that in your classroom. But the research that, you know, we're doing, and that other schools are doing now, the action research, you say, "Yeah, . . . I could change that. . . . Maybe I can do more hands-on projects. Maybe I could read out loud to the kids more." This just applies to your everyday teaching.

Down the road at UGA, Early Childhood Education professor Steve White was also thinking about research in a new way as he studied his own practice. "My training had been real quantitative," Steve explained. Through the partnership, he began interviewing, surveying undergraduates, and keeping a journal and lesson plans from his teacher education courses. These shifts in research paradigms, and in teacher/researcher roles, led to the next barrier we will discuss, feelings of inadequacy.

Building Confidence and Expertise

When Steve found himself in the middle of foreign research territory, he struggled at first. "It's been hard, very hard, and I don't always know what I'm doing. . . . I think a lot of us felt like we were just sort of doing it by the, you know, the seat of our pants." Joel Taxel, whose previous research was in analyzing children's literature, echoed Steve's self-doubts: "I have never done school-based research. . . . I have never seen myself as someone who is going to go out and take exhaustive field notes and triangulate and do all those neat qualitative kinds of things."

His school-based colleagues often felt the same way. We worried about various aspects of our ability to conduct research, especially the writing. As Cheryl Poponi put it:

> There were times when I thought, "What am I doing? You just don't know what you're doing. You're not a research person.

You can't . . . '' And then especially when it came to, ''Alright, well now that you have all this data, you can't write it up. You just, you just don't know how to do it. You're not that type of person.''

Cheryl discovered, as did Steve, Joel, and the rest of us, that research is a learning process. We are not, one day, nonresearchers and, the next day, researchers, any more than we are nonmusicians one day and musicians the next. We learn, practice, mentor, and are mentored, and we are in the process of becoming—all of us—confident and capable researchers.

Finding Time

The factor most often cited when we asked teacher researchers to respond to the question, ''What impedes your research?'' was time. We all had teaching responsibilities, other professional obligations, and families. Lisa Delgado explained:

> I mean all those things had to be done, and sometimes I would have to put my research aside and just not make my observational notes at that time, hoping that every once in a while if I saw something really neat I would try to write it down despite the fact that I just felt overwhelmed.

We as teacher researchers were not the only ones who found keeping up with our research difficult and time-consuming. Joel again worried about the new research role he had assumed.

> One of the things that I most regret and feel guilty about is keeping up my log and my notes and what have you. It is haphazard, at best. You know, there are times when I'll talk into a tape recorder after every meeting, and then I will literally go months without doing it because I just get so overwhelmed.

In addition to finding the time to keep journals, interview, analyze, and write, it became increasingly problematic for several of us to be away from our classrooms. We could request occasional substitutes for research time, and we began traveling to state and national conferences to present our research. We spoke to UGA classes, helped other schools with governance and action research through PSI, and served on UGA Initiative teacher education advisory committees, many of which met during the school day. We felt that our students suffered when we were away too often, although they may have gained from our increased professionalism. This is an issue that we still have not resolved.

Meshing as a Team

As with any large group of people with varied interests and needs, there were times when personalities impeded our team efforts. There were times of tension at all three partnership sites; we had to work to balance perceived authority and degree of contribution, personal preferences and needs, and writing styles. Although only one person spoke with us about this issue, we felt it was important to include, both in the interest of honesty and because we suspect other groups of researchers also negotiate personality differences. One member reported difficulty in coordinating meeting places, getting people to cooperate, and writing on a joint project.

> When you're working with a group of people, not everyone has the same idea on things. And I remember when we were doing the actual writing, there was some concern that it was going to be written as, I guess, not as I wanted it. I wanted my voice to be heard through it, and not just mine but the way that I think some of us felt and some of us felt that some of the chapters weren't coming out that way.

Does everyone get along terrifically now? Not always. But we can honestly say that we know each other better, that we talk with people we did not talk with before, that we have developed a healthy respect for differing points of view, and that we have a commitment to working as a team.

In the remainder of the chapter, we chronicle the avenues we traveled to come together. We describe the evolution of the Benton and South Jackson research teams as they developed both individually and together (during the summers).

EVOLUTION OF TWO RESEARCH TEAMS

The Benton Research Team (BRT) and the South Jackson Research Team (SJRT) both formed in September 1992. The BRT had 12 members, the SJRT six. We spent several initial meetings sharing our research interests, many of which had grown out of the questions and issues raised during

the 1992 summer analysis and reflection. Our questions included literacy development and achievement of students across a range of abilities
and settings; oral language development in new pre-kindergarten students; student drawings; engagement with literacy; assessment; inclusion of special education students; and the role of media specialists.

Developing Questions

We worried at the first meetings that we were too broad, too nebulous.
"I don't even know what my questions are," Holly fretted, "I just know
as a new teacher in this school, new to fifth grade, I do have lots of
questions, and I want to be a part of this group." Questions changed
considerably over time for some members and remained stable for others. Both schools pursued individual classroom research as well as
schoolwide research. The media study was not only schoolwide, but
also cross-school. Several people at Benton had questions about
whether a whole-school focus included students' views of themselves
as readers, writers, and learners; about learners' (and their peers') attitudes about being classified as special education students and going to a
resource room versus staying in their home classroom; and about the
long-term effects of student-centered, whole language instruction. Several of the teachers who had these questions decided to design a longitudinal interview study of five children from each grade level (see Chapter 11).

   During those early meetings we also discussed issues of developing
researcher skills and of finding (or buying) time for documentation,
reflection, meeting, analysis, and writing. We discussed research paradigms, including the pros and cons of using comparison groups. We
studied teacher research processes, including educative research processes (Gitlin et al., 1992). We kept in mind from the beginning the
issues raised the previous summer about audience, evidence, and products: Who might be interested in learning from our research, and what
form should it take for that audience?

Creating Supportive Structures

The BRT decided to meet one evening a month in different people's
homes. Meetings were 2 to 3 hours long, always included potluck
snacks or meals, and were well attended. Midyear, the team decided to
"hire" speech/language pathologist and fellow team member Marilynn
Cary as a school-based research coordinator; the SJRT didn't feel they
needed a formal coordinator, but Lisa Delgado agreed to serve infor-

mally. The BRT also decided that monthly evening meetings were not enough and that they would have weekly "briefings" to touch base with each other, just 15 to 30 minutes after school. The SJRT decided to meet only immediately following school because several members had young children and did not want to be gone in the evenings. In addition, both teams scheduled several monthly full-day individual research consultations with JoBeth, time to design surveys, discuss journal entries, brainstorm research techniques, analyze data, and talk about what we were learning.

Meeting regularly as a group was invaluable for both teams. For example, at the December SJRT meeting Terry Wood talked about studying her fifth graders' transition to middle school. She was interested in finding out how her students would do because she was concerned that "whole language might mess them up, and I want them to be successful." Several members questioned her. She explained that even though she saw definite improvement in her students' writing from their participation in writing workshops, and even though her students had specifically requested that they learn through writing rather than textbook exercises, Terry was worried that expectations would be very different in middle school. They would need to be able to do those workbook exercises, need to focus more on conventions than content, need to respond to teacher prompts rather than work to choose meaningful topics. Mary Leuzinger, from the district office, asked pointedly, "Is preparing kids for the sixth grade an appropriate goal? What if you learn that the way you are teaching *is* different; will you go back to textbook exercises? Is that best for the kids?" Another member asked, "Are you assuming that you should be the one to change?" We all thought differently about Terry's question as a result of the discussion. Similar discussions helped all of us shape our questions, purposes, analyses, and products.

Working together as a group not only made collaborative projects, such as the video interviews, possible; it also made reflection broad and interactive. All members of the group (not just those directly involved in the video project) developed and refined the questions, discussed interview techniques, and wrestled with problems. For example, a teacher brought up the issue of confidentiality, because one student said, "Is my teacher going to see this?" We had quite a discussion of teachers' rights to learn from the research, and students' rights to remain anonymous. We resolved it by making only the transcripts available and using pseudonyms. The video team also met separately from the whole research team; they helped each other immeasurably through group transcription and rough coding of several videotapes. Other collaborative researchers, like Jan Kimbrell-Lee and Terry Wood, met with and got feedback from the group, and also met by themselves regularly.

A very important aspect of group meetings was to learn from each other in ways that affected our practice immediately. We did not need to wait for a "final report" to learn drama strategies from Carol, portfolio processes from Linda, library collection needs from Mary Jane and Lisa, or a host of other information and insights that made us better teachers.

We also took time at meetings to celebrate personal and professional accomplishments. A highlight for the SJRT was Gwen Bailey's announcement that they had received a State Innovative Programs grant to start a publishing center. Gwen and another teacher, Melissa Brown, had written the grant and it was chosen as a finalist. When they arrived in Atlanta to make the presentation to the committee that would decide which proposals would be funded, they discovered theirs was the only one that had been written entirely by teachers and was being presented by teachers. The Publishing Center contains seven computers, a binding machine, a laminator, and other publication tools, and is staffed by trained parent volunteers. In its first year, the usage log showed 1,710 official visits, and 543 individual and class books produced; in addition, teachers used the center for a variety of purposes, including writing research reports.

We certainly had our problems. When school life got busy, research necessarily took a backseat. Several people dropped out of the group. Some people had difficulty transcribing their interview tapes; they decided it made more sense to have Julie Parks, our grant-supported substitute, transcribe so teachers wouldn't have to leave their classes. There were occasional conflicts over scheduling meeting times and places. Two teachers had three research projects going at once and were at times overwhelmed. However, through discussion, observation, and the joint creation of purposes and possibilities, our research was becoming more focused, our questions more specific, and our plans more collaborative.

Critical Time: Combined Team Meetings

We had stipends to meet together as a combined team for 2 weeks during the summers of 1993 and 1994. The group included 14 teacher researchers in 1993 and more than 20 part- and full-time teacher researchers in 1994, as well as administrators Patsy Lentz and Mary Leuzinger in 1993, and five faculty and graduate student university-based researchers and/or facilitators. We summarized our individual or group projects to familiarize everyone in the group with all the research, established goals and a working plan for the 2 weeks, and decided on what resources each project needed, for example, facilitators' time, articles, and so on. Every researcher had a copy of *The Art of Classroom Inquiry* (Hubbard & Power, 1993). In 1993, we talked specifically about data analysis, including data preparation, coding, indexing, writing research memos, the constant comparison method, and triangulation.

We worked for 10 days, some individually but most in dyads or small groups. Some groups worked at the university, some at the schools, and some in homes. We analyzed, wrote, revised, came together again to share findings, and went back to refine ideas and drafts. Facilitators helped as asked. Miraculously, on the tenth day that first summer we had respectable drafts (few final, of course) of eight projects (several other inquiries were still in process, and two other projects were still being analyzed and written). The final meeting of the team took place on JoBeth's back porch. For 3½ hours in 95 degree weather, we listened to what we all had learned. These are the chapters you will find in the remainder of this book.

Diverse Methods and Styles

The studies in this volume include description, interpretation, and evaluation. Most utilize some combination of participant-observation field notes; open-ended interviews with parents, students, teachers, or administrators; questionnaires; and documents (work samples, lesson plans, library circulation records) as data. As Erickson (1986) pointed out:

> Interpretive research methods are intrinsically democratic; one does not need special training to be able to understand the results of such research, nor does one need arcane skills in order to conduct it. Fieldwork research requires skills of observation, comparison, contrast, and reflection that all humans possess. In order to get through life we must all do interpretive fieldwork. What professional interpretive researchers do is to make use of the ordinary skills of observation and reflection in especially systematic and deliberate ways. [The] classroom teachers['] . . . role is not that of the participant observer who comes from the outside world to visit, but that of an unusually observant participant who deliberates inside the scene of action. (p. 157)

Several studies also make use of quantitative analysis to compare library circulation figures, standardized test scores, and so forth. Some are case studies of one classroom; others involve teachers and/or students throughout the school.

Like the teachers who conducted them, the styles of reporting in this volume are varied. Teachers chose how they would write based on their own educational research backgrounds, their primary audiences, and personal writing styles. When this book was accepted for publication, we had a specific audience and had to revise accordingly. For example, initially Jennifer White used a question-and-answer format about whole language to share with kindergarten parents at the beginning of school; they were her primary audience. Chapter 9, by White, is not only in more "book chapter" format, but her audience is now educators. In a different reporting style, Cary, Davis, and Benton (Chapter 10) initially wrote in a more formal research voice; they sent their report to the state department of education, having decided that the mix of qualitative and quantitative data would be most convincing. Co-authored pieces represented their own challenges, and the video interview study (Chapter 11) had many revisions. It also had many writers and voices, but we all agreed that the main voices we wanted our readers to hear were the children's.

GETTING OFF THE FREEWAY

In a classic song about getting out of the rat race, Guy Clark says, "If I can just get off of this L.A. freeway without getting killed or caught, I'll be down the road in a cloud of smoke to some land that I ain't bought . . . "; in other words, he would invent a new life for himself. As teacher researchers, we left the freeway, venturing off on the blue highways, but never alone. We supported one another, including our traveling companions from UGA, especially JoBeth and Frances, who attended all our meetings. The partnerships with the University of Georgia provided valuable support during the journey. Once we left the freeway—the one that told us it would free us from thinking and making decisions—we invented a new school reality for ourselves and our students. We created curriculum, redesigned programs, and became serious evaluators of our own effectiveness.

PART II

ACTIVE LEARNING,
INCLUSIVE TEACHING

CHAPTER 3

Teaching, Learning, and Partnerships: Strategies for Including Special Needs Students

Jan Kimbrell-Lee and Terry Wood

Terry is a fifth-grade teacher with 7 years experience. Jan has been teaching students with various learning difficulties (learning disabilities, emotional and behavioral challenges, and mild intellectual disabilities) for 8 years. We had "shared" students in the past as children traveled from Terry's homeroom to Jan's resource room, but we rarely had time to talk about, much less plan for, the students we shared. When we finally did talk, we decided that there might be a better way to meet the needs of our students. We formed a teaching partnership with the goal of including, rather than pulling out, students with special needs. We also formed a research partnership, with the goal of studying how this inclusion would affect our students. What follows is our story.

By the second week of school, things had already gone sour for Terry. The year began with 3 fifth-grade teachers, each having 18 students, but was reduced to two teachers due to low student numbers and money. The 3 fifth-grade classes were combined into two classes of 28 students each. Terry was disgusted, upset, and angry with the education system.

It was at this point that Jan approached Terry with a plan. Having experienced success using the whole language approach in the resource setting, Jan wanted to see if her resource students would transfer what they had learned into the regular classroom setting. She felt inclusion would be the best way to find out. Terry had been teaching using the whole language approach, and Jan felt they could have a strong partnership given their similar teaching philosophies and teaching styles. Jan asked, "Terry, how would you like to try a new teaching technique this year?" Terry thought to herself, "RIGHT." She was not familiar with the term *inclusion* yet, but had her own idea. In her mind, it would mean that her already oversized class of 28 students would grow even larger and her undersized classroom would appear even smaller. She did not realize this meant teaching students who were already in the class.

Jan persevered. She suggested starting small by combining Terry's fifth-grade students with her learners with disabilities during a writing workshop and co-teaching the class. Terry began thinking that maybe two heads would be better than one, but she had reservations. She had already tried many new teaching techniques. She told Jan she would give it a trial run, but as soon as the "mix" became a problem, the partnership would have to be dissolved. Terry gave it one week.

The following is our firsthand account of what did happen—of how we formed a teaching partnership with the goal of including, rather than pulling out, students with special needs, as well as how we formed a research partnership with the goal of studying how inclusion would affect our students.

HOW INCLUSION WORKED FOR US

At first, we focused on organization of the daily writing workshop. As the weeks progressed, the routine became set. Jan and her paraprofessional, Nancy Stringer, met in Terry's classroom at 1:10 each day. The learners with disabilities who normally would be pulled out of Terry's room to go to the resource room remained in the classroom, and five other children with learning disabilities joined the class. We had a total of 32 students, ages 10 to 14. There were 6 learning disabled, 1 mildly intellectually handicapped, 2 emotionally/behaviorally disordered, 3 gifted, 2 remedial/Chapter 1, and 18 students without handicaps.

During the 50-minute daily writing workshop, one of us led a mini-lesson or discussion while the other circulated and at times interjected ideas to enhance the lesson. We provided time during the period for students to work on their writing and twice a week scheduled in-class writing conferences with students. We wanted the students to see both teachers as equal—not the "homeroom" teacher and the "special education" teacher. We both worked with all the students.

Teaching Strategies

Throughout the year we tried new approaches to teaching on a regular basis. We found the following strategies to be very effective.

Double Up Teaching. One of us would lead a discussion or teach a mini-lesson on students' writing needs while the other acted as a secretary by writing ideas and concepts on the board or overhead projector.

Example: Terry used the brainstorming technique to help students develop their writing topics while Jan wrote the student's ideas and suggestions on the board. Both of us encouraged the students to make more suggestions.

Conference Days. Twice a week, both teachers as well as the paraprofessional conducted conferences with students to review their rough drafts and final copies of their writing. This strategy allowed students to speak directly to the teachers about problems specific to their needs. This helped the teachers to better determine where individuals were in their writing development and provide specific instruction.

Example: We used lists, on clipboards, of all the students in the class. Looking for strengths and weaknesses, Jan and Terry each held conferences with 11 students, and Nancy held conferences with 10 students. We exchanged lists of students on alternate conference days so all students benefited from the three teachers' ideas and suggestions. Any student who needed immediate attention was given the opportunity to confer between scheduled conferences.

Various Settings. Both teachers' classrooms were available for different groupings. This decreased distractions for those working on writing assignments.

Example: Those students who had finished their written work went to Jan's room to enter their final drafts on the computer and design their covers. Our rooms were located side by side, which allowed easy supervision and communication.

Media Center as a Resource. Lisa Delgado, our media specialist, encouraged students to work in the media center whenever they needed to. Use of this setting worked especially well with our learners with reading and writing disabilities, as well as with students experiencing writer's block.

Example: Because of differences in personalities and interests, two specific students (one with a learning disability and one classified as a high functioning learner) experienced writer's block when paired together. We suggested going to the media center to search for topic ideas. They returned with information about tarantulas that they both agreed they would like to write about.

In another instance, two students with learning disabilities (both nonreaders) chose to work together. They wanted to do research on lions so they could write about them. The students located information on lions in the media center, and Jan read the information aloud. The students then summarized the information while Jan dictated. This did not take away from the teaching of the class because Terry and Mrs. Stringer worked with the other students.

Utilization of Each Teacher's Strengths. We each brought different areas of expertise to the team teaching. When we planned, we used the strengths of each teacher to enhance the lesson or activity.

Example: Because of Jan's computer knowledge, she got the job of assisting students in entering final drafts into the computers. The other students continued working on unfinished pieces in Terry's room. Because science was one of Terry's strong areas, she provided students with science resources and information. For example, when we studied the ocean, Terry was able to share an abundance of information and meaningful examples, which the students used in their writing.

Teaching Units. We taught several integrated units during the year, most of which had a writing component and involved children's literature. We found that picture books enabled us to involve all students, including those who could not read longer books independently.

Example: Our unit on fairy tales worked particularly well. We read different versions and books written from different points of view. We used *The Three Little Pigs* as told by Paul Galdone and *The True Story of the Three Little Pigs* as told by Jon Scieszka. Each of us read one of the tales to the class, assuming the voice and persona of the different characters. After reading several other examples, we encouraged the students to write their own alternative version of a fairy tale. Using the picture books enabled the learners with disabilities to understand the vocabulary and the story, while everyone could relate to author styles and different points of view.

Positive Modeling. We modeled sincere disagreements in front of the class. When we had a difference of opinion about a skill or instructional direction, we would openly seek a way to compromise or accept the other teacher's view. This gave students the opportunity to witness how a disagreement could be handled constructively. We did not try to hide our differences of opinion. Instead, we modeled appropriate ways to handle them.

Example: While discussing a poem, Jan interjected her interpretation of its meaning, which differed from Terry's interpretation. Terry stopped the discussion to have Jan expand her thoughts on the poem. The students witnessed how two people can disagree and yet be open to other ideas. They also learned that each person responds to literature personally.

Sharing to Increase Self-Concept. Like the other learners, our students with learning disabilities were given opportunities to share their written work. This allowed other class members to see that disabled learners have creative abilities and are intelligent members of the community. This also increased the self-concept of the disabled learners and resulted in a much better rapport between them and the regular education students.

Example: One student stands out in our minds. He was very insecure about his abilities as a writer and extremely shy in front of a group. However, he had a terrific sense of humor, a trait he recognized despite his self-doubts. He shared one of his stories with his classmates, who obviously enjoyed the story very much. It consisted of only a few paragraphs but was read with great humor. The following is an excerpt from his story:

> I was born on November 26, 1982. I had brown eyes and light colored hair. When I was 2 years old I held a dead rat in my hands. I thought it was a puppy. One time I crawled up under the house and fell a sleep with my puppy. My mom called the police. Shortly after, I crawled out under the house and they found me. When I was 4 I went swimming naked because I was only little.

Heartened by his classmates' responses, he felt comfortable enough to tell how he planned to expand on his story.

Coordinated Discipline. Discipline problems were rare, but when they did occur, such as off-task behavior or minor disagreements, one teacher acted as a mediator while the other continued with the lesson or activity. It helped that we have similar ideas concerning discipline and that we consistently reinforced these ideas.

Example: While Terry was teaching a mini-lesson one day, Stephen was working on his writing and took the spell-checker from Maria, the student sitting beside him. Stephen and Maria began fighting over who would use the spell-checker. The rule was that students had to take turns quietly or lose the opportunity to use the spell-checker for the remainder of the period. Jan was circulating the room and interrupted the altercation. Stephen was dealt with without any interruption to the mini-lesson.

Comprehensive Planning. We were fortunate to have lunch together every day. During this time, we planned what we were going to teach and who would take what role. Unfortunately, this was our only consistent time to plan. We came to believe that a minimum of one hour each week is needed for joint planning.

Example: Here are some suggestions, gleaned from our experience, to help teachers make the most of team planning time.

1. Plan lessons to meet the needs of all learners.
2. Decide who will teach the lesson.
3. Decide on a time frame for the lesson.
4. Select materials needed for the lesson.

Peer Pairing and Tutoring. We used a pairing technique for many writing activities. Often we paired students with learning disabilities with nondisabled learners. The goal was to use both students' strengths to improve each other's weaknesses. In the following section we will show how this pairing strategy worked for two pairs of students.

TWO CASE-STUDY PAIRS

Our research on the impact of our inclusion-model team teaching will focus on the four students in these pairs. By using observational notes and students' writing samples, we analyzed how the students learned from each other when paired together. We were interested in

1. Student verbal and written interactions
2. Student responses
3. Problem solving
4. Self-monitoring
5. Improvements in weak areas for both paired students

Rusty and Eric

Rusty was a gifted fifth grader who had excellent ideas but often undeveloped written expression. He was easily distracted and often misplaced or did not complete work. His writing was usually disorganized and illegible. However, he knew how to use parts of speech, punctuation, and capitalization.

Eric was a fifth-grade student with a learning disability who had been retained twice. He kept his personal belongings and assignments organized and neat. He often did not complete assigned work because he worked very slowly. He was very quiet and usually stayed on task during activities.

The first 2 days of the pairing, both students were off task; it took them a while to figure out how to work together. By the third day, Rusty and Eric began discussing the main characters and plot for their story. They disagreed on a character's fate, but eventually worked it out. The following day the boys reverted to the off-task behavior. We intervened and redirected them. Jan read their rough draft and became concerned that Rusty was monopolizing the story, because some of the vocabulary was very sophisticated. For example:

> "That's all I need Mr. Ryu," then she turned off her phonovision.
> With precision teleportation, it only took one and a half hours for the ships to get to the bounty hunter.

But when she asked Eric about the meaning of "teleportation" and "phonovision," he did understand the words. Eric's response indicated the boys were communicating. The remainder of the period, the boys worked together to plan the attack. Since Rusty's writing was often unreadable, Eric wrote the final draft of their paper.

Using work samples and other data, we charted the progress Rusty and Eric made as a result of their pairing (see Figure 3.1).

Emily and Katie

Emily had creative ideas, but lacked organizational skills. When writing, she rarely used paragraphs and had difficulty staying on the topic. When trying to decide on story ideas, she often became frustrated to the point of physical illness. However, she always remained on task and turned in stories with few errors.

Katie often wrote whatever came to mind, an approach that resulted in choppy, incomplete sentences and fragmented paragraphs. She often rushed through her written assignments without any attempts to correct grammatical errors. She was able to maintain her topic throughout her stories, but her plots often lacked continuity. Katie had been classified as a high functioning student with a mild intellectual disability.

Once paired, Katie and Emily began working on their story immediately. They sat quietly as they discussed their topic while taking notes. Katie reminded Emily to focus on one idea, and Emily explained the importance of not repeating themselves in their writing. The following day, Katie wrote while Emily assisted with spelling and the wording of

Figure 3.1. Rusty and Eric: Writing strengths, weaknesses, and development.

RUSTY	ERIC
Areas where students had adequate skills before pairing:	
1. Semantic	1. Staying on task
2. Spelling	2. Recognizing his ideas as creative
	3. Organizing his belongings,work area
Areas where students needed improvement:	
1. Losing the reader because of poor organization	1. Punctuation
2. Failing to start a new line when using dialogue and quotations	2. Capitalization
3. Unclear flashbacks	3. Verb tenses
4. Difficulty with closure	4. Spelling
5. Failing to stay on task	5. Using quotation marks
6. Losing written work before completion	6. Sentence structure
	7. Story focus
	8. Work pace
	9. Confidence in writing abilities
	10. Completing assignments
Areas where students' work improved after pairing:	
1. Difficulty with closure	1. Punctuation
2. Losing written work before completion	2. Capitalization
	3. Sentence structure
	4. Story focus
	5. Work pace
	6. Confidence in writing abilities
	7. Recognizing his ideas as creative
	8. Organizing his belongings and work area
	9. Assertiveness
	10. Completing assignment

sentences. Katie added details she felt were needed. The girls used their time effectively and constructively.

After completing their rough draft, the girls eagerly shared their story with Terry. Terry noted that the story lacked an ending. Emily and Katie brainstormed ideas about the ending and toward the end of the week agreed on an ending. By the sixth day, the girls had edited their paper and were ready to type the final draft. We were especially pleased with this pairing because Emily did not show any signs of stress during the 2-week period. The final draft showed much improvement for both girls, as shown in Figure 3.2.

CONCLUSIONS AND RECOMMENDATIONS

Based on these paired case studies, additional observations, student feedback, and analysis of all our data sources (lesson plans, teaching

Figure 3.2. Emily and Katie: Writing strengths, weaknesses, and development.

EMILY	KATIE
Areas where students had adequate skills before pairing:	
1. Imagination 2. Sentence structure 3. Writing mechanics	1. Remaining on topic
Areas where students needed improvement:	
1. Remaining on topic 2. Organization 3. Forming paragraphs 4. Stress management 5. Writing information	1. Developing story content 2. Spelling 3. Avoiding incomplete and run-on sentences 4. Organization 5. Paragraphs 6. Sentence length 7. Providing detail
Areas where students' work improved after pairing:	
1. Organization 2. Forming paragraphs 3. Spelling 4. Stress management 5. Writing information	1. Content 2. Spelling 3. Avoiding incomplete and run-on sentences 4. Organization 5. Forming paragraphs 6. Remaining on topic 7. Sentence length 8. Providing detail

notes, student drafts), we concluded that co-teaching with the inclusion of special needs students was successful. Students in our whole language classroom progressed in both their writing and social skills. Positive interactions among students with and without disabilities improved the self-concepts of all students. We feel these interactions led to greater progress for all learners because each student had something unique to offer. In this final section, we reflect on a year of teaching writing in an inclusive classroom by sharing several cautions, disappointments, student successes, and goals for continued refinement of our teaching partnership.

Cautions

Inclusion is not for everyone. The first step is to determine the compatibility of the co-teachers. Self-reflection by both teachers should include questions such as

1. Do I mind sharing my room and materials with another teacher?
2. Do I agree with the philosophies of the teacher I will be working with?
3. Do I resist giving up my ideas for the ideas of others?
4. Am I willing to put forth the extra effort that team teaching and inclusion entail?
5. Do I have to be "head teacher" in my classroom or can I co-govern?

Our situation allowed us the choice to co-teach because our principal, Pam Johns, supported the idea. This may not always be the case. We learned from various inclusion workshops and articles that some teachers do not have a choice. They may be told they have to participate, or they may not be allowed to use co-teaching with inclusion. We also learned from colleagues that some teachers did not work well together. We believe it is important that a teacher have the option of using inclusion and the choice of teacher he or she feels will be a compatible partner.

Disappointments

All students may not benefit from teamwork in an inclusive setting. This does not mean that some students will be miserable in the class, but that they may choose to work independently. For instance, in our class one student with a learning disability who showed a lot of creativity in her writing showed little improvement during the year in her weak areas of spelling and grammar because she did not want to work with others.

Another disappointment we experienced was a lack of understanding and support from some parents. One parent was not open to the idea of inclusion. She commented that her child would not want to work with a child who was functioning below her level. However, her child was always eager to assist anyone who needed assistance. We are thinking about ways that we might increase parent understanding in the future.

Student Successes

The following are some ideas and suggestions for increased success in the inclusion classroom:

1. Allow all learners the same opportunities to respond in class so that no student feels unequal. Do this by rephrasing comments and questions.

2. When students give responses, listen carefully and focus on any part of the response that could answer the question. Encourage all students to participate.

3. Always use a supportive tone when responding to student remarks. Sarcasm is never appropriate.

4. Pair students who can complement each other. For example, a creative composer with poor writing skills could be paired with a writer with proficient conventions, but limited imagination.

5. When pairing students, make sure they are compatible in attitude and personality.

6. Just as teachers should have the choice, students should be given a choice whether to work with a partner or alone. However, students who always choose to work alone can be encouraged to do some work with a partner.

7. After a large-group mini-lesson, consider conducting a smaller-group mini-lesson for those who continue to have difficulty applying the skill.

8. Encourage the development of social skills during academic tasks, such as sharing materials, speaking quietly, and so forth.

9. Both teachers should assist *all* students. Treat all students equally. Focus on the student rather than on the label that has been assigned to the student.

10. On the first day of class, explain what you're doing and why you're doing it. Be sure students understand your expectations. Tell the students that both teachers will share the same discipline plan. If one teacher makes a decision concerning discipline, the other will uphold the decision.

Goals

From these observations, we developed the following goals for the next year:

1. We will begin the year by assessing the learning styles of each student.

2. Twice monthly, we will implement lesson plans that will feature cooperative learning activities to enhance continued cooperation among the students.

3. We will arrange a minimum of one hour each week to plan our lessons together. (Lunch time wasn't appropriate.)

4. After students have worked in a cooperative group, we will ask them to answer a short questionnaire about their partners. Some questions could be:
   a. How did you learn from your partner?
   b. How did you and your partner share the workload?
   c. What suggestions did your partner offer for making your completed work more interesting to read and/or share?
   d. Did you enjoy working with this partner?
   e. Describe any problems about your partner that you felt interfered with your learning.

We both were more than pleased with the students' progress academically and socially, and with their improved self-concepts. Students with identified learning difficulties, as well as those without, gained new strategies from their peers and from two teachers who had different strengths to share. Terry found that the hesitancy she experienced at the beginning of the year turned into satisfaction. "I saw with new eyes that the 'special ed kids' were not just more work. They were a real part of my class, and the challenge of including them helped all my students." We are looking forward to new challenges in the coming years, including teaming to teach science. But whatever we teach, we will be working together for the inclusion and benefit of all students.

CHAPTER 4

Being Somebody Else:
Informal Drama in the
Fourth Grade

Carol Carr Kieffer

"Being somebody else, I think, is the most valuable part. Because you're not yourself anymore, you're trying to play someone different than yourself. You're used to being yourself all your life and then one time you get to be somebody else." Quadrika was reflecting on a year of informal drama as part of the language arts program in my fourth-grade classroom. She was an average student, she read well, and she had wonderful support at home; but she struggled somewhat in math and she was still often a phonetic speller. "Being someone else" through various drama activities really helped Quadrika grow as a reader and writer during the school year.

In my classroom, literature was a daily focus. We had reading and writing workshops, students were involved in at least 30 minutes of silent sustained reading of their choice, and read alouds were important. Monday through Thursday evenings students had 15 to 20 minutes of reading homework, when they were to read and then record what they read. Four times a year they also had a home reading book project that they shared with the class. When new book orders came in, we examined them as a class and I recommended good literature choices. After a time, students began to make their own recommendations of books that they had read and enjoyed.

The focus on reading was important to me both personally, as reading is a basic survival tool and something that I enjoy doing, and professionally, because of my school district. The school district in which I teach is in a rural area; 56% of adults over the age of 25 years are considered functionally illiterate, and 59% do not have a high school diploma. Encouraging students to read and to enjoy school, as well as to feel successful and good about themselves, was an important task for me. I incorporated informal drama as an additional way to encourage reading literature and making personal connections with reading. I also saw it as fun, a criterion for school that is at the top of student lists (see Chapter 11), and as a way to promote positive self-esteem.

As I reminisce about my own days in elementary school, I remember my sixth-grade experience. We spent weeks planning and preparing a class play of *Animal Farm* by George Orwell after we had read it and seen the movie. Even with all the time and practice we put into it, the scenery all fell to the ground halfway through our presentation, much to our dismay. This was what I thought of, as well as other major productions such as those PTO plays, when I thought of classroom drama. Yet I found, through a class at Ohio State University taught by Dr. Cecily O'Neill, that informal drama was something that could be accomplished in 20 minutes during a regular class day. This idea seemed better suited for my busy classroom schedule. In fact, many of my initial ideas came directly from drama activities in which I had participated in her class.

I chose drama as one focus of my language arts program. Drama events and activities were selected in accordance with the literature I read aloud daily to the class. During the year, I used informal drama activities to enrich my students' experiences with five picture books and one chapter book. I chose this drama program as the subject of my classroom research study.

THE RESEARCH PROCESS

As a first-year teacher at my school, I was eager to join the newly formed research team. While others investigated evaluation, inclusion, and the use of the media center, I was most interested in looking at the impact of my drama program.

My initial question in my classroom research was how drama affected students' self-esteem, writing, and group cooperation. To collect data for this research project, I wrote reflective notes after each drama activity, jotting down what we did that day as well as recording student responses, activities, and comments; then I added my own personal observations of the day's events. I analyzed both audio- and videotapes of the year's final drama activity. Three focal students gave their perceptions in interviews with me at the end of the year, which I also recorded on audio- and videotape. These same three students worked collaboratively on a drama chart on which I listed activities and events, and they designated categories and the specific facts and ideas to put into those categories (see Figure 4.1). I collected student writing, such as samples of their responses to drama debriefing questions: What did you learn about the book (yourself, drama, others) through today's drama? What did you enjoy most (least) and why? I also collected samples of an end-of-the-year writing assignment in which they described themselves as readers, which I passed along to their fifth-grade teachers.

As I began to analyze my data, I developed four categories: What students learned about themselves, what students learned about drama, what students learned about text through drama, and what students learned about others. I used all my different sources of information to see what fit into each of those four categories.

DESCRIPTION OF DRAMA ACTIVITIES AND EVENTS

We used six different drama events throughout the year; most were repeated more than once. These events were

1. *Pantomime*—Students acted without words, using gestures to express themselves.

2. *Storytelling*—Students invented creative stories to share orally, retelling specific parts or elaborating on ideas or events presented. These stories were used as an extension of the text.

3. *Buddy conversations*—Pairs of students "gossiped" about book characters or events on the phone or over the fence, to share their ideas and understanding of the book and relate it to themselves.

4. *Class or town meetings*—Students role played characters such as classmates or townspeople for these meetings dealing with a conflict or an open-ended issue presented in a specific book.

5. *Talk show*—Students role played guests on a daytime talk show, with the teacher as the host.

6. *Tableaus*—Groups of students represented a specific event from a book by creating a frozen scene or photo.

Some literature activities used only one drama event, while others used as many as three drama events. Because of the repetition of events, students became familiar with them and better able to concentrate on

Figure 4.1. Drama activities and student learning.

Books & Activities	What did you learn about yourself?	What did you learn about drama?	What was your favorite thing in drama?
Molding imaginary clay	That you can make believe with clay.	That you can make things with your imagination.	When we sat in a circle and imagined that we had clay and shaped it into anything we wanted.
The Day the Teacher Went Bananas (buddy conversations and town meeting)	In class meeting we learned not to argue with people.	That you can help people with drama.	When we had the class meeting and tried to get the monkey back.
Would You Rather (storytelling and talk show)	What I learned is we can make believe what your house looks like.	That you can pretend to be anybody and live anywhere.	When we did the talk show. It was fun because everybody had different problems.
The Seal Mother (tableau)	I learned we have to stay in role.	When you freeze it's hard to be stiff.	When we did the tableau it was fun.
The Room (tableau)	That you could stop when you are told.	That it is hard to be stiff.	We had fun freezing when Mrs. Kieffer said freeze.
When The Relatives Came (buddy conversations)	I learned that when relatives come you need room for them to sleep.	You could act talking over the phone.	It was fun when we talked over the phone.
A Stranger Came Ashore (buddy conversations, town meeting and tableau)	We had people to do stuff.	That you can pretend to be anybody.	When we went to the committees and made plans.

added challenges I provided, such as focusing on the literature, or the development of their responses or reactions.

A Blob of Clay

The first week of school I introduced the students to an informal drama situation. Our first experience was with pantomime and focused not on a book but on observation and paying attention to others. We gathered in a circle and discussed pantomime as I pulled out a large piece of imaginary clay from my pocket. As I began to form a pair of glasses, I explained to the students that they could mold this clay into anything they wished when it was finally passed to them, but they could not tell us what it was with words. Their actions had to tell all. As we began, the students were tentative. They mimicked similar things I had done; for example, they made jewelry or objects you would find on people's faces or in their hair. But as the activity progressed, they became more confident, they took more time creating things with this imaginary blob of clay, and they loved the attention of everybody staring at them trying to figure out what they were doing. No one yelled out, "Oh! She just made . . . "; they were all intent on watching, and their reactions to each piece were wonderful. Their imagination and creativity were thriving; each student was involved. It was a simple, nonthreatening event that hooked each child on drama. Later that fall, before we shared our first literature for drama, I asked them if they wanted to pretend. They were excited and ready, thinking back to the day we pantomimed with the clay blob.

The Day the Teacher Went Bananas

While reading *The Day the Teacher Went Bananas* by James Howe (1984), a book about a classroom of students who accidentally received a gorilla as their teacher, we engaged in two drama events: the buddy conversation and a class meeting. I chose this book because it deals with the familiar setting of a classroom and sets up the conflict of their favorite teacher being sent away. This allowed me to try using the "mantle of the expert" (Heathcote & Herbert, 1985), where students are given the opportunity to take on the role of the experts, a change from the more common teacher–student relationship.

Students first called other classmates on their imaginary phones to share some of their feelings about this new teacher. They broke into pairs and began talking, and some mentioned how odd this teacher was compared with other teachers they had in the past. Others shared how much they really liked this teacher because learning was fun. All groups were talking about the book, but relating to it in different ways. They came back and shared stories and then we began a class meeting.

For the class meeting I modified the situation provided at the end of the book. Rather than keep the gorilla at the zoo, they were presented with the problem of convincing their parents, principal, and zoo keeper that this gorilla should be their teacher. The students began to get excited about the drama and thought of all sorts of ways to solve the problem. They yelled out their responses, interrupting each other and hurting feelings. We stopped the drama and discussed the problem. They returned to a calmer mode and decided to split into committees to work on different ideas for solving their dilemma.

When we concluded our class meeting, we sat down as a group and discussed what went well and what kind of problems we had. They saw there was a problem with the behavior during the class meeting, and from this one drama event the class as a whole came up with two guidelines for drama that we used in our classroom for the rest of the year. One of those guidelines was to stay in role. During the class meeting someone had wanted to be the gorilla. This caused a dilemma during the activity: The character of the gorilla had not been invited to attend the class meeting, since his role in the make-believe classroom was the conflict we were trying to solve. The class decided that while it was difficult, it was important to remember that you weren't yourself, you were someone else. Our second drama rule was that everyone needed to listen. Throughout the year we continually referred to these guidelines.

Would You Rather

We focused on two activities while reading John Burningham's *Would You Rather* (1978): storytelling and a talk show. His book, dealing with impossible scenarios that actively involve readers in decision making, worked well for students devising their own stories to explain the events they chose and allowed for a unique topic for our daytime talk show. His book begins: "Would you rather have a house surrounded by water? A house surrounded by snow? Or a house surrounded by a jungle?" I began to tell them a story about how I woke up that morning and found that snow had covered everything. It was so deep I could not even open a door! I had to climb out a window, taking a shovel with me. Then I began to dig out our dog from his house. Next, I hooked him up to a sled, and he was strong enough to pull me and the sled all the way into school. In fact, he was still outside waiting for me.

Then I asked if any of them wished to share what happened to them that morning and how they arrived at school. Rodney and Cynthia both shared that they had to climb through their chimneys to reach the roof because of the high water. The dialogue that followed began something like this.

Rodney: I climbed up a ladder through the chimney, and carried my
    bed up with me.
Another student: Why did you take your bed?
Rodney: I knew it would float. It was wooden.
Another student: How did you get a bed through your chimney?
Rodney: Oh, it was collapsible.

Another child mentioned having to carefully climb onto the back of a cheetah to ride through the jungle just to get to school. A third told of his adventures riding a shark to school that went something like this.

Tommy: I looked out my window just as a shark swam by. He got close
    enough so I just jumped out and rode him into school.
Another student: How did you get here without him eating you?
Tommy: I put a stick in his mouth so he couldn't eat me.

Our talk show was very similar to a class meeting, but as I was the host, it was more teacher-directed. Students came up with creative stories and solutions when faced with some kind of large animal entering their home. One child mentioned that while she was in the bath she heard a news report that animals were on the loose and shortly afterward an elephant came running into her bathroom and drank all the water from her tub, forcing her to get out. Another student had a hippo in his bed and shared how he put antlers on it and called in his father, who happened to be a hunter. His father, however, was a poor shot and the hippo-deer got away and was running through the city somewhere.

The Seal Mother

We used the event of tableau or frozen pictures with *The Seal Mother* by Mordicai Gerstein (1986). Gerstein's book is based on folklore; a seal sheds her skin and becomes a beautiful woman who marries and has a son, but then wishes to return to her seal family. After reading the entire story we looked at a final illustration, a family photo, and discussed how we could create a still photo with class members. We practiced with volunteers making a still family photo, commenting on positive drama actions such as their seriousness, being able to freeze when needed, and use of facial expression to create a feeling or tone for the picture. We split into two groups, and each group reviewed the beginning, middle, and end of the story and came up with an event that could be represented through a still photo involving everyone in the group. Retelling the story was important as were group dynamics; everyone had to agree on a story event, then decide on roles and practice. Before freezing, each group had 5 seconds to act out what was happening to provide clues to the audience. The practice was important for developing their actions and nonverbal expressions for this nonfreeze time. Pantomime or sounds were allowed during the nonfreeze time, but students could not use conversation to express what they were doing.

The audience watched carefully as each presentation unfolded. After the first performance, students instantly began to comment.

"That's where the boy goes and visits his family under the sea."
"I see the whole seal family down there. There's the mother seal."
"We almost chose that scene. I'm glad we didn't!"
"They did a good job acting. You could see them rowing the boat out to visit."
"Yeah, there was even a fisherman out there."
"What was Shawn doing? Can your group do it over again?"

There was a repeat performance before the second group shared. Their presentation encouraged similar responses.

The Room

Students really enjoyed creating tableaus, so we refined our skills with another Gerstein book, *The Room* (1984). In this book Gerstein introduces the reader to a single room for rent and the various tenants who lived there. As each page shows a picture of the room and the current occupants, along with a short text, it lent itself well to creating tableaus of new inhabitants. Students broke into two groups and were given the task of deciding who the new occupants were and how they used the room. Then, after practice, each group shared their page of the book with their frozen picture. The students began to see themselves as experts, critiquing their practice performances and trying to improve their scene with more well-defined actions and expressions. They also found it easier to freeze quickly and for a longer period of time, as they had their previous tableau experience to which they could refer. Again, they enjoyed discovering whom the other group decided to have inhabit the room by carefully studying their performance.

When the Relatives Came

Cynthia Rylant's *When the Relatives Came* (1985) provided another opportunity for buddy conversation. This book lent itself particularly well to the dramatic event of buddy conversations, as Rylant retells the attitudes, thoughts, and feelings of the participants in a large, extended family's summer gathering. Upon completing the reading, students engaged in a phone conversation, sharing events from a recent family gathering at their home or a relative's. Some pantomimed, others used rulers or other objects from the classroom as their phones, and one group even folded paper quickly to make cellular phones.

During a whole-class discussion about things that went well and things that still needed work, students made a variety of comments. Two students said they were calling each other at home from a pay phone and that they felt like they were two adults talking, not just kids. Another group mentioned problems with call waiting as relatives were phoning back to say thanks and that they arrived home safely. Another student complimented his partner for sounding so excited and telling a lot of details of the trip.

A Stranger Came Ashore

Our last literature book for drama was a chapter book by Mollie Hunter entitled *A Stranger Came Ashore* (1975). Hunter's suspense story deals with the folklore of seals taking human form. A stranger, Finn Learson, claims to be a victim of a shipwreck washed upon the shores of the island of Black Ness. I chose this book as a read aloud for the class as it was one of my favorites. I had not planned to extend it with informal drama. Yet as we began to chart the clues about this mysterious stranger washed upon the shore of the remote Scottish island, the students became involved with the story and drama grew as a natural extension of their excitement and interest. While we were still reading the story, I stopped and asked the class if they wanted to pretend. The conflict the stranger was causing among the townspeople of Black Ness was apparent. Some villagers saw nothing unusual about him, while others did not trust him one bit. There was something odd going on, but no one was really sure what. The students were eager to get involved.

We began with buddy conversations over the fence, as such a remote village had no phones. Students were to gossip with their neighbors. "Share what you have noticed about the stranger," I prompted. "What has your neighbor noticed? Can you figure out anything else?" Students then broke into pairs and began to retell the story, adding details and, for some, developing an understanding of the plot of the story. As one group began role playing, they drank tea and talked with an accent. It was interesting to see their seriousness and hear their descriptions and comments as they pulled and expanded upon ideas from the book.

Quadrika and Laurie carried on a very detailed and animated conversation about the stranger called Finn Learson, using events from the story to direct their talk.

Quadrika: It was strange but, well, that my mother told me that there was another man that came ashore. That you know, married . . .

Laurie: I think the man took Old Da's sister.

Quadrika: Yeah, but we don't even know if Old Da has a sister and plus he's dead.

Laurie: And I remember he was trying to talk about, when his very last speech, he was still living, he was probably trying to talk about, um, Finn Learson's gonna take Elspeth down to the kingdom under the sea made of diamonds and hair . . .

Both: Gold hair.

Laurie: . . . As the roof and that's the same color as Elspeth's hair.

Quadrika: Yeah, it's interesting.

Laurie: I think, and I think if Finn Learson never came ashore that Nicol would . . . (*pausing as Quadrika pours more tea in her tea cup*) Thank you. Nicol would probably marry Elspeth.

Quadrika: Um hum. That's the same thing I think.

Laurie: The only reason that I think she likes him is because he's strong. His hands are like steel and that.

Quadrika: Who? Finn Learson? I think it's because she thinks he's rich. That's what I think.

Laurie: That's another reason right there.

Quadrika: It kills me that Elspeth's footprint, Elspeth's footprint was in the ashes.

The class gathered on the carpet and we shared some of the conversations neighbors heard about Finn Learson. We also discussed what was good about their buddy work and what needed some improvement. Groups that felt they did well thought they had shared a lot of information. Those who felt they needed some improvement said that perhaps someone in their group was not helping out as well as she or he should, while others felt that their group was not staying in role; they were not remembering that they were Black Ness villagers. The guidelines for drama that they developed at the beginning of the year, particularly staying in role, usually came up for discussion each time we began or debriefed.

Next we started the town meeting. As the mayor, I explained that this emergency meeting was called because talk was traveling through town about Finn Learson. Many people felt we needed to take the matter in our own hands and get information about Finn Learson and his purpose on the island. Students quickly took an active part in the town meeting and provided many suggestions.

Quadrika: Talk to Robbie.
Many villagers in the meeting: Yeah! Talk to Robbie!
Quadrika: Robbie knows a lot. He can give you all kinds of clues.
Villager: He's been talking to Nicol a lot.
Quadrika: Yeah, about Finn Learson. And Nicol, I heard him when they
    were talking, that Nicol was laughing at what Robbie saw.
Mayor: Robbie? Did Robbie come to this meeting tonight?
Villagers (nodding heads and pointing their fingers at one student): Yeah,
    there's Robbie. Right there.
(student playing Robbie raises hand)
Mayor: Robbie? What do you think? This young lady right here, your
    neighbor, was saying you were telling Nicol some stories and he
    was laughing. That he thinks you're a little bit weird? Some people
    say you know a lot about Finn Learson. Is that true?
Robbie: Well, yeah. That first night that he was at my house when the
    storm came he was playing weird music on my dad's fiddle and I
    saw some weird shadows on the wall. Then when I went to the geo
    a couple of days ago I heard that same music from the seal pups
    and it kind of felt strange to me. Because, I mean, it was the same
    music.
Villager: Robbie, what do you think the strange shadows on the wall
    were?
Other villagers: Yeah? How did you know it was the stranger? What did
    the music sound like?

This lively exchange continued with villagers questioning Robbie about Finn Learson and Robbie getting his answers from his book knowledge and embellishing upon answers the author had not yet provided. The villagers decided that perhaps we needed to set up a committee to interview Robbie and gather as much information from him as we could. Committees began to organize as the secretary of our town meeting took minutes. One committee was set up to find the selkie skin, so five villagers took off to devise a plan to find it and decide what to do with it after they found it. Two women decided they wanted to take Finn Learson to lunch and very slyly ask questions to get information from him. Another group decided they wanted to spy on Finn Learson, following him for a day to see what he was up to, so they went off to work on a plan. The remaining villagers concluded that it would be necessary to warn the townspeople who could not make it to the meeting about the dangers of Finn Learson so they dismissed themselves to generate posters of warning to display in the town.

Committee work was interrupted by students needing to go to pullout (remedial) programs, so the dynamics of groups changed during their work time. Quadrika, who was interviewing Robbie, and Erica, who was planning to take Finn Learson to lunch, collaborated for a short while on questions to ask. The problem solving that occurred when these two girls joined together was impressive, and Quadrika's influence was evident when all the committees reconvened at the town meeting to share their plans.

Erica was proud of the fact that she planned to ask Finn Learson some riddles at lunch because in the story he was able to solve a riddle only islanders knew. She was curious to see if he really was a clever riddle solver or if he had gotten his earlier answer from another source. She also thought to ask him about where he would recommend that she go for her vacation as he claimed to have been to many distant places as a sailor on a ship. This led Quadrika to ask Erica about the question they had developed together.

Quadrika: What about the swimming question?
Erica: Huh? (*pauses*) Swimming? Say that again.
Quadrika: Remember the swimming question? When you were going to ask him if there's a good place to swim?
Mayor: Why would you ask him a question like that?
Quadrika: I know. To, like, if he's been there swimming or not.
Erica: A selkie has to swim!

When the committee to find the selkie skin shared their plan and the map that they had drawn, the villagers began a concerned discussion about their ideas, showing their problem-solving process and higher order thinking.

Villager: Shouldn't Robbie go? I mean, Robbie's the one who's the
most concerned around here. And he's the one who's been up to
the geo and you all haven't.

Tommy: If Robbie left the house Finn Learson would spot him because
Finn Learson is sleeping in the living room. We need Robbie to
stay with Finn Learson to make sure he does not go near the geos.
The reason why I think Finn Learson might go down there, because Finn Learson was about to check on his skin to make sure it
was still down there when Robbie was down there.

Finally, we shared tableaus from the book. Their frozen pictures
had to include every member of their group. Tableaus were a favorite of
the students. Many thought it was easy because "you just need to be good
at freezing," and others enjoyed tableaus because they liked watching
from the audience, trying to solve what part of the book their classmates
were sharing. The attentiveness of the audience as each group performed showed that they were involved in watching the facial expressions, body movements, and subtle clues the performers gave them.

Upon completing the drama activities for *A Stranger Came Ashore*,
students wrote about some things that they learned from the various
events. Felicia shared what she learned about the text itself: "When you
read the book it is kind of fun but when you act it out it is more fun."
Cynthia shared that what she learned about herself was "that I can act
as if I'm someone that I'm not."

WHAT THE STUDENTS AND I LEARNED

Reflecting upon the year, I saw a great deal of growth among my students as they participated in their extended drama events. Our first
town meeting, where students were problem solving the fate of their
gorilla teacher, was very chaotic and disorganized. Our last town meeting, regarding Finn Learson, ran smoothly. Students listened to others
sharing their ideas; they knew what they wanted to find out, and they
successfully organized themselves into their groups and took on the
various tasks they had created.

Looking at the data I had collected during the year, I concluded that
informal drama promoted the following in my classroom:

1. *students learning about text*
   connection of reading, writing, speaking, and listening
   higher order thinking

2. *students learning about themselves*
   confidence and self-esteem
3. *students learning about others*
   cooperation and respect
4. *students learning about drama*
   creativity and imagination
   enjoyment of learning (fun!)

Other educators studying the use of drama in their language arts curricula have observed similar areas of learning (Chenfeld, 1987; Hoyt, 1992; Nelson, 1988). Students grew in their ability to be attentive listeners; they were interested in what was happening, and they did not want to be left out. The students also became more comfortable with public speaking. Verriour (1985) notes the value of drama in allowing children the means to take control of their own language and thinking. The students appeared to organize their thoughts better as we continued with drama, because they needed to express their ideas and themselves clearly to their classmates. Providing students with opportunities to engage in discussions that adults might experience is important for language development (Halliday, 1975).

Most of the students made personal connections with their self-selected reading and classroom read alouds. Laurie shared:

It seems like I'm in the book, and other people in the class are. . . . I want to just act out the same parts that everyone in the book did.

Denise expressed the following:

I love reading! Sometimes when I read I pretend I'm the main character! Sometimes the main character has problems, I will stop reading and start solving the problems.

And Amber wrote:

I love to read because reading is fun and adventurest because you sometimes get to feel like your in the story and you get to be the main character or even just a plain character. Being or feeling like your in the book is real fun.

Students made writing connections during town meeting committee work, with their map making, question writing, recording of responses, and warning posters. Two students even wrote creative stories during writing workshop expanding upon ideas they had developed in our drama activities with *Would You Rather*.

Higher order thinking was developed as they questioned each other about the books or their roles in drama. They asked tough questions and expected reasonable answers, as we saw in the final town meeting. They expanded their understanding of the different literature selections as they embellished their responses and created plausible solutions.

Hoyt (1992) noticed that in her room, drama allowed for "powerful new understandings of story" (p. 582). During one buddy conversation event in my classroom, I saw a student go through this same process. Her understanding of the story increased dramatically after gossiping about the book. Vygotsky (1978) uses the term "zone of proximal development" for the difference between what a child can learn independently and what that same child is capable of with the assistance of a peer or an adult. The understanding this student achieved was related directly to the discussion with her peers.

As for confidence and self-esteem, many students flourished during drama. For example, Quadrika was quite competent as a leader during drama and more often than not she took on the leadership role when we were engaged in drama activities. I noticed it also increased her confidence and creativity as a writer. She wrote a poem during writing workshop that won "Best Overall Piece" for the fourth grade at our elementary school.

Drama really helped some of those students who were a bit lower academically. It was a very successful way for them to share their knowledge of the books without struggling with the difficulties of getting their ideas across with pencil and paper. Students returning from a pull-out language arts resource program usually needed to be coaxed into working quietly on an individual project and not disrupting other students. However, these students were always eager to participate actively in the drama activities as soon as they re-entered the classroom.

Students also became risk takers during our drama activities. While they were somewhat hesitant in our initial experiences with informal drama—concerned about others' reactions and comments—as the year progressed, they quickly and excitedly engaged themselves wholly in their drama.

Regarding the development of cooperation and respect, Erica mentioned to me one day that the class kept getting better and better at drama because they were doing what they needed to do. With many strong personalities in my classroom, the collaboration that came naturally with drama gave students the opportunity to work through conflicts. Arguing was always a concern with the students when they did group work, and by the end of the year many thought they had come a long way in cooperating and respecting others and their ideas. They learned that they could really work with others in the room and not argue. One student stated, "We did it together and had fun with it."

Students became noticeably more creative and imaginative. I observed this in their writing, as some students began to show more creativity in developing their stories. One child spent a month on a piece about gnomes that was so well done and imaginative that it was the focus of one entire writing workshop sharing time. This gave other students the enthusiasm to attempt unique forms, including fantasy, with their writing.

Just being able to transform oneself into an inhabitant of the island of Black Ness required imagination. The pair of girls who felt they needed to use a British accent and "take tea" as they gossiped generated those ideas on their own. Another student who was very serious and quiet was able to unleash himself and take on a whimsical quality within our drama experiences.

Finally, it was obvious that the children had fun and enjoyed learning. Quadrika would always clap her hands and comment, "Yeah, drama!" whenever I said, "Let's pretend." In fact, in her interview she commented that she wanted to tell people coming into fourth grade next year that they would get to do drama and drama was "really, really fun."

For all these reasons, I valued drama as a part of my curriculum. But I was even more convinced that drama was an important component of my language arts program when three students reflected on what they saw as the value of drama. Quadrika stated that "being somebody else is the most valuable part." Tommy explained, "A kid learns how to use his imagination." And Laurie said, "It helps you learn and it helps you, I mean when you read, it, it's helping you read."

Just like that imaginary blob of clay that each student molded into a unique use the first week of school, drama experiences became something different for each child. After a year of shaping and reshaping their experiences, they had something important that they could take with them into the future.

CHAPTER 5

The Playground Experience

Ruth Rowland

I was lost in thought one day at recess, staring at the old rusty slide. Joshua raced by, then stopped and asked what I was doing. "I'm analyzing our playground because I'm on a committee to plan improvements." I had joined the task force at a PTO meeting in the fall. This group of parents and teachers would decide on how to improve the present playground and what new equipment should be purchased. Joshua quickly began making suggestions. "You would make a good committee member," I told him. "You should join the committee!" He was excited and began looking around the playground with new eyes, commenting on existing and anticipated equipment. This attracted other members of the class. By the time we returned to the classroom my whole fourth-grade class wanted to join the adults on the task force. One child commented, "After all, the playground is for kids so we should help plan it."

BRAINSTORMING AND PLANNING

The project began in earnest as we brainstormed together ways to study this topic and make informed decisions. Because I had not preplanned this project, our discussions were really give and take. By the end of the day, we had generated many opportunities for integrated learning. This project would involve cooperative learning, math problem solving, interviews, researching and data collecting, letter writing, and public speaking. As it turned out there were even more opportunities than I originally thought. The experiences continued to evolve as the year went on, and they gave us a meaningful, real-world foundation on which to build our learning (Wigginton, 1985).

We knew immediately that for our recommendations to have substance we needed to know what the rest of the school thought about this project. In small groups the students worked to develop interview questions that we felt could be used for all grades. I wrote all the suggestions on the board. We discussed the clearest way to word the questions; several students copied the information so that I could type it as a formal interview sheet. We planned to use the interview questions not only in our school but also in other schools where there were playgrounds we wanted to visit and evaluate.

This was our final list of questions.

1. What is your favorite piece of equipment on the playground?
2. Why is it your favorite?
3. What piece of equipment do you dislike?
4. How do you like the size of your playground?
5. What would you do to improve your playground?
6. Do you need more space for games on your playground?
7. What would you like to add to your playground? Why?
8. Do you have shade on part of the playground? Do you think it is necessary?
9. Do you think a fence is important for a playground?
10. What equipment do students most likely get hurt on?
11. Do you have a water fountain on your playground?

INTERVIEWING STUDENTS AT OUR SCHOOL

There were 22 students in my class so I divided the class into seven groups, letting them select the grade level that they wanted to interview. Each student interviewed three students per grade level, since in our school there are three classes of each grade. They recorded responses on the interview sheets. It was more difficult to arrange interviews with the fifth grades, because they changed classes for different subjects. My students ended up interviewing them at fifth-grade recess. Usually, however, we used the writing workshop time to conduct the interviews and to do much of the writing throughout this project.

Observing the students compile the information from the interviews was especially interesting, because that process gave me new insights on how my students learned. They were surprised that even younger students had definite opinions of what a good playground should have. They enjoyed sharing their findings in their grade-level groups and then with the rest of the class. I modeled graph making by recording the information by grade level on large chart paper that we saved as documentation.

Through discussion, graphing, and summarizing, we learned that

the primary grades had different interests and favorites from the intermediate grades. There seemed to be a need for two playgrounds or at
least two areas according to the ages of the classes. When we finished
collecting all the information, we summarized it across the grades with
a graph showing favorites (see Figure 5.1, a computer reproduction of
the large chart).

During this initial part of our project we took a field trip to Gainesville to attend a ballet. Our picnic lunch was at a community park that
had a beautiful playscape with multiple colors and activities. The students played on this equipment with great enthusiasm and fell in love
with the spiral slide. Everyone decided that this was a must for our new
playground.

COMMITTEE WORK

Interviewing students and examining equipment gave us the basis to
begin committee work to summarize our thoughts and findings. I pro-

Figure 5.1. Playground survey graph.

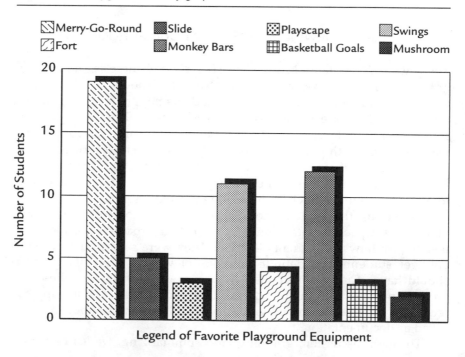

Legend of Favorite Playground Equipment

posed four groups with individual tasks: Group 1—analyze all the phases of the park playground; Group 2—examine many catalogs with all types of playground equipment to get ideas and costs; Group 3—make individual graphs for each grade level to share with interested parties; and Group 4—take the information from our previous investigation of the size of our playground and sketch possible areas for activities and equipment. Students chose which group they wanted to join, with some suggestions from me to ensure groups that had the likelihood of succeeding.

The group that analyzed the Gainesville playground had to go by memory so they discussed it with members of the class informally. Then each member of the group wrote a summary report. The brainstorming that occurred among the group members and with members of other groups helped them write with clarity. They shared their summaries orally with the rest of the class.

The group that made the graphs (Group 3) used large chart paper and bright colors. Each member made two graphs, being careful to have even spacing and accurate labeling. We had done graphing before but this experience seemed to be more meaningful to them. Not only were they recording information that they had collected, but they wanted these graphs to support their suggestions when they were presented. All members of other groups stopped by to look at the graphs as they were made.

The group that chose to sketch the playground (Group 4) didn't have the same success as the other groups. They were busy drawing pictures of swings and slides without using the information we had collected. As a math lesson the whole class had measured our existing space. We had averaged the findings so this group could use the information. But the group had difficulty staying on task and keeping in mind the ultimate goal. They drew underground tunnels and swimming pools. I realized that because I allowed each student to choose his or her preferred group, this one lacked a range of ability and discipline. They needed more guidance from me than I could give while managing four ongoing groups.

Group 2 really got into researching the playground equipment catalogs. They found one fantastic playscape after another and eagerly shared their discoveries with others. They compared prices for similar equipment. I observed mental math in action as they subtracted rounded numbers in their head. I made a note to myself at this point that all the students would benefit from such an opportunity to construct knowledge in a meaningful way. When the group finished, the catalogs were littered with self-sticking tags. Throughout the rest of the year this group was our resource when we referred to the catalogs.

SHARING OUR FINDINGS

The first opportunity to share the information with anyone outside our class came at a Local School Advisory Committee (LSAC) meeting. This organization of parents, community members, teachers, and administrators has strong input into school-system decisions. Seven students volunteered to present the information at this evening meeting attended by the superintendent, parents of my students, other parents, teachers, and Pam Johns, our principal. They worked very hard during writing workshop, drafting, conferencing with each other, and revising their speeches. They focused on content revision, rather than editing, since they were reading their speeches; otherwise I would have had them correct their spelling. Carrie's speech from the catalog research group is a good example.

> Hi my name is Carrie. We took the information we learned from the surveys and looked in the catalogs. We were looking for pieces of equipment that were the favirotes and safe for children. There are several major companies that sell playground equipment. The slide support tube is an additional saftey and convienance feture that only burke offers. A support tube helps children prepare to slide down safely. Almost everyone likes spiral slides. Landscape Structure Inc offers spiral slides 72" heigh. The playbooster is loaded with sevaral play events and activity panels. The play booster has alot of shade under the arched roofs. It has two sets of talking tubes that provide alot of fun. we have these catalogs that the comittee might like to look at. All the companies offer equipment that can be added onto in phases, as the money is raised. Thank you for listening to my speech.

I made suggestions to make sure that they included all the information they wanted to get across; at the same time, I wanted to be sure that their voices came through in the writing. For example, Lynsay reported:

> Hi. My name is Lynsay and I'm here to tell you what the third forth and fifth graders like on our playground. We've got a couple of things we've noticed. . . . The fifth grade has a very strong preference for the swings, We feel the reason they do is because they're bigger than the other students and don't get hurt as easy. The fourth grade was the only students that liked the playscape, but we have no idea why.

This brought laughter from the adults because she was so sincere and natural. I was pleased to see how poised these students were in speaking to this large audience. They knew what they were talking about and were eager to share it. I showed slides of the present playground, the park playground we visited, and scenes of students measuring the perimeter of our playground. It was apparent as these adults listened intently that my class was now a viable part of this task force.

VISITING OTHER SCHOOLS' PLAYGROUNDS

The next phase of our project was to visit other schools to ask their opinions about their playgrounds and give us an opportunity to test out those playgrounds. The students eagerly looked forward to playing on the playgrounds. We decided to use our original interview questions. I arranged to visit two schools in the next county; both schools had playgrounds designed by the architect we planned to hire, Lawrence Steuck. Teachers at both schools were very cooperative and arranged to have students available to be interviewed. Winterville Elementary School was our first stop. They had two separate playgrounds, a primary one with both a wooden playscape and a vinyl coated metal playscape, and an intermediate playground that included a large wooden playscape, a basketball court, and a fitness trail. We were really impressed by the facilities and the host students who escorted us around and answered questions. There were representatives from each grade who behaved like professional guides. These students were candid during our interviews, which was very helpful later on when my students spoke with the playscape architect.

After a visit to a pizza place for lunch, we headed for the next school. Rain cut short the play on the two wooden playscapes. We then interviewed two fourth-grade classes. Some of my students had less than successful interviews, which seemed to be a good lesson in itself. They carried on politely even though they weren't getting the cooperation they expected. Suggestions by these students were, however, very valuable when we talked with the architect. He learned what the students thought of parts of the design that he had believed to be successful. His concept of a playground was that it should be educational. Students wanted it to be fun.

Before we summarized our interview data, students wrote thank you letters to each school. They were actually eager to write and took pride in using their best handwriting; they could picture the people who would be reading their letters. It showed me that this type of

letter-writing activity—to real people for real purposes—was most beneficial. A few students even searched vocabulary word lists from their
reading journals to find the best words to express themselves, without
my suggesting it! Figure 5.2 shows Crystal's letter.

We worked as a class to organize the new information. I made large
charts representing each school we had visited. A committee of parents
came to our classroom to listen to our findings. This time six students
who had not spoken at the last meeting volunteered to share the information. They didn't write down what they would say but did a great
job explaining in a spontaneous way. I was especially pleased when one

Figure 5.2. Crystal's thank-you letter.

Dear Mrs. Sturdivant,

Thank you for letting us come to your class. You had some students that were very helpful. Your playground is very nice. We will assuredly use the information when we plan our playground. Your school was a lot bigger than I imagined. Your school was very neat and tidy.

Yours Truly,
Crystal D. Racney

student with behavioral problems stood up and spoke to the group. This opportunity helped him receive the recognition that meant so much to him.

GRANT WRITING

At one of the LSAC playground meetings a parent brought in a pamphlet from Target Stores about grants to nonprofit organizations. She wondered if my class would consider writing a grant proposal to help fund the playground. The next day, Lynsay approached me and asked if she could write the grant. An excerpt from her learning log states:

> One day I was at an LSAC meeting when one lady was talking about a Target grant. So I decided to ask Mrs. Rowland about writing the grant. I was kind of scared, but when Mrs. Rowland suggested that I get another person to help me I said alright. When Joshua got to writing we decided to get Crystal in so that's how it happened.

These students began 2 months of hard work—brainstorming, writing several rough drafts, and conferencing with me, the Curriculum Director of the county who is an experienced grant writer, and Pam Johns, our principal. They used the computers in the school's Publishing Center to write the grant. I was so proud that I never had to touch the computer to help them. They did all of their own corrections and additions, too. The proposal, as they wrote and submitted it, is in the Appendix.

We learned during the summer that we did not get the grant (in fact no grants were awarded to public schools). However, the local store was so impressed with our students that it gave us $50. We are now looking for other places to send our proposal.

THE LEARNING PROCESS

The opportunities for learning that occurred during the year were more numerous than I had anticipated. Integrating math, social studies, and language arts gave the students real reasons for learning, made more efficient use of class time, and helped students discover how these subjects are related (Greenleaf, 1990). I saved all the paperwork, from the first day forward, which has given me documentation of how the project developed and how the students grew in knowledge and confidence. I made charts each step of the way as we brainstormed, collected information, and analyzed it. For example, the students' LSAC speeches gave me insights into their ability to summarize and interpret information, to draw conclusions, and to write an informative paper, as Andrea's speech on "Student Dislikes" demonstrates:

> We found that the fort was on every dislike list. We feel that this means that alot of students do not play on it. The younger grades did not like the Monkey Bars probally because the students are too small to use the one we have. The younger grades said they dislike our swings. Again we think it is because they are dangerous. In the younger grades 4 students did not like the merry go-round. Perhaps the base ground under the merry go round should be safer. The older students mentioned the tires. We feel the tires need to be removed from the playground.

Any time there was an opportunity to have a math lesson pertaining to the project I tried to include it. Planning our field trip required work to decide costs of lunch, bus expense, and film for taking pictures of playgrounds. The class worked in small groups, then shared their information with the rest of the class. As Figure 5.3 shows, we had an averaging lesson when we measured the playground. Since each group got different measurements for the dimensions of the playground, we figured the average. We also had a quick application of rounding numbers (e.g., 69 to 70) and figured the area in square meters.

The variety of writing opportunities ranged from making notes in individual groups to the formal grant proposal. Students had many experiences as they wrote to learn (Greenleaf, 1990). One of the most challenging was writing the responses as they were interviewing other students. I observed intense concentration in their faces as they took their job very seriously. Writing with real experiences motivated even the disinterested students.

STUDENT REFLECTIONS

By the middle of the following year, the students were playing on their new playground. Because of the students' sustained interest, research, and hard work, the adults on the committee moved quickly and secured donated materials; many parents, students, and teachers worked on the

Figure 5.3. Joshua's averaging worksheet.

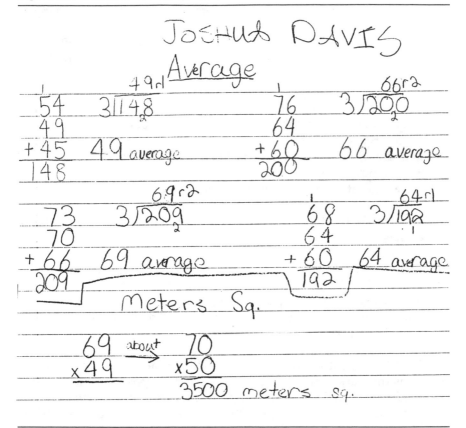

actual construction. We now have two beautiful, inviting playgrounds, one for the younger students and one for the older ones. Based on our students' research, and their advice to the architect, the upper grade playground has many movement activities, including a swinging rope bridge. The students rush to play on it every recess; I'd estimate that more than double the number of students (especially the girls) play on it instead of just standing around as they used to do. Even without the grant, we have a really successful playground for $4,200. The children are still waiting for $3,000 more to be raised, so they can get the spiral slide. We all feel a tremendous sense of accomplishment, and everyone is amazed at the level of responsibility and quality of work of our students. One mother, a member of the LSAC committee, told me, ''It has been a wonderful experience for my child to see something go from an idea into a reality, and to be such an important part of making it happen.''

At the end of the year I asked the students to write briefly their impressions of this project. The replies reinforced my belief that students enjoy learning through active involvement.

"The project was alot funner than opening my math book."
"The best thing I like abot this was visiting the schools."
"I liked interviewing kids."
"I liked doing graphs instead of doing pages of math because we learned how to do them."
"I hope we can still continue this in the 5th grade."

Students also learned how to take responsibility, and they were proud of themselves.

"It taught me how to find things out about accomplishing projects."
"Taking part in this has made me feel responsible."
"I like to have a voice and a part of this."
"This was hard work and we are still not finished. This is important to me to have a voice in this."

Another benefit of the project, which spread across most of the year, was the class unity and sense of shared purpose that developed. One student reflected, "I think doing this playground work brought the class more together." I was especially pleased that every student had an important role, regardless of ability.

This project has had a lasting effect on my teaching. It taught me not to underestimate what students are capable of doing, but to give them the chance to learn and prove what they can accomplish (Wigginton, 1985). I believe that real experiences are so valuable for students. I am always looking for new opportunities that we can investigate as a class.

APPENDIX

**South Jackson Elementary
School Grant Proposal**

*Written by
Crystal Rainey
Lynsay Roberts
Joshua Davis
Students of Mrs. Rowland's Fourth-Grade Class*

Project Description

We are a fourth-grade class from South Jackson Elementary School, located between Jefferson and Athens, Georgia, on Route 129, in Jackson County. South Jackson is a rural school with 371 students. It is a community center for surrounding homes and families. South Jackson has an after-school program and is beginning a Pre-K class for 4 year olds.

Our school is in definite need of safer and newer playground equipment. The playground is inadequate, or not very fun. We have 15 pieces of equipment, which include two boring old slides that came from the Navy School's old playground. A home made fort which often has boards that come off making it unsafe. In fact, one-third grade student fell off and broke her arm last year. The swings we have are metal and are sort of caged in, with two bars in the front and two in the back. Two of the bars in front are used to get the swing going. Often as you would try to swing or try to stop, you continuously would hit your head. "OUCH." The other pieces are just as unfit as the ones described above. We have one small playscape, and the rest of the stuff is rusted and squeaks whenever it moves.

Supporting Documents

We joined the playground task force Local School Advisory Council as student representatives. Our goal is to redesign and rebuild our playground. Three or four kids get hurt on our playground each year other than cuts and scratches. We want to improve the safety record of injuries on our playground.

Our class interviewed a sample number of students in each grade of our school. We made graphs to show their favorite playground pieces, and their dislikes. We then visited two schools in Clarke County that have well-equipped playgrounds. We interviewed students at both schools and compiled this data to gain ideas about what to build on our playground.

We want a nice big playscape with a spiral slide and other fun activities. We have a vision of getting a "Fun 'n' Fitness" area on our playground. Our group searched through catalogs and found several choices of playground equipment that will fit this need.

Our new playground hopefully will be used as a community park for families in this section of Jackson County. It may draw more kids to the after-school program with newer and safer equipment. It would make the parents of the students at South Jackson happy because their children would be safe at school and be having fun too, if we got new playground equipment. We would like to get finished with this project by August of 1994, the start of the new school year.

Our proposed budget is $18,000 dollars, so we can get an adequate playscape with a safe base. We are having fund raisers such as faculty/ parent basketball games and selling flower bulbs. If Target does not approve this grant, it will take us many more years to fund the new playground.

As fifth graders we plan to interview parents and students at the meetings to see how much they use the new facilities. We plan to make posters now, and use the posters when we get the new facilities. We will use these posters to encourage the people of Jackson County to use our playground as a community center. When we get the new facilities we will keep track of how many kids get hurt to see if the amount of injuries is lower.

Closing Statement

We want a cyclone slide which costs around $4,000.00. The playscape we are planning to get costs around $15,500.00. When we get the new facilities, we plan to make posters to encourage the people of Jackson County to use our playground as a community center. We hope to get this grant!

Business Donors

S.C.T. Yarns gives the school $1,000.00 per year for educational needs. Bell's in Jefferson gives food items for different occasions, like Field Day, and the Spring Fling. The PTO playground task force works to get money for our school. The PRE-K grant for $2,000.00 will be used for the younger student's playground equipment. The school's general fund is giving us $1,000.00 toward our playground this year.

PART III

AUTHENTIC ASSESSMENT

CHAPTER 6

A Schoolwide Study
of Assessment Alternatives

Gwen Bailey

I began this study with the question, "Should assessment be designed to match instruction, or should instruction be designed to match assessment?" The faculty at South Jackson became involved in developing alternative modes of assessment once we realized that the standardized assessment instruments, especially basal tests, being used did not match our instructional methods. The school had changed from a traditional textbook approach to a whole language philosophy of teaching. We began to look at portfolios as a means of assessing students in the area of language arts, so that assessment would match instruction. Standardized modes of assessment show which child knows more, while alternative modes of assessment show what an individual child knows. As elementary school teachers, we need to know what each child knows so we can plan instruction to focus on individual needs.

MOVING FROM BASALS TO WHOLE LANGUAGE

For years, teachers at South Jackson Elementary used a basal text for the teaching of reading and a program called Individualized Language Arts (ILA) for writing. The ILA program involved such teaching techniques as story starters for creative writing, and slotting techniques where students filled words in blanks in sentences. As we studied whole language, teachers began using more tradebooks or "real books" for reading instruction and writing workshops for writing instruction. Although we had changed the instructional methods, the district still required the basal testing program for reading.

Because we were dissatisfied with this incongruity, we decided to form an evaluation task force (ETF) to explore alternative modes of assessment that would more closely match the whole language approach to teaching reading and writing. One representative from each grade level took part in this task force, and I was elected chairperson. Once the task force developed a proposal, the next step was a faculty vote; this is a required procedure established by our school governance process. We needed at least 80% approval from the faculty for implementation.

A major goal of the ETF—to have meaningful instruction and assessment occurring together—can be summarized by Valencia's (1990) statement: "Teachers and students do not have to take time from real reading for assessment. Real reading is used as an assessment opportunity" (p. 338). We began our search for alternative means of assessment that reflected this belief. We examined examples of portfolio assessment used by the Bellingham (Washington) Public Schools. After a year of research, UGA workshops, and numerous grade-level meetings, the task force made several recommendations to be implemented the following school year. We suggested a checklist of skills, as shown in Figure 6.1, to take the place of the basal testing program at each grade level. In conjunction with the checklist, teachers would keep portfolios for reading and writing. The task force also recommended a list of items to be included in the portfolios. This list is shown in Figure 6.2, the letter we used to report back to our faculty. We wrote to the superintendent requesting a waiver of basal testing in order to field test the alternative assessment processes (Figure 6.3). With over 80% faculty approval, and permission from the school district administration to conduct a pilot study, we began using portfolio assessment in place of basal testing the next school year.

ASSESSING ALTERNATIVE ASSESSMENT

As chairperson for the ETF, I was given the responsibility of studying the effectiveness, strengths, and weaknesses of the new procedures during the pilot year. I determined the usefulness of these new assessment instruments through teacher interviews after the first grading period and from an evaluation questionnaire consisting of the following questions:

How have you been using portfolios this year?
What are you including in the portfolios, and how did you decide?
What information does the portfolio give you that you need to evaluate and grade the children?
What information does the portfolio *not* give you that you need to evaluate and grade the children?

Figure 6.1. Initial second grade reading checklist.

Second Grade Reading Assessment					
Student_____ Below level					
On level					
/ - skill taught, X - mastery Above level					
GRADING PERIOD	**1**	**2**	**3**	**4**
READING STRATEGIES/COMPREHENSION				
Distinguishes between fantasy and realism				
Learns, understands and utilizes new vocabulary				
Recognizes explicit: __main idea __details __sequence __cause-effect				
Recognizes implicit: __main idea, __details, __sequence. __cause-effect				
Identifies main character(s)				
Makes predictions				
Follows written instructions				
Classifies and categorizes words				
Interprets syntactic and semantic relationships				
Recognizes auditory similarities and differences in words including single vowel sounds and rhyming patterns				
Uses word families, consonant and single vowel letter relationships in word recognition				
LITERATURE				
Recognizes various literature forms: fiction, nonfiction, poetry				
Recognizes that literature reflects human experience				
Responds creatively to literature				
REFERENCE SKILLS				
Uses book parts, including title page, table of contents, and glossary as information sources				
READING PARTICIPATION				
Chooses books willingly:				
self-directed				
with teachers guidance				
Demonstrates interest in various genres				
Reads a variety of materials				
Sustains interest in a book				

Figure 6.2. Task force report to faculty.

To: The S. J. E. faculty
From: The evaluation task force

The evaluation task force has been working on reading and writing portfolios for the 1992–1993 school year. We have developed a skills checklist for writing and reading.

Writing: We would like to include the following items in the writing portfolios.

1. The writing evaluation checklist
2. Five writing samples: one from the first week of school, and one from each quarter. This should represent the student's best work for the quarter
3. A self-assessment (examples will be given for you to look over, of course you can make up your own self-assessment)
4. Anecdotal notes

Reading: Many teachers would like to do away with the magazine test. We are proposing to use a reading assessment checklist instead of giving the test. This checklist would be part of a reading portfolio with the following items included.

1. The reading assessment checklist
2. A reading log (age appropriate)
3. Responses to literature
4. Self-assessment
5. Any teacher made test
6. Anecdotal notes

With faculty approval, the evaluation task force will present the above suggestions for reading evaluation to the central office staff. Our intention is to waive the use of the magazine test for the 1992–1993 school year. One area which Dr. Guerke says must be addressed is the reading level of the child. You can see on the checklist that an area has been left for checking above, on, or below level. She is concerned about students transferring to other schools. We must be able to put the reading level (such as 2.5). How can we come up with this level if we are not giving the basal test? Any suggestions for addressing this problem will be welcome. Please let us know what you think of the above proposals for portfolio assessment. We will discuss all of these areas at a faculty meeting during post-planning. If we do not receive a waiver on the magazine test, we would not expect you to keep the reading checklist. However, if we do receive a waiver, you would have to use the checklist if you do not give the magazine test.

Gwen Bailey
Chairperson E. T. F.

Figure 6.3. Request for school district waiver.

Dear [Superintendent],

For the past two years, the South Jackson Faculty has worked on the implementation of whole language teaching strategies. Teachers have observed students spending more time reading, reading for enjoyment and information, as well as challenging themselves to read harder books. As teachers began to use children's literature to teach reading, they became aware of the inappropriateness of our current evaluation techniques (the basal magazine test). Assessment should correspond to the teaching method being used in the classroom. The basal tests tend to force teachers to focus on skills separate from the context of real reading.

During the 1991–1992 school year, the evaluation task force (ETF) worked on alternative assessments to the basal test. The ETF developed a reading checklist for each grade level. The checklist would be a part of a reading portfolio which would include the following items:

1. The reading assessment checklist
2. A reading log (age appropriate)
3. Responses to literature
4. Self-assessment
5. Any teacher made test
6. Anecdotal notes

The faculty would like to request a waiver of the magazine test for the 1992–1993 school year. By being free to use an alternative assessment instrument, we believe we will have a better indicator of our students' abilities and will allow more time for actual reading. If we receive a waiver, all teachers who do not use the magazine test would use the reading checklist and portfolio. The 1992–1993 school year would be a pilot year for the alternative assessment methods mentioned. As the year progresses, the ETF would take feedback from the faculty on the appropriateness of the checklist and revisions would be made as needed.

As chairperson of the ETF, I would like to request a meeting with you to discuss the above waiver. I have enclosed a copy of our checklist for your review. Because of vacation plans, I will not be available to meet with you until August the fourteenth or at preplanning. I will call your office for an appointment.

Sincerely,

Gwen M. Bailey

Did the information you collected in the portfolios affect your instruction in any way? If so, how?
What other information have you gathered for evaluation that is not in
the portfolio?
Do your students evaluate their own work? If so, how?

Strengths: More Information About Readers and Writers

The responses teachers provided indicated areas of both strengths and
weaknesses in the portfolios and checklist. Teachers were using the
portfolios in a variety of ways, but the majority were including the
items recommended in the ETF guidelines. These early portfolios were
primarily a collection place for samples of students' work, tests, language arts surveys, checklists, and anecdotal notes on students' progress. One teacher noted that she collected work students ''feel proud
about.''
Teachers used the portfolios to show the progress a student was
making and to provide feedback to students and parents. When it came
to using portfolios for the purpose of evaluation and grading, teachers
indicated that portfolios showed the amount of progress a student had
made, as well as ongoing reading and writing strengths and difficulties.
Teachers were able to document even gradual progress, which was especially important when working with students with learning disabilities.
One first-grade teacher said that she could determine where students were in reading by the difficulty of the books they read, as well as
from information gathered on the reading checklist and from her anecdotal notes. She was able to use these sources of information to gauge
her students' reading expression, decoding skills, and growth in vocabulary. Other teachers reported that the assessment processes helped
gather evidence of comprehension issues, word order, sentence order,
and grammatical usage. Overwhelmingly, teachers found the extensive
information they were gathering helpful in developing a fuller picture
of their students as readers and writers, and much preferred these
teacher-developed procedures to the basal testing program.

Concerns: Grading and Self-Evaluation

There were, however, some areas of dissatisfaction. Teachers noted that
they had some problems using the reading checklist. The checklist was
double work because information was being transferred from anecdotal
notes and work samples at the end of a 9-week period, rather than

serving as an on-the-spot method of recording literacy behaviors. Teachers recommended revising the scoring system on the checklist; they also felt the checklist was too long.

The teachers' primary concern with the new assessment techniques was with translating the wealth of information into a single grade. The county requires all teachers to assign grades. There were no clear-cut A, B, C, D, F guidelines to go along with the new assessment procedures. A first-grade teacher summed up the frustration of many when she wrote: "The portfolio is helpful in evaluation, but not grading. It goes well with the checklists on report cards, but I still have difficulty assigning a grade."

Other teachers looked at the grading issue a bit differently (although almost everyone found grading problematic). A fourth-grade teacher noted that the portfolio provided a "reference point for where they [the students] began and offers substantiation for what could be a very subjective grade." The samples of student reading and writing, along with related teacher observations, show parents the progress their child is making in school. Several parents indicated their appreciation to teachers. Similarly, teachers in Rolling Valley School in Springfield, Virginia asked parents about portfolios and found that parents "felt that portfolios as a tool allowed them to see the basis for the grades in the same way the teacher saw them" (Areglado & Dill, 1992).

Many of the teachers at South Jackson would prefer not to assign grades; they would prefer to use a report card that was more developmental in nature. However, letter grades are required by the county. The same year the ETF was formed, the county organized a committee to revise report cards for the five elementary schools in the district. The ETF submitted samples of nongraded report cards to the countywide committee for consideration. Our school's representative on the report card committee shared our views concerning the use of nongraded report cards, especially in the primary grades.

The views of South Jackson (and Benton) teachers were not the predominant ones on the committee. Although they changed the first-grade card to a more developmental report, the second- through fifth-grade card continued to report the traditional letter grades for each subject. Since all schools within the county must use the same report card, and the countywide report card committee determined that traditional report card grading was most appropriate for the majority of schools in the county, we had to continue with a system that did not match our new assessment strategies.

Another concern was with students evaluating their own work. Although some teachers were involving students in self-evaluation, the

involvement seemed limited. Some teachers held private and peer conferences to increase students' involvement in evaluating their work.
One kindergarten teacher used conferences with a small group of students to help them pick their "best" writing samples to keep in their
portfolios. A few teachers responded that their students were not involved in the evaluation process, but that they would like to learn more
about how to work with students on self-evaluation. However, for the
most part, teachers were the primary evaluators.

Revisions: Improving the Checklist

It was clear to us that we needed to revise the checklist and that teachers
needed further guidance on student involvement in portfolio assessment. What we had developed was more like an assessment folder than
a true portfolio. Teachers made very helpful suggestions for change,
including condensing the checklist, adding a comment area, revising
the scoring system, eliminating divisions of the checklist by quarters,
and focusing on what students need to be able to do when they read
versus mastery of specific skills.

   Once I completed the interviews and summarized the questionnaire
findings, the task force began to meet again to determine how best to
address the problems we were having with our new assessment. The
biggest concern, assigning letter grades, could not be changed at the
school level, so we added an area to record an estimated reading level
and how the teacher determined the level. Most of the work of the task
force focused on revising the reading checklist. We added an observation area so teachers could use their own scoring system and make
comments. We devised a three-time asterisk system (/, x, *): The teacher
added a slash each time she observed the student using the skill, so the
first observation she made one slash (/), the second she crossed it (x),
and the third she completed the asterisk (*). A strategy was considered
mastered when students correctly demonstrated its use in three different observations. Although many reading strategies were still included
on the checklist, we broadened its scope and condensed it based on
specific teacher feedback, as shown in Figure 6.4.

   The work of the Evaluation Task Force is ongoing. Although we
have worked for 2 years to develop alternative modes of assessment,
the task force will continue to refine assessment procedures. Several
areas still need to be addressed. We are still concerned that many students are not involved in the portfolio process and engage in very little
self-evaluation (see Chapter 7 for a notable exception). This aspect is
critical to the use of portfolios (Graves & Sunstein, 1992), and we are

Figure 6.4. Revised second grade reading checklist.

Second Grade Reading Assessment

observation 1   /
observation 2   X
mastery (3)   *

Student_____

	Observations	
READING STRATEGIES		

Applies a variety of reading strategies:
   sounds out unknown words
   uses context clues		

Self-correction: does not self-correct stops at unknown words goes back & self-corrects successfully attempts to self-correct		
READING COMPREHENSION		

Reads with understanding:
   main idea
   logical predictions
   follows written instructions
   retells/summarizes
   discusses aspects of book		

READING PARTICIPATION		
Chooses to read		
Sustains interest in a book		
Chooses appropriate books		
REFERENCE SKILLS		

Identifies and uses:
     title page
     table of contents
     glossary
     copyright date
     book summary		

Instrument	Date	Reading Level

hoping to grow in our ability to involve students. In addition, we need to determine, as a school, specifications about which portfolio items should be sent on to the next teacher. The task force will continue to meet to discuss these needs and to refine the evaluation process.

CONCLUDING THOUGHTS

I began with a question, "Should assessment be designed to match instruction, or should instruction be designed to match assessment?" When teachers used whole language instruction to teach reading and a basal assessment tool to evaluate reading, they spent a great deal of time in assessment procedures. This not only frustrated students and took time away from actual reading, but also provided little meaningful information to guide instruction. Anecdotal notes, checklists, conferences, and portfolios provided much of the information needed to assess progress and were much more directly related to instruction.

Perhaps a more appropriate question would have been, "What is the relationship between assessment and instruction, and how do they influence each other?" What became apparent is that assessment and instruction are not separate entities but directly affect each other. Portfolios made teachers more aware of student needs. Anecdotal notes from conferences provided teachers with guidance for the planning of class mini-lessons as well as for individual instruction in subsequent conferences. One special education teacher noted, "My instruction is based on the needs exhibited in the work samples contained within the portfolios." Because portfolios containing a broad range of assessment measures provide an ongoing picture of a student's progress, teachers are better able to plan appropriate lessons rather than teaching a lesson simply because it is the next chapter in the book ("If this is March, we must be doing adverbs").

The action research of the ETF had a direct impact on the daily lives of both teachers and students. We have eliminated countless hours of inappropriate testing. Because we documented the usefulness of our alternative assessment procedures, and then revised them based on teacher feedback, the district granted us a variance to continue using our methods rather than the basal tests. Now we are ready to explore assessment in depth, at the classroom level, with our students.

CHAPTER 7

Developing Portfolio Processes:
"If You Don't Have Anything in There,
You Can't Do This"

Linda Morrison and Ronald Kieffer

For 2 years, Linda Morrison, a second-grade teacher, and Ronald Kieffer, a language education professor, have asked each other questions
about authentic assessment. We have come to believe that assessment
information, embedded within the context of the classroom community,
is more authentic when it involves gathering evidence from multiple
sources, such as work in progress, observation, self-evaluation, peer
evaluation, and collaboration. The process becomes even more authentic when we listen to and document the voices of teachers, students,
peers, parents, and other observers. These multiple voices, in concert,
tell rich stories about learners' growth over time, goals, and experiences. They can provide an account of students' performance, progress,
self-awareness, and change.

The assessment process is not static, but shifting and dynamic, and,
for both of us, a portfolio can become a possible container for information that supports teaching and learning. Portfolio processes, that is,
expectations, questions, collection, selection, containment, organization, and reflection, encourage and support authentic assessment of
reading, writing, speaking, and listening (Faust & Kieffer, 1993). Portfolios—systematic collections of student work that represent individuals
as learners—are possible formats for authentic assessment when students are immersed in rich literate environments with connected goals,
experiences, and purposes for reading, writing, and communicating
(Belanoff & Dickson, 1991; Graves & Sunstein, 1992; Rief, 1992; Tierney,
Carter, & Desai, 1991).

Linda teaches in such an environment. In her second-grade classroom, students are connected with reading, writing, listening, and
speaking every day. Choice is a central element as students use self-
determined reasons and relevant purposes to decide on their work and

interactions. Classroom members provide positive response and support for peers' ongoing plans and ideas. The students and the teacher also collect evidence of learning for student portfolios. The portfolio process has added breadth, depth, and richness to experiences, connections to self and others, and opportunities to reflect on learners' questions and concerns.

PORTFOLIO PROCESS

The subtitle of this chapter comes from an exclamation by one of Linda's second-grade students about the portfolio process: "If you don't have anything in there, you can't do this." We agree that portfolios are collections of items for various purposes that represent human beings as learners, critical thinkers, and problem solvers. The process starts with putting things "in there," as Linda's student noted, but it does not stop there.

Collection, Selection, Reflection

The portfolio content does play a role in the assessment process, but the content is only part of the process. Not everything that is produced by a student is chosen for the portfolio. Selection depends on the purpose of the learner's portfolio. With selection come reflections of worth or value that justify an item's inclusion. Learners reflect on items in process and listen to what others have to say about them, but the process doesn't stop there either. Collection, selection, and reflection are merely directives within a greater portfolio process involving the potential for powerful engagement with self-evaluation, questioning, creation, lifelong learning, and self-awareness.

Building Classroom Ethnographies

In Linda's classroom, the portfolio is part of the learning process. The students and the teacher learn from each other. In a way, the students and the teacher become researchers, and the stories that they tell build an ethnography, a story of a classroom culture.

From an anthropological point of view, John Van Maanen in his book *Tales of the Field: On Writing Ethnography* (1988) describes the concept of an ethnography as "a written representation of a culture (or selected aspects of a culture)" (p. 1). When teachers and students are viewed as researchers in their classrooms, the day-to-day existence, observation, and record keeping that the teacher and students compile represent the fieldwork, and the culture under study is the classroom community. A portfolio ultimately represents a creation of self, a whole-life portfolio. Its contents, like items in a scrapbook, are tangible pieces of the story. They are ways to remember. A portfolio becomes an ethnography of the person, an ethnography of the teacher, an ethnography of learning.

Before the idea of portfolio assessment was conceived, Barbara Hardy (1977) proposed that narrative is "a primary act of the mind transferred to art from life" (p. 12). We believe that a portfolio can be viewed as an ethnography or story, a "narrative of the mind," as Hardy suggests.

> For we dream in narrative, daydream in narrative, remember, antici-pate, hope, despair, believe, doubt, plan, revise, criticize, construct, gossip, learn, hate, and love by narrative. In order to really live, we make up stories about ourselves and others, about the personal as well as the social past and future. (p. 13)

Hardy (1977) elaborates by saying that "we tell stories in order to change" (p. 14). Each life is one long story. And for some the story continues after death as their lives are relived through family stories. An important question to ask young children might be: "What story do you want to tell people about your life?" or "What story do you want others to tell about your life?" In classrooms, we might ask them, "What stories do you want to tell about your life in the second grade? What can we put in the portfolio that will help you tell those stories?" An equally interesting question for teachers to ask themselves might be, "What stories can I tell about my students that will assess their growth and change over time?"

Hardy (1977) adds that "we do not grow out of telling stories" (p. 14). This is certainly true for both of us. We have always told stories to our students, our families, and our friends, and even to occasional strangers. In writing this piece, we have told each other countless stories, in an attempt to search for answers to questions that do not necessarily have answers.

In this writing, we want to continue telling stories about our families, our students, and ourselves. First, we will tell two stories about our family literacy. Linda will continue with stories from the classroom. Finally, we will tell our updated and continuing story of what we believe now about portfolio assessment, and end with goals for the future and revision plans for next year's story.

PARENT STORIES

Ron's description of a literacy event he observed and noted follows:

> My 13-month-old daughter, Kelley, amazed me again.While I
> was sitting at the kitchen table, Kelley handed me her "Teddy
> Bear." I moved "Teddy" in a circle on my knee and sang:
> "Teddy Bear, Teddy Bear, turn around. Teddy Bear Teddy
> Bear, touch the ground. Teddy Bear, Teddy Bear, shine your
> shoes. Teddy Bear, Teddy Bear, how old are you?" Kelley
> smiled and walked out of the room. She returned with a small
> book of rhymes. She helped me turn to the page that had
> "Teddy Bear" and I read it to her. She focused intently on the
> page and smiled again. I then read the rest of the book—twice.
> Shortly after celebrating what I considered a pivotal literacy
> event, I wrote the following entry quickly in a log:
>> 2/11 7:31 a.m. I did "Teddy Bear" with KEK [Kelley
>> Elizabeth Kieffer] in the kitchen. She then went into the
>> living room and got the Pat-a-Cake book which has "Teddy
>> Bear." I read it to her and then read the rest of the book.

As a parent, I hope to capture these important moments in my
child's life. I hope that Kelley's teachers can tell similar stories to me
about pivotal experiences in her school life. These moments build an
ethnography of Kelley's life as a human within a world community;
they help define her as a learner, artist, reader, craftsperson, writer,
problem solver, artisan, mathematician, and citizen.

Parents often keep informal portfolios of their children—a special
drawer, a bulletin board or the refrigerator, or a memory book. What
follows is a special memory Linda kept.

> It wasn't the "moment" I'd expected; the great literary event
> in my daughter's life happened one ordinary Sunday after-
> noon. She'd been occupying herself quietly at her table as I
> wrote nearby, and her request for some tracing paper barely
> interrupted my train of thought. As she talked quietly to her-
> self, my curiosity was aroused; just what was she so engrossed
> in? As I peered over her shoulder, I could see that she was
> tracing drawings from a current favorite book, *Julius, The Baby
> of the World* [Henkes, 1989]. She turned to me, saying, "I love
> this book so much that I want to have the drawings all for
> myself. I wish I could copy this book right now so that I could

have it forever!'' With that, she cradled the book in her arms, exclaiming, ''I just love this book so much that I want to hold onto it all the time!''

What a powerful connection my 7-year-old had made, and how thankful I felt to have been witness to it! Her personal connection with literature means much to me as her mother. Had this same experience happened while she was at school, chances are I would have missed it entirely. As a second-grade teacher, I want those same experiences for my students and want to be able to share those ''moments of connection'' with their parents. Traditional assessment, whether in the form of standardized test scores, end-of-unit tests, or report card grades, hasn't allowed me to share such moments with parents. Portfolios provide students and their parents with concrete memories. Many parents have kept ''portfolios'' of special learning events, letters and notes to Mom and Dad, school papers, and treasured moments like my daughter's deep attachment to a favorite book. As a teacher, I am helping children and parents preserve these meaningful events.

LINDA'S CLASSROOM STORIES

As I worked over the past 3 years to create a whole language reading and writing program in my classroom around children's literature, I became frustrated with traditional assessment. Instruction that was driven by outside assessment did not allow me to document my students' literacy growth. I have rejoiced with my students when they've made connections with the literature they've read. I saw this as proof of growing literacy, yet had no way to include such growth in traditional assessment. I wanted to document their progress as readers and writers, and to share this progress with parents. Portfolio assessment provides a means for sharing this growth.

My ''gut'' feeling, reinforced by my own children's literacy learning, has always been that children learn to read by being read to and by reading. However, until 3 years ago, that feeling wasn't reflected in the way I taught reading. The literature I exposed my students to didn't extend much beyond what was included in the basal reader, and my instruction was governed by the prescribed basal sequence of skills. Although I wished to create the joys of personal connection with literature, there just didn't seem to be time to spare during the course of our busy days for something ''extra.'' In spite of my own love for reading, *teaching* it wasn't something I particularly enjoyed. I found the basal lessons tedious to teach and spent a good bit of time and energy keeping students busy with monotonous "seatwork" while I taught a small group. I realized that many of the lessons were dull and isolated; reading groups weren't very exciting. I felt frustrated when some children made little or no growth as readers in spite of my carefully orchestrated lessons. I also remember feeling guilty if the principal walked in when I was reading to the class. How could I justify what I was doing if the children weren't busily filling in a workbook page? Reading aloud was nice, but was seen as a "frill" that took away from the important task of "teaching" reading.

Why did I begin to change the way I taught reading? Like most other teachers, I was a cog in the larger wheel of the entire school. I was influenced not only by the way I had been taught as a student, but by the culture of my school. I taught reading with a basal because that was the way my peers taught. The school system had gone to great expense to provide these materials, and I was expected to use them. I wasn't aware of much beyond the world of the school in which I taught and didn't question what I was doing; what other alternatives were there, anyway? Wasn't this the way everyone taught reading?

Literacy Beliefs and Actions

I began to change when the culture of the school began to change, as detailed in Chapter 1. With the support and guidance of our university colleagues, we struggled to create literature-based reading and writing programs and to define goals and expectations for our school and students. As I began to read and learn more about literacy, my own philosophy about how children learn to use language began to crystallize.

1. Children learn to read by *reading*.

2. A "significant adult" can create a supportive atmosphere in which a child "blossoms" as a reader. The support, encouragement, and attention of that adult invite the child to become part of the literate community.

3. Children are competent language users in the context of their own communities. Schools traditionally haven't recognized this; the language of the mainstream has been the standard by which we judge children's success. Therefore, many children have been condemned to fail.

4. Children want to read and write for their own purposes; they want to choose their own books and write about topics that have significance for them.

5. Reading and writing are *social* activities; they bind us together and remind us that we are part of the larger community of humankind.

6. Children strive to create meaning when they read.

7. Children become readers at different ages and in different ways. My task is to offer support, guidance, and instruction that will build proficiency toward becoming successful readers.

8. Children will take risks if they are encouraged and supported in their efforts.

9. Reading and writing are connected; one supports the other.

10. Schools should strive to create independent learners, rather than passive, dependent, answer-oriented students.

In addition, watching my own children's emerging literacy served as a powerful example that reinforced what I was learning. I realized that the way I was teaching no longer fit for me. It was time to make the change toward teaching reading and writing with literature, and discard the basal and workbooks. What I didn't realize, at the time, was that this would also require a shift in assessment. My understanding of it, how I assessed myself and my students, and the tools I used would change.

Today, there is a feeling of activity, excitement, and engagement during reading time in our class. Children are scattered throughout the room—in the reading corner, at tables, on the floor. A constant hum pervades the room. Some children are sharing a big book; one child may take on the role of "teacher" and point to the words as he or she reads the book to the "students" gathered nearby. Pairs of children may be reading a book together, taking turns reading to each other. Others may be listening to a favorite book on tape. One or two children may go to the reading loft in the media center. Individuals may be curled up with books, reading alone. There are many choices about how, where, and what to read.

The decision to create a literature-based reading and writing program wasn't easy to implement. Working without the "safety net" of the prescribed skills listed in the basal was intimidating at first. For someone who was very skills oriented, making decisions about what to teach and how to assess learning required some adjustments! Fortunately, county administrators were willing to allow those teachers who were interested in developing alternative assessment tools to work together to do so (Chapter 6). Because of my participation in this project, I no longer was bound to teach or test the skills listed in the basal continuum.

STUDYING PORTFOLIO POSSIBILITIES

During the 1992–93 school year, as a member of my school's research team, I decided to focus on how assessment affected my instruction. Specifically, I was interested in furthering the use of portfolios as assessment tools in my classroom and in studying the process. Ron Kieffer had expressed an interest in investigating changes that occur when teachers explore alternative assessment techniques and portfolio use. Our shared interest prompted me to invite him to visit my classroom. He accepted the invitation and visited often to observe, interact with children individually, and read to the class.

The predominant ways in which assessment informed instruction were shown in my reflective teaching journal and in the changing portfolio processes that evolved during the year.

Informing Teaching Through a Reflective Journal

One of the most important tools for data collection was my teaching journal. I originally structured it as a three-part record, with reflective, theoretical, and methodological sections. The reflective section turned out to be the most informative and was the only one I kept all year. I spent the majority of my data collection time watching my students, recording their responses and activities, asking myself questions, and reflecting on what I saw happening. Examination of this information led me to plan lessons, restructure ideas, and reorganize lessons and units for the following school year.

Recording my observations provided me with a rich source of information about how my students were developing as readers and writers. Often I was able to share with the entire class some of the strategies I saw children using in their reading and writing, or to plan mini-lessons around what I observed. I found that assessment informed instruction in four ways: The information guided my instruction during one-to-one conferences, in "stop the class" instant lessons, in planning lessons for following days, and in revising plans for the following year. Development of a chart enabled me to keep track of instances that led to instructional changes (see Figure 7.1).

Reading "looks" different than it did when I taught it in a more traditional way. I have seen children engage with literature and have heard them talk with one another about connections they've made with what they've read. I needed to find assessment techniques that would match the whole language instruction that was occurring. Simply recording some of the spontaneous conversations that happened was one technique that proved insightful. The following conversation was taped and then transcribed. My notes indicate that Hannah and Christina were working on a letter to me about their favorite book of the week. They seemed concerned about how to spell "The Twits." Jared heard their conversation and brought the girls his copy of *The Twits* (Dahl, 1991).

Jared: Here. Look at the cover and you'll know how to spell it.
(*Gillian has been watching and listening with curiosity*)
Gillian: Why *The Twits*?
Hannah: It's funny. It's about this old man and old woman; they're nasty.
Jared: Oh, man! Mrs. Morrison read it when you were in Bermuda. She'll have to read it to you 'cause of all those chapters in it.
Christina: They're both married. She put worms in his spaghetti.
Jared: They put hug-tight glue on the trees 'cause he liked bird stew.
Christina: No, bird *pie*.
Gillian: I gotta get this crazy book!
Jared: Yeah. Mrs. Morrison could let you borrow it, and your Dad could read it to you.

The above exchange showed me that Jared had figured out a strategy for finding the spelling of an unknown word and could share it with others. I also saw his powerful connection with a favorite book. His enthusiasm was contagious; Gillian was eager to get the book. Jared also offered her another strategy to ensure her successful experience with the book: to have her father read it to her. My teaching journal notes indicate that I planned a mini-lesson for the following day. I shared Jared's strategy for finding help in spelling a word. After we listened to the tape, a spontaneous discussion ensued in which we talked about what made a successful group-sharing experience.

Figure 7.1. How assessment informs instruction.

One-to-One Conference Instruction

2/15. Gillian DOESN'T want me to write correct spelling on her rough draft; she doesn't want to make a final copy! I offer to put correctly spelled words on a Post-It note and give it to her. I tell her she can stick it on her rough draft or final copy, so I'll have a record of what she needed help with. This became an acceptable option for the rest of the class.

2/23. Mary's not happy with the title for her book; doesn't fit. I conference with her about this; she comes up with a title she's more satisfied with, then asks if she can share this change with the class. Class discussion on fitting title with story follows.

"Stop the Class" Instant Lessons

2/22. Reading *Abiyoyo*; pointed out how I liked the word "zoop." We talked about weird words. Someone suggested *The Amazing Bone*. I suggested we think about a unit on books with "weird words." Unit planned for week before testing.

3/4. Color poems; classroom guest reads Christina Rossetti's "Colors." Jerry writes his own "color poem" after this. Julie suggests that others try this after she hears Jerry share his. Whole class rereading of "Colors," followed by discussion of other possibilities for "color" poems by several students.

Plans for Following Days

1/28. "When I Was Little" stories unit for writing workshop; idea came from a child's story. We discussed the idea as a class, and decided to start this unit.

2/22. Hannah's "When I Was Little" story is five pages long! She has trouble reading it, loses the "thread" of the story. Plan a mini-lesson addressing this.

3/2. Math: Back up and redo lesson tomorrow. Hand out centimeter and inch squares; using the rulers was too hard (observation during lesson)!

Plans for Following Year

1/29. Reworked letter writing unit for next year; noted in plan book. Several children expressed frustration during independent writing. (Had four conferences, and *all* four children weren't at all sure of how to go about writing their own letters. I don't think I was very *clear* during my mini-lesson.)

2/6. Nutrition unit; children had trouble copying my "food wheel." Next year, make a ditto for them to cut out and paste on a paper plate. Noted in plan book.

Shared reading experiences are a pivotal part of our reading program. Daily engagement with quality literature builds a familiarity with "book language" and reinforces the joy of interacting with books. This is an enjoyable time for us as we discover new books and return to old favorites. We also use literature to create a shared chronology of our time together as a "community of readers." When students are actively involved in listening to stories, there is ample opportunity to ask questions that promote higher order thinking. Recording and reflecting on the ways students respond to what we read together allows me to witness the connections they are making with literature.

These are some of the comments made during and after a shared reading of Paul Galdone's *Little Red Riding Hood* (1974) (they were noted by Ron, who was observing while I read to the class).

Julie: This kind of sounds like the real one. (*This refers to the traditional version of the story that she is familiar with*)

Christina (*remarking on the voice I use when I read the parts spoken by the* wolf): Good wolf voice!

Gillian (*asking about the word* forbidden): Does that mean she can't do it?

Hannah: I know why you read that; 'cause we're studying the forest.

In my classroom, the focus is not on giving correct answers to teacher questions. We share responses that are connected to what we read. By documenting responses such as these, I am able to remember an important focus of my reading instruction. In addition, I have evidence of my students' growth as readers in a way that goes beyond a score on a workbook page.

Observing the behavior of children as they read together offered insights, as the following entries from my reflective journal illustrate:

Amber and Hannah are reading to each other. They take turns reading a page at a time. They offer help and support.

Amber (points): You were right here. (*When Hannah loses her place, Amber supplies a word for her; this seems to keep the pace "flowing"*)

Hannah (encourages Amber): Just guess what that word is. I don't know it either.

Amber (turns to me): Is it "disappointed"? (*When I affirm her guess, both girls smile*)

Linda: How did you know what that word was?

Amber: I just read the whole thing [*sentence*] and when I looked at the beginning of that word, I thought "disappointed" was it.

After this observation I was able to record Amber's successful use of a reading strategy on her reading assessment form.

The following example shows how more successful literate students often supported those who weren't yet as successful. I noted this on Frank's reading assessment form.

Frank is reading *The Magic School Bus Inside the Human Body* [Cole, 1989]
    to Rob. When I ask the boys to tell me how it's going, they say:
Frank: I'm reading with my voice, 'cause Rob and I really like this
    book. He's reading with his eyes right now.
Rob: Yeah. We were just talking about how he [the illustrator] draws
    these pictures. We both think he's a good artist!

Both boys' roles were seen as equal; both were actively participating as readers and were interacting about their shared experience. It also provided me with documentation that Rob could discuss aspects of a book. I found these and numerous reflections throughout the year to be valuable to my understanding of literacy development, as well as to my instruction.

Changing Portfolio Process

My initial understanding of portfolios was rather limited. I saw them as merely collections of student work that were to be saved for evaluation, presumably by me. In essence, they weren't much different from the folders in which I'd collected student work, to be shown at parent conferences. Initially, I was the one who was doing most of the selection, deciding which pieces of writing showed "best effort," or which "projects" would be most impressive to be shown to parents. Writing portfolios were the only ones I attempted to use. Reading portfolios were just too much to think about.

During the 1992–93 school year, my thinking began to change. I wanted students to begin to get involved in self-assessment of their writing. Rather than doing the selecting myself, I asked my students to make selections every 2 weeks. As I conferenced with students, I noted what they had said in response to my two questions: (1) Tell me why you chose this piece; and (2) What do you think you did well in this piece? I made these notes on "Post-its" and stuck them on the piece of writing. At the end of the quarter, I was able to share with the students what they had said about each piece of writing they turned in. I also had a record of how the students were answering those two questions and how their answers changed as the year progressed.

I noticed that some children never had difficulty choosing pieces and that others would not make selections unless pushed by me to do so. Frustration led me to wonder why some children had such difficulty. I began to ask the children who were choosing pieces with ease to share with me reasons why they chose the pieces they did and what they thought their pieces showed about them as successful writers. Their self-assured and confident responses were insightful. I tried pairing up these children with those having difficulty and asking them to explain to their partners what they had already explained to me: why they chose the piece they did, and what that particular piece showed they were able to do successfully as writers. A conversation between Amber and Chad, recorded in my teaching journal, illustrates the richness of this kind of sharing.

Amber: Well, I picked this one 'cause I liked the title—it goes good with the story. I told more about my dolls; like I put them in a row and play school, and I'm the teacher. I thought it was a real good story, 'cause it's what I really do at home.

Chad: Yeah. I like that part about the dolls, too. (Turns to me) I can just see Amber being the teacher, can't you? Your picture is nice, too. Those dolls are all sitting on the bed.

Amber: Yeah, that's like their table at school. They all sit together.

Chad: I might pick that story about my trampoline. That's what I do a lot after school.

Listening to Amber describe her reasons for selecting a particular piece of writing served as a far more powerful example for Chad than anything I could have said. He took away an idea for his own selection; Amber's piece gave him an idea that will facilitate his own selection.

The kind of daily, informal assessment that goes on now in my classroom serves to strengthen and confirm my beliefs about literacy and portfolios. I continue to learn as I watch the children I teach. The following list represents my beliefs about portfolios:

1. A portfolio is a collection of items that represents a student at a particular time, in the context of a particular classroom community.
2. Portfolios facilitate the demonstration of growth over time.
3. Portfolio use can encourage development of active, involved decision making, rather than reward the search for ''the right answer.''

4. Literature-based reading and writing programs lend themselves to portfolio use.
5. Portfolios aren't something you can "do" instantly. Their use evolves over time and changes as the teacher learns more, observes the children he or she teaches, and allows time for reflection and growth.

LAYERS OF TEACHER CHANGE

There are several layers to the change that is going on at South Jackson Elementary. First, there is a real movement toward whole language philosophy as evidenced by teachers allowing students the opportunity to choose materials for reading and writing, allotments of time to engage with whole texts, literary demonstrations in the form of mini-lessons and conferencing, and sharing of books read and written by students.

Second, there is a move beyond traditional forms of assessment toward authentic portfolio assessment, as documented in Chapter 6. Although Bailey pointed out in that chapter that in general teachers are not satisfied with the amount of student ownership and self-evaluation, many are convinced that involving students in the process of assessment is beneficial not only to the students themselves, but to parents, students' peers, and the teacher. In fact, although we originally implemented portfolios as a teacher-directed assessment tool, we are now questioning, "Whom is the portfolio really for?"

This has led to a third layer of change: Teachers are moving past writing portfolios and thinking about process portfolios where reading and writing are connected. We are integrating across content areas. Since students generally are engaged in writing on a daily basis, there are sufficient written documents to select from for portfolio assessment. A focus on reading assessment has been much more challenging, but we are finding ways to document rich evidence about reading engagement.

The real challenge has been to think about reading in a more authentic way. With reading assessment, it's a real challenge to move past having students write about their reading. Checklists of standard reading behaviors, tape recordings of students as they read, and written running records of students' on-line reading strategies provide bits of evidence about students as readers. Standardized tests such as the Iowa Test of Basic Skills seem to carry less and less weight. Informal reading inventories that are tailored to a particular classroom continue to provide useful information. But there are other rich stories to be told—stories not easily captured and that have meaning only in the context of the classroom environment, the community of readers, writers, thinkers, and learners.

GOALS AND FUTURE DIRECTIONS

My goals for working with portfolios are ongoing, as is our view of the portfolio process itself. Specifically, I want to continue to explore the changes that occur as I work toward use of alternative assessment methods and continue to document the links between assessment and instruction. I would like to mesh the rich information in my teaching journal with portfolios. Communicating my perceptions about individual students as readers and writers through letter writing is a possibility. Students could write to me, to their parents, and to their peers. Parent voices also could be included in our classroom community in this manner.

Moving toward true portfolio use requires student involvement and ownership. I would like to involve my students in assessment more fully. I will continue to document their reasons for inclusion of items in their portfolios and help them to see the progress they make as readers and writers. I hope that portfolios will assume a central role in my classroom and that they will contain evidence of the unique voices within that community.

In future collaborative research, we will focus on the broader elements of portfolio process. Our goal is to explore ways that portfolio assessment can be extended toward connecting the literate activities of reading, writing, listening, and speaking. Ultimately, we want to connect portfolios across the curriculum and extend them over a period of years, so that we can build whole-life portfolios that really represent individuals as learners. We hope to develop the portfolio as an ethnographic story.

We envision the following possibilities:

1. Portfolios that are a central part of the classroom context.

2. Portfolios that contain multiple voices—reflections from the student; peers from the classroom, school, and community; parents; other teachers from the school; and possibly community members.

3. Portfolios that contain multiple stories of what individuals can do within the language arts—reading, writing, listening, and speaking— and across the curriculum.

4. Portfolios that serve as a way to communicate assessment information to parents, schools officials, and the public.

5. Portfolios that document change—student and teacher.

6. Portfolios that allow student ownership and responsibility.

7. Portfolios whose purposes vary according to the individual learner.

8. A portfolio process that not only matches instruction but also meshes with the ongoing, dynamic, and shifting learning process.

We see this chapter primarily as a description of a teacher's journey toward creating authentic assessment and how it matches the instruction in her classroom. It is the beginning of an ethnography of a teacher's steps toward using portfolios as part of that authentic assessment. As teachers, we have rich stories to tell about students that can be documented in portfolios and that are very different from most assessment information. We believe that narrative, as a metaphor for portfolio assessment, has the potential to solve many of our difficulties with evaluation, testing, and assessment.

PART IV

ENHANCED COMMUNICATION

CHAPTER 8

Whole Language, Media Centers, and Classroom Libraries: Research in Action

Lisa James Delgado, Mary Jane Hilley,
Melvin Bowie, and JoBeth Allen

School media centers in many parts of the country are undergoing important changes. With movement toward flexible scheduling, collaborative planning and teaching, and whole language instruction, media centers are truly the heart of schools. Media specialists provide a constant supply of books, media, ideas, instruction, and support throughout the school. Media specialists in the past read to each class once or twice a week and then helped children find books to check out. Today's media specialists are more likely to interact continually with individual and small groups of students as they move in and out of the media center daily to read, discuss, research, and compute; and with teachers as they gather materials for thematic teaching, look for just the right read aloud, gather multiple copies of books for a literature circle, pull together an author study, or consult on a professional matter in the teachers' resource section. Media specialists are dedicated to the principle of "service at the point of need" (American Association of School Librarians, 1988), and teachers and children in whole language classrooms have a constant need for good books, good ideas, and good collaborators.

Such new roles are not uniformly accepted, nor does this desired synchrony occur overnight. Stanek (1993), through interviews with teachers and librarians in schools moving toward whole language, found that many schools are struggling with this transition, and teachers and media specialists too often find themselves in conflict rather than collaboration. Whole language teachers cry for "more books!" in their classroom libraries, and in some schools there is misunderstanding and discord rather than the desired synergism of classroom and school libraries (Hansen, 1993). The current study grew out of two media specialists' desire to create media centers that would be the hub of whole language learning and complementary to growing classroom libraries. Through studying teachers' needs, they hoped to provide support for both teachers and children in flexible, collaborative relationships.

The two media specialists in this project, Lisa Delgado and Mary Jane Hilley, wanted to play a vital role in their schools' transitions to whole language. School and university faculty designed ongoing inservice on whole language instruction and on children's literature; Lisa and Mary Jane participated in the planning as well as in each session for 3 years. At the same time, the state and national guidelines called for flexible scheduling of school media centers, which Lisa and Mary Jane saw as very compatible with whole language instruction. Both schools began inquiry into how students were growing as readers, writers, and learners; Lisa and Mary Jane decided to study the role of the media specialist in a whole language school. They formed a research team with Melvin Bowie, a UGA professor in instructional technology with particular expertise in school media centers, and JoBeth Allen, a UGA faculty member who had worked with them on whole language instruction.

ACROSS-SCHOOL RESEARCH DESIGN

Our questions about school and classroom libraries came from several sources. All school personnel had been interviewed twice a year beginning in February 1991 about their evolution as whole language teachers. In these interviews, teachers often expressed concern over not having enough books to teach effectively; they referred to their classroom libraries most frequently, but also occasionally to the media center, specifically in reference to books for thematic units. Lisa and Mary Jane also participated in the interviews, where they noted more extensive use of the library by both children and teachers and increased circulation. They also raised concerns, such as increasing their collections to meet teachers' needs, and getting an on-line catalog that both teachers and children could operate more independently.

Questions About School and Classroom Libraries

As a research team, we began a series of dialogues to generate, prioritize, and refine our research questions. From 24 original questions, we decided to investigate the following:

School Media Centers. Since the advent of whole language instruction and flexible scheduling at the schools:

1. How do students use the media center? What facilitates or hinders their use?
2. How do teachers use the media center? What facilitates or hinders their use?
3. What role does the media specialist have in a whole language school?
4. How adequate is the media collection for the thematic units teachers most frequently teach? How can teachers and media specialists work together to analyze the collection and purchase books and other resources that support whole language instruction?
5. What suggestions do teachers and students have for improving the media center?

Classroom Libraries. Since the advent of whole language instruction:

1. How do students use classroom libraries, in comparison to how they use the media center?
2. How do teachers use classroom libraries, in comparison to how they use the media center?
3. How have classroom libraries changed? Where do teachers get books, and how do they incorporate them?
4. What suggestions do teachers and students have for improving classroom libraries?

Definitions

Rather than a universally agreed upon meaning for terms, we sought local definitions—how terms are defined by the key players. Mary Jane and Lisa provided the following definition of *flexible scheduling*: Teachers sign up each week as they need the media center. They come with a specific purpose in mind rather than being assigned a time. The advantage is that teachers and students can use the center throughout the day, as often as they need to. Media specialists serve as instructional resources.

Teachers at the two schools had complex and varied definitions of *whole language instruction*, but elements that ran across definitions included the following: teachers integrate writing and reading, and often bring children's literature and writing into the study of science, social studies, and thematically organized units; children read and write daily for meaningful purposes, including enjoyment, gaining knowledge, and expressing feelings; children make choices, depend on each other, and are responsible for their own learning; and teachers and children are all learners. Whole language, while not uniformly adopted throughout both schools, is now the predominant teaching philosophy in special education as well as regular classrooms grades K–5, although each teacher designs whole language instruction differently.

Gathering Information

We designed four ways of collecting data to address the questions.

1. *Circulation records*. Mary Jane and Lisa kept monthly circulation totals of the number and kinds of books and media checked out by teachers and by students. They also kept anecdotal records of school and community events that might affect circulation totals.

2. *Evaluation of Resources for Thematic Units* (ERTU). In a previous study (Loertscher, Ho, & Bowie, 1987), Melvin and colleagues designed a collection mapping and development technique that we adapted for this project. Teachers used the ERTU form (see Figure 8.1) to evaluate six qualities of the materials available for various thematic units they taught from January to June, and to record how many books they used from the media center, from their classroom library, and from other collections. On the back, they wrote comments and listed titles they wished the media specialist to purchase. The initial return rate was low, but it increased when media specialists gave book fair coupons and free books as incentives.

3. *School and Classroom Library Survey*. Teachers completed a 23-item survey during an after-school meeting in May 1993 (see Figure 8.2). We provided the incentive of hardback books contributed by university faculty. Nearly every teacher, including special education and Chapter 1 teachers, participated.

4. *Classroom Library Analysis*. Teachers analyzed their collections for the number of books provided by school district funds, those donated, and those purchased with personal funds. Students discussed (and teachers recorded) four questions concerning how they used the media center and their classroom libraries, and how each could be "even better" (see Figure 8.3).

Figure 8.1. Evaluation of resources for thematic units.

Teacher's Name   Unit Title

Grade   Dates

Number of books from media center used for this unit: _____

Number of books from classroom used for this unit: _____

Number of books from other collections used for this unit: _____

List sources: _____

Number of A-V materials used for this unit: _____

	Rating	Comments
Range in Readability Were there enough easy-to-read, average, and challenging texts for your grade level?		
Variety in Perspectives Did materials present different cultural, social, and political viewpoints, if applicable?		
Variety in Format Was there enough variety, such as picture books, fiction, nonfiction, filmstrips, videos, etc.?		
Currency Were the items current enough?		
Availability of Items Were items from media center available when you needed them?		
Student Interest Did students seem to find the items interesting?		

Figure 8.2. School and classroom library survey.

I teach _____   Date_____

  1a. Describe how and why your students use the school media center.
    b. Do they tend to use it individually, in small groups, or with the whole class? Why?
    2. What facilitates and encourages their use of the school media center?
    3. What hinders or discourages their use of the school media center?
    4. Describe how and why your students use your classroom library.
    5. What facilitates and encourages their use of the classroom library?
    6. What hinders or discourages their use of the classroom library?
    7. Has the role of your media specialist changed as you have become a whole language school, and if so how?
    8. What could the media specialist do that would further support whole language teaching and learning?
    9. Compare your classroom library 3 years ago and today:
  10. Compare *student use* of the media center with the old, fixed scheduling and the recent flexible scheduling.
  11. Compare *your use* of the media center with the old, fixed scheduling and the recent flexible scheduling.
  12. Describe the role of your classroom library in your instructional program.
  13. Rate how *important* your classroom library is to your instruction.
          1..........2..........3..........4..........5..........6..........7..........8..........9..........10
          not at all   somewhat   essential
  14. Rate how *adequate* you feel your current classroom collection is for instructional purposes (including self-selected reading).
          1..........2..........3..........4..........5..........6..........7..........8..........9..........10
          not at all   somewhat   totally
Questions 15–18: please compare use of the *school media center* now with 3 years ago (before whole language and flexible scheduling).
  15. My students use it now
          1..................2..................3..................4..................5
          much less   some less   about same   some more   much more
  16. I use it now
          1..................2..................3..................4..................5
          much less   some less   about same   some more   much more
  17. My students now use it more for_____finding a specific topic, _____finding a specific author, _____finding a specific book, _____ general browsing, or _____.
  18. I now use it more for_____finding a specific topic, _____finding a specific author, _____finding a specific book, _____general browsing, or_____.
  19. Who selects books for the school media center? By what criteria?

Questions 20–24: In thinking about *your classroom library,*
  20. Where do you get books? (include any use with other teachers)
  21. At a given time, about _____% are your permanent books, _____% are books from school media center, and _____% from regional library.
  22. Who selects the books for your classroom library? By what criteria?
  23. About how much of your own money do you spend yearly on books?
  24. **What specific suggestions do you have for upgrading your collection?**

Figure 8.3. Classroom library analysis.

name_____

How many books have been purchased with school or district funds?

How many books have been donated to your classroom?

How many books have you purchased with personal funds?

Other (number and sources)

Student Survey (You could read the questions to students and have them write their responses, or hold a class discussion and have someone take notes.)

At our school, we have books and magazines in our classroom, and in the school media center. Sometimes you get books from our library, and sometimes you go to the media center. Think about how you use each.

1. Describe how you use our classroom library.

2. What does our classroom library need to be even better?

3. Describe how you use the school media center.

4. What does the school media center need to be even better?

Analysis of Information Sources

The primary purpose for our study, like other teacher research, is the improvement of educational practice. We posed questions that were important to us regarding teaching and learning in our own classrooms and schools. We collected information that contributes meaningfully to investigating these questions, analyzed and interpreted the data in ways that made sense to us and furthered our own understanding, and shared what we learned with other teachers.

In this study, we analyzed data in a variety of ways to gain insights into our original questions. The ERTU forms were most valuable in giving specific information about a collection on one topic. However, we also analyzed the ERTUs collectively to look for general strengths and weaknesses in our collections (e.g., currency, availability). We averaged, graphed, and charted circulation data from a variety of perspectives. On the survey, we tallied frequency of certain responses, created averages of numerical figures, and conducted a qualitative analysis of open-ended responses. We then grouped all data sources according to which question they illuminated. We worked through each step of the analysis as a group, discussing various interpretations. Throughout the analysis, we kept as our primary focus, "What does this tell us that we can use to improve the media center, classroom libraries, or the services of the media specialist?"

FINDINGS

We learned many things about students, teachers, and their interactions with libraries. The following section highlights those findings that were most useful to us and to our students and faculty.

Media Centers

Student Use of the Media Center. Since the partnership began, media specialists and teachers have reported increased use of the media centers at both schools. Of 34 respondents, 31 teachers indicated that students use the media center "much more" (21) or "some more" (10) than they used to. At Benton, circulation statistics bore out teacher observations, with student use increasing from 21,348 in 1990–91 to 33,645 in 1992–93 (Figure 8.4).

At South Jackson, student circulation remained stable across 3 years (see Figure 8.4). This led Lisa to investigate factors that might have affected library use. She found that many students were more concerned than in the past with finding books they could actually read; teachers reported that some students kept books out longer (and thus checked out fewer). Another factor that limited student circulation was student access to the media center. Although teachers were encouraged to send students to the media center individually or in small groups, most of the teachers at South Jackson still preferred to bring their class as a whole group so students wouldn't miss class instruction. Further, many students used their classroom libraries daily, and increased teacher use of the media center made books available to students through their classroom libraries.

When surveyed, students reported using the library about equally for pleasure reading there and for checking out books to take home or back to their classrooms. The second and third reasons for using the media center were doing research and using the computers and other learning centers. Teachers reported almost identical perceptions of how the students used the media center, with one exception: Students re-

Figure 8.4. Annual library circulation statistics, 1990–93.

	1990-91	1991-92	1992-93
Benton			
Students	21348	35147	33645
Teachers	8320	15063	18925
TOTAL	29668	50210	52570
South Jackson			
Students	15633	15667	15905
Teachers	4369	8171	7688
TOTAL	20401	24692	24118

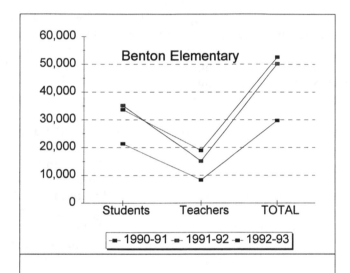

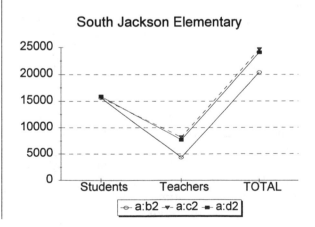

ported many other uses, such as for book fairs, reading magazines and newspapers, to learn, and "to leave the room." (You always suspected as much for one or two, didn't you?)

Teachers thought media center use increased because students were more interested in reading; this was gratifying to all members of the partnership, because "increasing interest in reading" was the primary goal established by both schools. Students were reading books daily in most classes, in reading workshops, thematic studies, and literature circles; in addition, several classes had reading buddies or frequently read to other classes. Teachers pointed to the wider variety of books and other materials in the media center (compared with their own rooms) and to teacher encouragement and recommendation of specific books and authors. Another important element was the inviting atmosphere of the media center, mentioned in specific terms of friendly staff who help students, and the reading loft at South Jackson.

When asked what hindered use of the media center, teachers reported that time was the biggest issue. All but two teachers liked the flexible scheduling better than the previous set schedule, but it too had problems. Some teachers had trouble finding a time during the day when their whole class could come; sometimes the only time one teacher could find had already been reserved by another teacher. Individuals and groups of three to four children could go to the media center at any time, without prior arrangement, but larger groups had to be scheduled because of other activities going on at the same time. Both media centers have limited space, and not enough personnel to work with more than one group at a time or to help individuals and still conduct a group lesson.

Students had uniformly positive things to say about their own use of the media center; when asked, however, they did have some advice for how it could be even better. They wanted more books (again, we were thrilled with this response as an indicator of student interest in reading). Some of the students were very specific about what they wanted: particular genres (poetry, biography), specific topics (from sharks to antique airplanes), and favorite authors (Mercer Mayer, R. L. Stine). Mary Jane and Lisa noted that for many of the children this specificity evolved over the past 3 years. Previously, when children came to the library to request help finding a book, they asked in general terms, like "a thin book" or "a chapter book." Even the topic requests were more general in the past—primarily joke and riddle books, books about sports, and "how to draw" books.

Students also wanted more computers, especially those with CD-ROM; more centers; and more games like Geo-Safari, Trivial Pursuit, and chess. Students had additional suggestions for the physical setting. They wanted more book displays, more comfortable places to read (pillows, couches, etc.), a computer card catalog (yea!), more shelves, more duplicate copies of books (so they could read the same book as a friend); one child even suggested turning off the lights and reading by candlelight. Student responses showed us that students were indeed using the media center flexibly and that the media center was a special place for students outside the classroom.

Teacher Use of the Media Center. Teachers also reported using the media center more regularly and more extensively in the past 3 years. On the survey, 89% of the teachers said they used the media center more than 3 years earlier. They reported using it most for finding books on a specific topic (89%) in connection with planning instructional units, including themed studies and author studies. Teachers also used the library more frequently to find a specific book or a specific author. Almost all of the teachers reported liking the flexibility of being able to come to the media center any time, to check out read alouds, help children choose books for research projects or thematic studies, and just browse. Teachers' increased use of the media center is reflected in the circulation statistics. At South Jackson teacher circulation doubled when teachers began using whole language instruction in their classrooms. Lisa and Mary Jane attribute the subsequent leveling off in circulation to the tremendous growth in classroom libraries.

The Role of the Media Specialist. Teachers defined the media specialist's most important role as locating materials. They responded that the media specialist "assists me in finding books for my units" and "is very aware of related books appropriate to themes," "coordinate[s] books between grade levels," compiles "sets of books," "suggests types of media," and "is more involved in what is going on in the classroom" since the advent of whole language and the flood of literature into the curriculum. Requests for materials come in a range of specificity, from "everything you have on oceans" to a list of specific titles.

A few teachers see the media specialist as a "teacher" who helps "students find information about their research . . . [and] demonstrates how to use the computer to find information. She also teaches lessons in the library." There is not yet as much collaborative planning and teaching as either Lisa or Mary Jane would like, although some grade levels do include the media specialists in half-day quarterly curriculum planning sessions. Some teachers still seem reluctant to draw the media specialists into the planning of units that integrate information access skills such as using the card catalog, posing questions and conducting research, and accessing various resource materials. Time for joint planning may be a crucial factor.

One of the main questions Lisa and Mary Jane wanted answered was, "What could the media specialist do that would further support whole language teaching and learning?" They received several concrete suggestions and uncovered a few misconceptions that they can now address.

The most frequent suggestions concerned acquiring more media, including multiple copies of novels and informational books, computer software, books on tape, filmstrips and videos, and the most frequent response—more books. Several teachers suggested creating thematic instructional resources, such as lists of books and media related to various topics; and continuing summer workshops on new books and resources. Some teachers also had suggestions for specific interaction with children, including book talks, storytelling, role playing book characters, and readers' theater.

Teachers also raised policy issues, alerting Mary Jane and Lisa to decisions that needed to be addressed by the faculty as a whole. An issue at one school was how long materials can be checked out. Some teachers think that books should be checked out for longer periods of time and that the media specialist should "not be so strict about overdue books and the number of books we are able to check out." Others believe the media specialist should "not allow a grade level to keep the same books for long periods of time." This is a common problem in a school where teachers often teach similar units, do author studies, and use literature to enhance seasonal and yearly topics, such as dental health and fire prevention. Lisa and Mary Jane agreed that the issue of how many books, and for how long, should be brought up within their shared governance systems.

They were also alerted to some misconceptions. For example, one teacher wrote that she wished the media specialist would "allow students to come to the library to just sit and read." Both librarians encourage individuals and small groups to come to the media center as often as they wish, to browse, research, or "just to read." The media specialist who received this comment was able to talk with teachers and clear up the misperception.

Overall, teachers and media specialists appear to enjoy positive relationships. When asked how this relationship could be improved, one teacher commented, "Continue to monitor our needs with assessment questionnaires" like the one used in this study. Teachers at these schools seemed to appreciate action research that solicited their insights and responded to their needs.

Since the purchase and gathering of materials for instruction was what teachers identified as most helpful, Mary Jane and Lisa are able to make that a priority when the many tasks of a media specialist compete for their time. They are better able to meet teachers' specific requests because of the way they gathered information, as reported in the next section.

Teacher Evaluation of Resources for Thematic Units. As teachers incorporated more literature into the curriculum, and learned more about the range of children's literature, they had more requests of the media specialists. Writing about the value of using a variety of resources in whole language instruction, Lamme and Ledbetter (1990) stated

> Thematic studies in whole language classrooms are grounded in high-quality fiction, nonfiction, and poetry and process writing. . . . It is the literature that forms the framework for explorations into the content. Textbooks in the content areas simply cannot match the flexibility, depth, or quality provided by trade books. (p. 736)

Lisa and Mary Jane, in an attempt to learn specifically what teachers needed, assessed the quality and adequacy of supporting materials with the ERTU form (Figure 8.1). We gathered data on 56 different units over 5 months. Teachers rated the items on a four-point scale, ranging from Poor (1) to Very Good (4), on six qualities: range in readability, variety of perspectives, variety of format, currency, availability, and students' interest.

The primary use of the ERTU forms was individual and ongoing. Lisa and Mary Jane used them in creating their yearly book order. They ordered all the specific books and materials teachers listed on the back of the forms. They also planned orders based on general unit needs. For example, a second-grade teacher who evaluated 38 books and three videos for her unit on Africa was pleased with the variety, currency, and degree of student interest. However, she wrote that there were not enough easy-to-read books, especially informational books, and that she would like "books told from perspectives of African people." Lisa added to the collection based on these two requests.

Examining category averages was helpful in letting us know generally what the collections' strengths and weaknesses were. For example, teachers were much more concerned about variety in format than variety in perspectives. Several of them commented on the absence of videos, computer software, filmstrips, and picture books. Teachers suggested, and we subsequently ordered, specific titles for media in these categories.

Classroom Libraries

Student and Teacher Use. In classrooms where the curriculum was primarily based on textbooks, the classroom library (if it existed at all) was used primarily for independent reading, often only for students who completed their work ahead of the rest of the class. Now at these two whole language schools, most children use the classroom library throughout the day. When teachers described how students used the classroom libraries, two categories predominated: reading related to instruction, and individual pleasure reading. Most teachers indicated that classroom libraries were vital to their instructional programs. Within instruction, students read widely during reading and writing workshops and thematic studies. Nearly every teacher listed one or more instructional uses of the classroom library, including book comparisons, research, literature groups, author studies, reading to the teacher or a friend, developing reading skills, and categorizing books within the library. Three-fourths of the teachers who responded also noted that students chose books from the classroom library for self-selected "free time" or "pleasure reading." Two special education resource teachers pointed out that classroom libraries are especially important for their students because they have students only for 50 minutes, making travel to and from the library very difficult, and because some of their students "are too shy to come to the media center."

Students listed almost all of the same reasons for using their classroom libraries as teachers did. The most frequent response was "to read books." They read these books for reading workshop, at center time, to look at the pictures, for homework (several teachers asked parents to read with children for homework), and of course for pleasure—or to find "the perfect book," as one child said. Students noted several ways they learned from books in their classroom libraries, including categorizing by genres, spelling a word, using books as models for their own writing, learning to read, finding new words/building vocabulary, and our favorite, noted by four children: "to get smart."

Changes Since Whole Language. Classroom libraries have changed along many dimensions as a result of their increased use for instruction. The most dramatic change is in the number of books. Nearly every teacher reported that she now had more books. One went from "one box to five boxes," another from one crate to "five crates and three bookshelves," and a resource room teacher who once had only about 15 books now has "over 450" at any given time. Teachers reported an average of 336 books in their libraries at the time of the survey (May), with an average of 188 there permanently. Teachers also reported more variety; they buy books on themes they study and other books related to student interests. They reported more comprehensive libraries, with varied genres, reading levels, and more picture books.

Processes for using classroom libraries have also changed in some classrooms. One teacher noted what we have observed in many classrooms: "Books are available to all students now, not just those who finish their work early." Although one teacher noted that "the really good [books] disappear," some classes have developed checkout systems so they do not lose as many. Fourth-grade students Shumira and Becki created a database of their classroom library that included author, title, genre, and a picture book/chapter book distinction. They then created databases for two other teachers in the school and taught a third-grade student how to set up one for her classroom.

Sources of Books. Where are teachers getting all the additional books? Most books they buy themselves from bookstores, garage sales, flea markets, class book drives, and school book fairs. Teachers use book club bonus points regularly. Teachers estimated spending an average of $137 of their own money each year on books for the classroom library, with 8 teachers spending less than $50, 21 spending $50–200, 12 spending $200–400, and 3 spending over $400 a year. Teachers decided which books to order based primarily on instructional themes, student interests, and reading level. Other criteria included age-related characters, favorite authors, award-winning literature, teacher preferences, availability, price, and quality of literature and illustrations.

The school or district provided the next largest number of books, averaging nearly 100 per classroom. Most of these books came in the form of Scholastic's Bridges classroom libraries. However, there was a big discrepancy in the number of books supplied for individual classes. Two primary teachers had over 200 books from the district; a resource teacher and a speech teacher reported that the district had provided no books for their classroom libraries. The survey was valuable in pointing out this discrepancy and in documenting needs in district requests for funds.

In terms of other sources, teachers reported that at any given time, about one-third of the books in their classroom libraries were on loan from the school media center. Some teachers also got books regularly from the regional public library, and many classroom libraries also included student published books.

Facilitators. When we asked teachers what facilitated and encouraged use of classroom libraries, their responses grouped around three important factors. First, children were likely to use the libraries based on their interactions with teachers and peers. Students read together, talked about books, looked up information, and chose books to read to other classes. Teachers also influenced students when they read aloud to them, helped them find a book, encouraged them to read both in school and at home, and provided daily time to read library books. Second, use was facilitated by easy access and constant availability. The children like having multiple copies to read with friends, favorites for rereading, and a range of levels so everyone can find something to read. Third, teachers indicated that books are read because they are interesting, colorful, and current.

Suggestions. Teachers had one main suggestion for upgrading their classroom libraries: They would like the school district to provide more money for books. Teachers rated their classrooms as only "somewhat adequate" in the number of books. More than half the teachers wrote that they did not have enough books to meet the range of reading abilities, student interests, and themes studied. Some noted a troublesome loss of books due to age or mistreatment.

Whereas during the early days of whole language teachers had simply requested MORE BOOKS, they now had specific requests. They wanted more age-appropriate books, books about specific themes, multiple copies, read-along books and tapes, hardbacks, and award-winning books. They needed more nonfiction and more poetry, and several wanted to extend or create collections of authors' works.

Teachers suggested that money could come from the school district budget for consumable texts (workbooks), which they do not use. Benton teachers wrote an official variance request to do just that. Other suggestions included conferring with other teachers to trade more and combine orders to take advantage of discounts. Lisa and Mary Jane learned that teachers also wanted to learn more about new books, find guidelines for filling out certain genres, and develop effective checkout systems—all possible topics for their summer media workshops.

When students were asked what would make their classroom libraries even better, they too had specific suggestions. Their two most common ideas had to do with more books and with the physical environment (which teachers mentioned relatively infrequently). Students of all ages requested "new books" most frequently and made many specific suggestions.

1. They requested specific topics, including survival, adventure, action, whales, animals, sharks, horses, wrestling, boxing, transportation, drawing, and holidays.
2. They requested genres, such as poetry, biography, joke, mystery, nonfiction, and a new set of encyclopedias.
3. They requested specific authors and titles, for example, Encyclopedia Brown, Ann Martin, and Judy Blume.
4. They requested types of books, such as "colorful" picture books, "exciting" chapter books, hardbacks, and books with read-along tapes.

Students also had many specific suggestions for enhancing the physical setup of the classroom library. Their interests support Morrow's (1991) studies demonstrating that the way a classroom library is designed has an impact on its use. The students wanted a comfortable and inviting setting, with pillows and bean bags, small tables and chairs, quilts, and a teddy bear to read to "like the one in the media center." Several thought they needed more bookshelves, and crates to hold books by genre. Other suggestions included bookends, rules, a card catalog, and "bookmarks to keep in the book and write if we liked it."

CONCLUSION

Frequently, the isolation of teaching makes communication among teachers and media specialists difficult. There were tremendous shifts in roles and resources as Benton and South Jackson moved toward whole language. Such change created even more potential for miscommunication. However, our research created communication channels during that change process. Teachers and students have told us what they need, and we have responded.

Like most action research, what we learned is most important to us as a way to improve our own educational roles. Moreover, our findings are consistent with those of other researchers. For example, Hughes (1993) studied the impact of whole language on four elementary school libraries. She found similar implications for the need for more books, collection development, a changed role for librarians, as well as some shared concerns such as limited budgets, time to meet growing needs, and providing multiple copies of books.

The data we collected were, for the most part, easily incorporated into the everyday life of the school and the media center. The information we gained has been invaluable in planning and building the media center collection, communicating with teachers and students, and examining the relation between the media centers and classroom libraries. Teachers have benefited directly, and one even urged us to continue methods such as the survey. We intend to.

Studies such as this one demonstrate that media specialists are not only a school's greatest resource, but also models of research in action.

CHAPTER 9

A Communication Triple Crown: Making Home–School Connections Among Parents, Students, and Teachers

Jennifer White

Making home–school connections has always been a big focus for me as a teacher. I enjoy parents knowing what's going on in the classroom and I want to know what kinds of literacy experiences the child is having at home. This interest in home–school connections is probably so important to me because I'm both an educator and a parent. Another reason I have focused on home–school connections is because I want the child and the parents to feel comfortable about the learning taking place. I encourage parents to visit the classroom and become a part of their child's learning. As fellow kindergarten teacher Bobbi Fisher (1991) pointed out, when there is positive communication between home and school, parents are better able to support their child's social, emotional, and academic development.

GATHERING INFORMATION AND ASKING QUESTIONS

As I became interested in researching my own practice, I decided to study home–school connections in order to understand them better and make changes where needed. For 2 years I collected data through student interviews, parent interviews, parent surveys, response journals, and the class mascot journals. I saved everything that might possibly be of value. Teachers are notorious "pack-rats," and I fit that description. Once at the grocery store the bag boy commented, "You must be a teacher. My mother was a teacher and her car was always full of books and games, too."

Each summer, I spend time looking through all the data I collected over the year and ask myself just what I'm looking for. As I read through data from the past 2 school years, I asked myself several questions: What information did I learn about students and their families? What information did parents learn about their children and my classroom through our home–school activities? What information did I learn about my own teaching? What did students learn about the reading and writing process? How did students develop as readers and writers?

In the following sections I will describe the ways I have encouraged home–school communication, using two broad categories: meetings with parents (parent orientation, town hall meetings, and the ABC Circus) and consistent channels for home–school dialogue (response journals, weekly progress reports, and the classroom mascot journal). As I describe them, I will include what I learned from my analysis.

MEETINGS WITH PARENTS

As we made significant changes in our curriculum, we wanted to explain our whole language instruction and get feedback from parents. We agreed with Regie Routman (1988) that whenever there is a major change of curriculum, teachers need to help parents understand the changes. Routman noted that at her school, "Many times, we have found that parent and teacher expectations are out of alignment" (p. 160). The kindergarten teachers at Benton designed several kinds of meetings with parents.

Parent Orientation

The first time I met with parents was at the parent orientation. All the kindergarten teachers wanted time to meet just with parents; in the past we had an open house, but that did not give us a chance to talk with parents, listen to their questions and concerns, and tell them in detail about our classrooms. So we decided to have a parent orientation just for parents; later we had the traditional open house, for children to come in and get familiar with their classrooms, when we could focus on the children. We informed families about the parent orientation during spring kindergarten registration in a letter listing many activities to help prepare their child for kindergarten, and in August we sent postcard reminders.

We had a great turnout for the orientation; nearly every family had someone there. I began with my philosophy of teaching, which is a whole language philosophy. For the most part this was the first time parents had heard the words "whole language" so I explained about teaching reading and writing as a daily process. In order for students to understand reading and writing, they need to begin reading tradebooks (actual literature books, not a reading series) and start writing stories as soon as possible. I explained how I focus my instruction around whole group activities, rather than putting students in ability groups (we do not test children at the spring registration, because we feel heterogeneous grouping is more educationally sound). Through this arrangement, I told parents, children learn from one another, and I have the opportunity to conference individually with children to address their specific needs.

Next, I explained how I integrate curriculum units, and the daily routines of reading and writing workshops (Routman, 1988). Reading workshop incorporates real literature through daily components, including the teacher reading aloud, a mini-lesson, free choice silent reading, and students sharing. In writing workshop I emphasize having the students express something in writing every day. Some key components of the writing workshop involve my reading a book to students, a mini-lesson, students writing, conferences, and time for oral sharing. I also talked with parents about how they might expect their children to develop as readers and writers. I showed samples of writing from the previous year, including books (both individual and class) the students had published.

Other aspects of home–school connections that I explained during orientation were the weekly progress reports, response journals, and the concept of a class mascot. All our kindergarten teachers and parents found this orientation most helpful, and we are definitely looking forward to continuing it in the following years.

Town Hall Meetings

Town hall meetings met a schoolwide goal that the faculty set for the year to focus on improving home–school connections. Because we wanted to make our PTO meetings more beneficial for parents, the faculty came up with the idea of town hall meetings held on alternating days 3 times a year, by grade level (e.g., fifth grade on a Thursday, third on a Wednesday, etc., so parents with more than one child could attend). Traditionally, PTO meetings have been presentations to parents; we designed town hall meetings to be more interactive. We wanted parents to be able to ask questions about their child's classroom learning. Parent orientation served as our first town hall meeting, and the next meeting was in the winter. The kindergarten teachers put together a video of the various components of our kindergarten classrooms. We felt by showing a 5-minute section of reading workshop, writing workshop, calendar time, and free centers we could give parents a better feel for their children's day. The parents watched the video and then we opened the floor for questions or comments that parents might have about their child's education. Unfortunately, parents didn't ask questions or make any comments, although I felt there probably were some.

Next, I went to the fourth-grade town hall meeting, but this time as a parent. My daughter's teacher opened the meeting by explaining activities the students had done recently and what activities would be coming in the future. Then she too opened the meeting up for a question-and-answer section. Being disappointed at the lack of discussion at the kindergarten town hall meeting, I started the group off with a question. Then other parents began talking and discussing questions and concerns with the classroom teacher and with other parents. Several parents mentioned that their children no longer had time to read for pleasure. One parent suggested that the teacher assign so many minutes each night of free reading. The teacher was very open to all suggestions that the parents made to improve the learning experience for the children. The town hall meeting had an immediate effect in the classroom. The teacher began assigning less homework and encouraged children to do more reading.

I felt the fourth-grade town hall meeting was very beneficial to me as a parent. It helped me communicate not only with the classroom teacher, but also with parents who shared the same problems or concerns with children of the same age. Parents I talked to later really appreciated the communication that took place, and the fact that the teachers acted on our concerns and valued our perspectives as parents.

ABC Circus

The ABC Circus is a favorite family activity. It is the "grand finale" of an integrated unit on the circus with major components of literacy and drama. The students and teachers read a wide variety of alphabet books; then they make and publish their own ABC big book focused around circus acts. Each kindergarten class takes a certain number of letters of the alphabet and students brainstorm together about what they could do with a letter to be an act in the kindergarten circus. Then the students make a page for the ABC Circus big book, which is read during the circus show the night of the performance. For example, the "F" page read "Fire Jumpers are jumping over fire." During the show one student would read that page in the book, then the "fire jumpers" would come out on the floor for their act. For the past 2 years the ABC Circus has been standing room only in our large gymnasium.

CONSISTENT CHANNELS FOR HOME–SCHOOL DIALOGUE

Orientation, town hall meetings, and the circus are the main times that parents and teachers communicate face to face. However, we "talk" several times a week in other ways.

Response Journals

When I asked Lori's mother what she thought of the weekly reading and writing journal they did together at home, she replied that reading and writing together "motivates her [Lori] more and she's more interested in doing it." Isn't that our job as teachers, to motivate students to want to learn? What better way to motivate students than to carry the motivation home and back again. Response journals are opportunities to build on literacy from both home and school settings. They give families a somewhat structured way of reading and writing together.

As our school moved toward whole language, our goals included increasing students' ability to read and write. With response journals, I knew I was also increasing reading and writing at home. Often parents read bedtime stories to their children, but I wanted to encourage dialogue about the books. I introduced the response journals with a very positive attitude during orientation; the parents kept the enthusiasm when they witnessed the enjoyment in their children during this shared reading and writing time.

Implementing Response Journals. Mrs. Adams, our paraprofessional, and I made the journals by stapling 10 sheets of white paper between laminated sheets of construction paper. I sent the journals home every Monday and collected them every Friday. This allowed the parents to have the journals 4 nights a week so they could decide on which 2 nights to read and respond with their child. Over the weekends, I read and responded to each journal. Some children brought their response journal in daily because they wanted me to see their responses immediately. I was pleased with the students' enthusiasm, so in those cases I praised the child, and gave him or her a sticker for the response. However, I didn't respond until the weekend because I couldn't find time in the teaching day and I wanted to send them home every night. In charting the children's responses for each week I was very pleased; I asked for at least two responses and many children and their families wrote three or four.

Interacting with Two Students and Their Families. I chose two students, a boy and a girl, for more in-depth journal study over the course of the year. I wanted to know what impact reading together, talking about books, and writing in the journal might have on these families, and particularly on each child's literacy development. It was especially important to me to develop good communication with these families, since these were children I worried about, although for different reasons.

Lee. I chose Lee because he was a child who really needed some attention. He enrolled for school 2 weeks late and showed some signs of neglect. I conferenced with the mother on several occasions. I gave her suggestions on activities that she could do at home that would help her children. The Department of Family and Children's Services was also called on by this family, and they too offered help.

Communicating with Lee's parents was difficult because the family didn't have a telephone. One day, after Lee had been absent several days, I decided to make a home visit. Lee's mother was very nice and inviting with regard to my unexpected visit. I told her that I had come out because we missed Lee in the classroom. I also asked her if I could interview her for my response journal research project, since I was already there. She agreed. As I sat down she explained how she had been using some of my suggestions to help Lee. I had suggested that they read together and talk about the letters of the alphabet. She had gone one step farther and put up each letter of the alphabet on the living room wall on white index cards. Lee's schoolwork was also taped to the wall. These were the only objects on the wall. I found this very touching and assumed it was rewarding for Lee.

Lee took a while to adjust to a structured learning setting, even one with a great many options for choice, movement, and working with friends. He did not have the chance to go to preschool and he had never had rules to follow, with consequences to deal with. Despite Lee's problems, he seemed to enjoy school tremendously. He seemed to be very happy and to thrive on the attention he received from me and the other staff.

Lee was the only student who responded almost every night in his journal; he actually had 28 responses during March, even though I required only two entries a week. He was very proud of his response journal and I was too! I still remember the look on his face every morning when he would hop into the classroom, breakfast all over his face, with his journal in hand. He couldn't wait to show me his response from the night before. Then he would return his book to the classroom library. Every afternoon he would get another book to take home to do his reading with his mother and to write another response.

Because of my home visit to Lee's house, I found out early on in the year that he didn't have any books at home. He checked books out from me and the school library and never lost a book. It was amazing and rewarding to see how far this particular family went because of our home–school connection. The family was very open to suggestions and help.

In March, Lee's father came to the school and informed me that Lee would be transferring to another school in the county because the family was moving. I really tried to convince his father to leave him at our school for the remainder of the year. The father even talked to our bus superintendent about any possible way to transport him, but it wasn't feasible. I called Lee's new teacher and discussed his progress with her and talked about the possibility of her continuing with his response journal, but she wasn't interested. She said, "Kindergarten students are too young for response journals." I couldn't convince her otherwise.

Lori. Lori and her family had just moved to the area when school started. Lori had a lot of adjusting to do. She really seemed to be a loner at first. Even at recess she wouldn't play with the other children, although toward the middle of the school year she really came around and made friends well. I think the response journals served an especially important role in helping this child and family become part of our community.

Lori chose books from the school library as well as her home library. At the beginning of the year, her parents read to her and then asked, "What do you want to say about this book?" Lori drew a picture in the response journal and copied the title and author; then her parents wrote down what Lori said.

Early in the fall, Lori contributed her own writing, using beginning sounds and words copied from books and her parents' writing. As the year progressed, Lori often started the responses with her own sentence, and then her mother would continue the response for her by taking Lori's dictation. Lori once wrote an entry herself, with her mother adding to it on the back of the page, noting that Lori had taken ownership of the entire front of the page.

One response really showed a connection between reading and

writing, and Lori's growing sense of herself as an author. Lori had chosen a book she had written and illustrated. I felt this was a significant task for a kindergartner and was even more pleased when she took the book home to read to her parents. Her journal entry was, "I rote this book. I am the author. Emily [her sister] liked this book." Emily, like other younger siblings of children in my class, also enjoyed and benefited from these family book sessions.

I used the journal to encourage Lori's progress as both reader and writer. On one occasion, I commented when Lori first used a period in her own response, and praised the way she was really starting to sound out words. Later that same week I wrote to Lori's mother and father about how pleased I was to see Lori taking on more ownership of the response journal.

On occasion, Lori's responses reflected mini-lessons from the classroom. In one response Lori's mother wrote, "She told me about the front cover, title page, and back cover." It was helpful to me to see that Lori was transferring classroom information to her home reading, and it was helpful to her mother to learn what was being talked about in the classroom. Soon, Lori was a full participant in the classroom.

One of the things I learned from studying Lori's journal, as well as the other children's, was that classroom discussion and lessons often did find their way home, as in Lori's comments about the parts of a book. In addition, as I will discuss in the following sections, I learned other valuable information about my students as learners and myself as a teacher.

Integrating the Curriculum. Several times throughout the year the opportunity arose to make connections across curriculum areas by reacting to something in the journal. I reacted with comments and questions to the parents and child. Once Andrew and his mother drew ice cream cones to illustrate their response to a book, and the mother discussed in the responses how Andrew could use shapes to draw ice cream cones. I wrote back, "Did Andrew tell you we are studying shapes? I'll have to share this with the class." Later, I did share this response and others with the class. Students took obvious pride in the responses as they were shared with the whole class. Another time, I noticed Andrew and his mother responded to a book that used positional words, and I commented that it sounded like a good book for me to use in the classroom when we focused on positional words. I recall many incidents when the students wrote about books that tied in well with our curriculum, and I used those books later as I taught various integrated units.

Encouraging Risk Taking. As a teacher I encouraged literacy development through risk taking. I often suggested to parents that they should encourage their child to do some of the writing in the journals. In early May, after several dictated responses, I wrote to Scott, "Thanks for your response. I sure hope you write the next few responses by sounding your words out. Show Mom and Dad how well you can write sentences! Thanks, Mrs. White." In the next entry, Scott responded to a book about ducklings out for a walk: "I Like iT because The Dokse Got A aiway freme aL THE Degor [danger]." For the rest of the year, Scott wrote all the responses except one.

Examining My Teaching Role. Through my fall oral interviews with parents about their children's response journals, I learned that the children really enjoyed it when I posed questions in the responses. I was glad to know this because I hadn't been asking many questions at the beginning of the year. I then decided to increase my questions. I asked the children, "Who reads my responses?" For the most part the parents read them to the child. However, Scott told me, "Sometimes I do. I sound out the words."

Lori was a child who always answered my questions. Once I asked Lori's mother if Lori herself read the book to her mother because I knew she had read it for me at school. Lori's mother wrote that she had. Later, Lori herself often wrote that she read the book. Not all children were such good correspondents; often, my questions would go unanswered. However, the parents said my questions and comments were important to their children, so I continued the practice even when the children did not respond directly.

I often learned something from the journals that informed my teaching, and my assessment of individual growth. In March, Lori wrote, "I can read this book." The more I looked back over the students' journals the more I realized this was a significant pattern. "I can read this book" was a proud announcement somewhere in almost everyone's journal. Bryan wrote in his journal, "I love this book because I can read it. It is so good. that I can read it." Kevin's mother wrote, "Kevin liked this book because he could read it by himself." The next night she wrote, "Kevin also read me this book." Children and their parents were delighted by their growing independence as readers, and, through the journals, they shared these important milestones with me.

Parent and Student Perspectives. I interviewed three students and their parents about the interaction at home with response journals. I learned that parents were already listening to their children read. Parents still tended to read to their children more, but all of them mentioned that their children also read to them. When I asked the children how they liked this time with their parents, they all responded that they really liked it. Scott said it was "Real good. I read with my mama and my daddy and my sisters. Real fun because I miss them because I'm at school."

Everyone mentioned reading stories at bedtime. Two of the three students also mentioned reading at other times of the day, too. When I asked who chose the books they read together, Scott said, "Me, from the library, and at home on the shelf in the living room and my room." Lori also mentioned, "I do from my bookshelf in my room." Lee replied, "Mama just gives me a book." Lee's mother says they don't have any books at home so they read the book Lee selected from school. It was important to the children, to their parents, and to me that they took home books they really wanted to read.

When I asked parents how they and their child decided what they would write about, I was pleased to hear them mention the ways I discussed during the parent orientation in August. They talked and wrote about how the book made them feel, whether they enjoyed the book or not, or what the book reminded them of. There were other kinds of responses also, and I always accepted whatever the child or parent wrote. Still, the journals occasionally caused frustration. Parents and children both mentioned that the most difficult aspect of writing in the journals was the frustration for children of sounding out words.

Over the past 2 years of using response journals I have had an overwhelming success; however, every year there's been a child whose parents have not participated in the journals. For these few children, Mrs. Adams (the paraprofessional) or I tried to be his or her partner.

Benefits. There are many benefits to the response journals. After interviewing the children and their parents, I found the home interaction helped increase the children's abilities as both readers and writers, and helped me establish ongoing communication with the parents. I wanted reading to become a regular part of each child's life, and I think it did. Scott's mother remarked that one Sunday afternoon, Scott chose to stay in to write a story instead of going outside to play with his siblings.

Teachers at both Benton and South Jackson learned about home-school response journals from Betty Shockley, a local first-grade teacher. She found that many parents used the journals to communicate with her about their children's literacy development, and she had extended written dialogues with them (Shockley, 1993). This did not occur as frequently with the parents of my students, because we already had a channel for communicating about how their child was doing—the weekly progress reports.

Weekly Progress Reports and Class Letters

Our county school system requires that all teachers send home weekly progress reports. There are two standard forms for teachers to choose from, a checklist by subject area with a section on behavior, or an open-ended form that has a place for teachers to comment on how the child is doing both academically and socially. I chose the open-ended commentary where I wrote what I had observed that week, with room for the parent to comment and sign the report. In addition, I wrote a class letter each week that went home with the progress reports. This letter described all the activities that were going on in the classroom. Reports went home on Tuesday, and children brought them back on Wednesday.

Sometimes parents simply signed the reports, but often they wrote questions, information about the child, or concerns. For example, in Scott's progress report I once wrote, "Scott is doing very well. He writes his numbers well and he's sounding out words beautifully. I'm so proud of his progress." Then his mother responded, "Scott so much enjoys his class and learning. He read *Caps, Hats, Socks, and Mittens*— except for the last seven pages—all by himself. I think he got tired of reading. (It took 30 minutes.) Thanks for all you do for him!" An example of a concern was when Lori's mother wrote, "Lori will not tell me the reason but she does not want to participate in Olympic Nite on 17th. She starts crying when I say she will participate. Try to find out why, okay?"

Parents really valued these two-way communication vehicles. In 2 years, every child has returned every single report. Some were a few days late, but they always came back before the next week. At the end of each year every child had a file folder full of dialogue between me and their parents. The progress reports are nice for parents to save for their child because the year's reports are all stapled together in one file folder. It's also a great way for a child to look back at his or her kindergarten year.

Classroom Mascot

My idea of using a classroom mascot came from my reading of *Joyful Learning*, a very helpful book by Bobbi Fisher (1991), as I was preparing for my transition from teaching fourth grade to teaching kindergarten. "Dino" was our first class mascot. He was a stuffed nylon dinosaur. I made sure to purchase something that was machine washable. This helped to cut down on germs. Parents threw Dino in a pillow case and washed and dried him anytime he needed it.

Dino went home with someone different every night, and the children played with him and then wrote about their time together in his journal, although parents usually did the actual writing. Every morning we read Dino's journal aloud to the class. The children loved to hear all about Dino's journeys. It was a great way of teaching new vocabulary and getting to know the students and their families well. We learned about siblings and other family members, friends, after-school activities, and bedtime routines. All parents commented that Dino was a good idea and said their children enjoyed his visits home. On a parent survey, parents remarked that the Dino activity "helps the kids to learn about reading and writing and about sharing things they do," it "teaches them responsibility and also gives them a chance to express themselves with creative ideas in writing about their time with Dino," and it "encourages creative interaction between parent and child." Parents also noted that it encouraged writing at home, set a foundation for understanding sequencing, and gave the teacher a feel for after-school activities. Most important, though, "Dino is a good friend to the children and with their stories, he comes alive."

At the end of the school year, I discussed with my students what we could do with Dino. The students wanted him to go to first grade with them, but I explained how they would all be in different classes. So as a class, we decided to put Dino in the school media center in the reading corner on the new dinosaur bean bags for all to enjoy. We talked about how they could go and read to him whenever they got a chance.

The next school year I chose another mascot for my new group of students. This dinosaur, Spike, was loved just as much as Dino. The students always seemed to get great joy out of our class mascot, and parents enjoyed the excitement it brought to their child's kindergarten learning experience.

The mascot journal writing was another way that let me know about the home life of the children and gave the families a way to get to know me and Mrs. Adams, since we both take the mascot home, too. For example, we learned that Natalie had 35 baby chicks to care for, Katie's mother went to school at Athens Tech and had homework, Anne's father was driving a "Big Truck" to California, and Spike was a big Braves fan—he even learned how to do the "Tomahawk Chop."

In deciding which class mascot journal entry to include in this chapter, I chose Jessica. While her family did not write in the response journal, they usually did write in the mascot journal. This entry is rather short compared with most of the responses families wrote, which were often two (and sometimes three) full notebook pages in length. Two days before school was out in June it was Jessica's turn to take Dino home. Although it was Jessica's parents who usually responded in the mascot journal, this response was written by Jessica and her older brother, who was in third grade at our school. It was great to see that Jessica had another interested family member.

> Surprise wasn't the word when Ken picked my name and Kari read it. I'm sure Dino was so excited as me. We rode home together on the bus and I excitedly showed him to my brother, Donald, as we came home. Once at home Dino almost leaped out of my arms as he saw my younger brother Stewart and Mom. Joy raced across his face as he was passed from arm to arm. Daddy wasn't at home when we got there but came in later. Boy was he surprised that Dino was back. Together we all set down and watched TV. Daddy works at nite and Mom had recorded "Call of the Wild" on the VCR for him to watch. Dino had never seen it before last nite so he watched it with Daddy. However half way through me and Dino fell to sleep. We finally went to bed, so we would be rested for school the next day.
>
> Someday I hope to have maybe one of Dino's brothers as my very own, but until then I can enjoy Dino's company whenever it's my time. Thank you class for this experience.
>
> Jessica T.

AN INVITATION

Mrs. Adams gave me both the poster, which hangs in my room, and the book *All I Really Need to Know I Learned in Kindergarten* by Robert Fulghum (1986). One thing Fulghum learned in kindergarten is that we need to "share everything." That's true for teachers, too. We need to share among ourselves to help the children of the future have the best education possible. I feel that I have a better understanding now of how important kindergarten is, not only to students but to their families. I also have reinforced my belief that each student and each family is unique and offers us opportunities to expand our knowledge as teachers. I really enjoy researching my teaching practices to help benefit the students and improve my teaching. I write about my research in the hope that my experiences will be helpful to someone else. I encourage other teachers to take time to look at their classroom and identify questions they have about teaching. It has been really helpful to me to interview students and parents, do surveys, examine journals over time, and think about how I might improve my home–school communication channels. I encourage other teachers to indulge in the rich data that students have to offer, and then to write about what they learn so that the rest of us can share it. That is how we build the knowledge base for teaching.

PART V

STUDENT PERSPECTIVES

CHAPTER 10

New Pathways to Literacy: A Reflective Look at a First-Year Pre-Kindergarten Program

Marilynn Cary, Lori Davis, and Janet Benton

Look with us into a pre-kindergarten classroom of 4- and 5-year-olds. Chad and Ellen share a picture book in the reading corner. Ted, a fifth grader, reads to a small group of students. Jim, Kevin, and Janna build a castle in the block area, using a book cover as a model. Nina, using invented spelling, is taking orders with a crayon and scratch pad in the housekeeping area as she pretends to be a waitress at a "fancy restaurant." Bobby and Lisa fold paper for their invitations to a teddy bear tea party. The teacher, Lori Davis, moves among the learners—looking, listening, questioning, and smiling as she watches the children on their pathways to literacy.

Giving young children the opportunity to explore literacy in a developmentally appropriate classroom environment became a reality in 1992 when Georgia implemented its first public pre-kindergarten program, and our school became one of the pilot sites. This chapter is a close look at the impact of the new program on its first class of students.

PLANNING THE JOURNEY: PROGRAM ORIGIN

In the early 1990s, the state of Georgia specified criteria to identify a group of 4-year-olds whose individual needs required attention not generally provided prior to their first days of kindergarten. The pre-kindergarten program was intended to enhance the students' early elementary school years with opportunities for success. Through this program, it was hoped that schools might become places for growth rather than institutions of disappointment.

During the Jackson County school strategic planning in 1992, members of the school community formally identified the need for a pre-kindergarten program and developed a tentative plan of implementation. When the governor of Georgia, Zell Miller, proposed a pilot program for ''at-risk four-year-old children and their families,'' the proposal expanded to include cooperative services through the Jackson County Human Resource Council.

The Georgia Department of Education determined the eligibility criteria for the pilot program. A child must meet these criteria.

> A. Four (4) years of age on or before September 1 of
> the school year and either
> B. Participants in or income eligible for one of the
> following:
>   1. Medicaid
>   2. AFDC/Food Stamps
>   3. Women, Infants, and Children (WIC)
>   4. Child Nutrition Programs
>   5. Subsidized family housing *or*
> C. Referred by an agency serving children and their families other than the above agencies. Such agencies include, but are not limited to, United Way, Health Department, Migrant Program, Homeless Shelters, Salvation Army, or local Department of Family and Children Services. (Georgia Department of Education Office of Instructional Services, 1992, pp. 2–3)

Many families in our area met these guidelines. A sociodemographic description from our pilot program application (Benton Elementary School, 1992) provides insights into the general context and particular needs of certain families.

> Jackson County is a large, rural county of 342 square miles with 2/3 of the population living in unincorporated areas. In 1990 there were 432 4-year-olds, half of whom were at-risk. . . . In 1988, 22% lived below poverty level. In 1991, 618 children received AFDC benefits, and 603 received Medicaid. . . . Between 1988 and 1990 there has been a 293% increase in the number of reported child abuse cases. In 1990 the Health Department reported 33 low birth weight babies and 32 four-year-olds being served through the WIC program. (n.p.)

The pre-kindergarten program we proposed would meet the needs of those children the state called at-risk 4-year-olds.

CLEARING THE PATHWAY: PROGRAM DESCRIPTION

The pre-kindergarten program at Benton consisted of twenty 4-year-olds with birth dates ranging from 10/19/87 through 8/8/88. There were 13 boys and 7 girls at the beginning, with one boy and one girl leaving the program during the year. As with any group, there was a wide range of personality types, developmental levels, and family backgrounds. Lori Davis, the lead teacher, and Kelli Ingram, the support teacher, worked daily with the children. Rebecca Lindsay, the family services coordinator, worked together with the teachers, children, and their families.

The preschool curriculum met the guidelines of the National Association for the Education of Young Children (NAEYC). The program, designed to provide learning opportunities and enhance childhood, offered rich and developmentally appropriate learning experiences. Materials and activities enabled children to solve problems, develop science and math concepts, improve self-expression, practice cooperation, enhance social skills, and learn language skills. Firsthand experiences with equipment, materials, and various environments helped these young learners develop concepts, form opinions, make choices, and organize ideas.

The pre-kindergarten program linked the school with the child's family and the community. As part of the program, Mrs. Lindsay and Mrs. Davis made home visits and offered family workshops throughout the school year. The program also helped families access service agencies and focused on adult literacy issues by helping parents complete their high school educations.

Parents volunteered to help with classroom activities and projects, went on field trips, visited for lunch, and attended various workshops providing information on enhancing parenting skills. We sent home periodic informal progress reports and held parent–teacher conferences to give feedback about children's experiences in the classroom throughout the year. Additionally, monthly family council meetings furnished opportunities for families to come together at school, with the school providing baby sitting. During council meetings we discussed issues including nutrition, health services, effective discipline, and choosing age-appropriate books and toys.

The pre-kindergarten class met Monday through Friday, from 7:30 a.m. until 2:20 p.m., in conjunction with regular school hours at Benton Elementary School. The daily schedule included breakfast and lunch, manipulative and circle time, group sharing, rest time, and small-group activities. The teachers and students engaged in free exploration through learning centers, stories, finger plays, and creative movement. The students participated in physical activities and large motor activities through outdoor play and gym time. Language experiences and peer reading by older students added to the daily routine.

The teachers drew from community resources for learning experiences by taking the students on field trips to the post office, library, fire station, pet shop, local parks, grocery store, museum, chicken hatchery, swine farms, greenhouse and nursery, and the shopping mall and local restaurants. The teachers integrated these activities with classroom literacy experiences.

The physical environment of the program included a wide variety of manipulatives for both large and small motor development. The classroom consisted of areas known as centers for exploration. The areas included "at home," with housekeeping items, medical kits, grocery store, and dollhouse; "at work," with a miniature workshop complete with tools, hollow blocks, duplo building blocks and various other blocks, vehicles, and a motor mat; and "at play," providing a wide variety of puzzles, games, legos, activity cards for lacing, peg boards, play dough, stencils, paper and pencils, and markers. Other areas in the room were "library and listening area," which contained over 100 books, audiotapes, videotapes, puppet theater and puppets, musical instruments, and records; "I made it," containing paints, easels, and various mediums for creating arts and crafts; and "my big world," with science and earth manipulatives, toy animals and insects, plants, an aquarium with fish, a balance and scale set, sand and water table, and a place for objects brought in by students to observe. During the latter part of the year, items were added to develop a computer center, with Touch, Tell, and Discover games, My Little Computer, and Alphie. Another area, the large motor area, contained tricycles, a wagon, climbing and playhouse slide, basketball goal, balance board, ball, hoops, and bean bags.

Children came to school with their parents or on county buses with other Benton Elementary students. An after-school daycare program existed in a private home for those children whose parents worked; between three and six children attended this program throughout the year.

INTERSECTING PATHWAYS: PROGRAM INTEGRATION

One of the important changes that took place was the acceptance of a new pre-kindergarten program into the existing school community. This integration took place on several levels. The fact that the pre-kindergarten students followed the same daily schedules as the rest of the school aided the integration process. The students ate breakfast and lunch in the lunchroom with other classes and had recess on the playground while other classes were there. The children visited the school library weekly to choose and check out books. The pre-kindergarten students also participated in schoolwide activities such as the Olympic field day and program presentations.

Additionally, other classes invited the pre-kindergarten students to programs in their rooms, and students from other grades came to the pre-kindergarten room to demonstrate literacy activities, which included choral readings and mini-plays. For example, as part of the fifth grade's unit on community awareness, the students in one class submitted job applications to work in various areas at Benton Elementary. Mrs. Davis interviewed and "hired" two fifth-grade students to work as readers in the pre-kindergarten class. They reported weekly and read to small groups and individuals. The overall school climate at Benton further aided the integration of the pre-kindergarten program. Our program was very consistent with Benton's literacy initiative, including changes in teaching, in methods of assessment, and in curriculum adaptations. The school has become accustomed to change and educational diversification. Further, there is a strong sense of community here, and our desire to be an active part of that community was welcomed and facilitated.

On a professional level, Mrs. Davis, Ms. Ingram, and Mrs. Lindsay participated in the self-governance structure of the school by serving on cluster groups and on task force committees. They also attended the elective staff development classes held on a regular basis at the school. All of these activities made it possible for the pre-kindergarten program to be integrated successfully into an existing K–5 school. Mrs. Davis was interested in studying the impact of the program and joined the Benton Research Team, which led to further communication and integration across classrooms.

FOOTPRINTS ON THE PATHWAY: SUMMARY OF FINDINGS

Because this was the first year of a new program, as teacher researchers we felt that it was important to examine and document the benefits of the program and to see how it affected the learners as individuals and as a group. Quantitative and qualitative data were collected and analyzed in an attempt to map out the progress of children in the program.

The blending of quantitative and qualitative research strategies allowed us to incorporate multiple perspectives into the group and individual descriptions of students in this pre-kindergarten classroom.

Summary of Quantitative Information

During the 1992–93 school year, members of the district's psychometric staff administered the Bracken Basic Concept Scale (1984) and the Social Skills Rating System (Grasham & Elliot, 1990) as pre- and post-test measures to the pre-kindergarten class. Since these measures are used by the district in program evaluation, we wanted to interpret them and include them in our own research. Additionally, we wanted data that would convince policy makers that our program was effective. The data most often requested by policy makers are test scores. Analyses performed on the data outlined broad pictures of the classroom. Where percentile ranks were compared, pretest measures used beginning-of-year norms, and post-test measures used end-of-year norms.

We asked Cliff Gardiner, a graduate student, to do a statistical comparison of the pre- and post-tests. A comparison of pre- and post-test performance on the Bracken Basic Concept Scale, an instrument measuring concept acquisition, revealed a substantial improvement at the whole-group level. The Bracken Basic Concept Scale is concerned with the child's acquisition of certain concepts deemed important for school readiness: color, letter identification, numbers/counting, comparisons, shape, direction/position, social/emotional, size, texture/material, quantity, time/sequence. The national mean on the total score is 100, with a standard deviation of 15, placing the Bracken Basic Concept Scale scores on a scale shared by many current measures of intelligence and achievement. The pretest mean for the class was 84.1, and the post-test mean was 89.2, making the average gain during the year 5.1.

A related samples t-test was run on the pretest and post-test group means of the Bracken Basic Concept Scale standard test score. There was a significant improvement between pretest and post-tests (see Table 10.1). Mr. Gardiner also performed a related samples t-test on group mean percentiles between the Bracken Basic Concept Scale pre- and post-tests. The mean percentile rank on total standard score for the pretest was 17.9; the mean percentile rank on total standard score for the post-test was 29.3, showing a significant gain in percentile ranking.

The Social Skills Rating System allowed the classroom teacher to rate each student in terms of the frequency with which he or she manifested certain social behaviors. For this program the teacher rated each student in two domains. In one domain, social skills, the teacher as-

Table 10.1. Pre- and post-test scores of a pre-kindergarten class.

	Bracken Basic Concept Scale		Social Skills RatingSystem		Problem Behaviors	
	pre	post	pre	post	pre	post
n	18	18	18	18	18	18
Mean	84.0	89.2	97.6	116.1	45.9	81.2
S.D.	9.0	11.6	14.4	11.8	30.0	20.6
Min.	66	66	70	83	2	13
Max	103	105	118	130	88	98
t	2.80		8.00		6.51	
p	0.006		0.0001		0.0001	

sessed common behaviors such as cooperation, assertion, and self-control. On the first measure, performed early in the school year, the mean standard score for the class on the social skills component was 97.6. On the second measure, performed toward the end of the school year, the mean standard score for the class on the same component was 116.1, indicating substantial improvement in the children's social skills. A related samples t-test comparing these pre- and post-measures revealed strong evidence of improvement, as shown in Table 10.1.

The second domain of the Social Skills Rating System used by the teacher was the problem behaviors component. In this domain the teacher assessed behaviors such as inappropriate verbal or physical behavior toward others, behaviors indicating internal qualities like anxiety and poor self-esteem, and hyperactivity. On the premeasure, the class mean was 45.9. On the postmeasure, the class mean improved substantially to 81.2, indicating a reduction in the children's observable problem behaviors. A related samples t-test on the pre- and postmeasures showed significant improvement, as shown in Table 10.1.

While the quantitative instruments provided evidence that students showed improvement in the areas of school-related knowledge and social skills, we were not able to construct in-depth insights into the behaviors of the children from these measures alone. To enhance the quantitative data and to better describe the experiences of the students, Mrs. Davis and Mrs. Cary collected qualitative data through observations and video interviews.

Summary of Qualitative Information

We analyzed the video interviews conducted as part of the schoolwide longitudinal research project (see Chapter 11). However, for the pre-kindergarten segment of the study, Mrs. Cary and Mrs. Davis did not choose the pre-kindergarten students by ability groups. Mrs. Cary interviewed 10 of the 18 children in the classroom for the qualitative research component of the study; parents' willingness to permit participation was the primary criterion for the selection of these students. Mrs. Cary used roughly the same interview protocol used with K–5 students (see Figure 11.1); however, she modified the wording of questions for the younger children.

Mrs. Cary and Mrs. Davis, along with Janet Benton, a university research assistant, reviewed the transcripts of the videotaped pre-kindergarten interviews and found that the students' responses to the questions could be grouped into various categories. They then reviewed and collapsed these categories into three overarching themes. One theme was the children's view of themselves as readers and writers in relation to our perceptions of their literacy development. The second theme evident throughout all interviews was that much in the children's responses about educational experiences related to family and home experiences. The third theme was the children's association of positive learning experiences with play. General, overall patterns and themes emerged; from this analysis came the in-depth portraits of four students, highlighted against the backdrop of the broader quantitative data.

When the researchers compared the interview data about the children's views of themselves as readers and writers with their actual classroom behaviors and performance on testing instruments, they noted that the children who scored higher on the Bracken Basic Concept Scale based their ideas about themselves as readers and writers on conventional definitions of literacy. The children who scored lower made reading and writing claims based more on preconventional definitions or made unrealistic claims. For example, when Mrs. Cary asked Kim, who had a concept age of 3-8 (chronological age 4-11), "What will your pre-kindergarten teacher tell your kindergarten teacher about your reading and writing?" Kim said, "I can write my name. I'm a reader in preschool." On the other hand, Charles, with a concept age of 5-11 (chronological age 5-6) responded to the same question with, "I don't know no reading. I like to learn reading." These definitions fit with Sulzby's (1985) finding that emergent readers often think of themselves as readers when they tell stories about the pictures, but many reach a "refusal" stage when they say they can't read, which often directly precedes the beginnings of conventional (print-oriented) reading.

As expected, the children's conversations about educational experiences also related to family, home, and recent school experiences. For instance, when asked about future impressions of school, children tended to draw from their recent experiences as well as those of their older siblings or other family members. When asked the question, "How do you feel about going to kindergarten," Will responded, "I feel good. [I will] make a fish. My sister painted a fish yesterday in kindergarten." Our findings reaffirm the assumption that children's perceptions of school tend to be built on their past experiences with family, home, and previous structured learning experiences.

Another trend developed during the interviews when children were asked, "What did you like most about pre-kindergarten?" Charles answered this question by saying, "Housekeeping . . . I play with food, beds, baby dolls. You can do some pretending in housekeeping." When asked, "When do you feel smart at school," 8 of the 10 children interviewed made positive statements about playing; direct references also were made to "playing" in the hands-on center activities. The interview data corroborate Piaget's (1950) philosophy that children's work is play.

THE EXPLORERS: PORTRAITS OF FOUR LEARNERS

Based on interview data and observations, Mrs. Cary, Mrs. Davis, and Ms. Benton selected four learners to spotlight in individual portraits. They purposely selected these four students to represent differences in school-related performance behaviors and gender. These glimpses into the lives of Kendra, Will, Ellen, and Chad enhance an understanding of their worlds, both inside and outside the pre-kindergarten classroom. The names of the students have been changed to ensure confidentiality. Sources of information used, in addition to the teacher researchers' classroom participant-observations, are the Bracken Basic Concept Scale, the Preschool Social Skills Rating System (completed by both teacher and parent), Creative Curriculum's informal developmental assessment, transcripts of videotaped student interviews, and students' drawings.

Kendra

The year was an exciting one of awakenings for Kendra and her teacher. This cute little girl with brown hair and brown eyes entered the classroom with wide-eyed wonder, very few social skills, and virtually no academic readiness skills. Her Bracken Concept Scale pretest given in January, 3 months after her entrance to the class, revealed a concept age of 2-6 (chronological age 4-7) and a standard score of 73. Her Social Skills Rating System pretest yielded a standard score of 78. Kendra appeared unkempt and had few grooming or self-care skills. She did not demonstrate proper hygiene when eating and toileting. Her speech and language abilities were below age level. She had difficulty with both receptive and expressive language tasks. Early in the year, she failed a hearing screening, and the school audiologist referred her for medical care. She also exhibited behavioral problems such as hitting, kicking, spitting at others, temper tantrums, and refusal to follow directions.

Kendra's family situation was challenging at best. Her family lived in a small mobile home and consisted of mother, father, and several siblings under age 10. The family had moved several times because her father's work led them to various places. One of Kendra's older siblings was identified as learning disabled. She mentioned this sibling often as being abusive to her. Many of her conversations were about her family and various situations within the home that made her uneasy or upset. In her video interview, Kendra mentioned past experiences and family members when answering questions. Her interview was very hard to interpret; because of her poor language skills, she often had difficulty understanding and answering questions. When asked about what she liked to do at school, she would relate home experiences like playing "boogie man" and "Nintendo." When asked what made her feel smart, she answered, "When my brother is mad, it smarts [hurts]."

As the year progressed, many encouraging events took place. With the guidance of her teachers and peers, Kendra's social skills increased. She also began to have a passion for books, wanting someone to read to her frequently in the large group, small groups, and individually. Her mother reported that Kendra had started to request books instead of other treats when allowed to purchase items. On two occasions, Kendra hid books in her locker to take home or to look at during nap time. This new appreciation for reading was very exciting for Mrs. Davis. When asked during the video interview, "What would your teacher say about your reading," Kendra replied, "Fine . . . I can read one book, a frog book." She claimed reading skills and writing skills throughout the interview, stating that she "could write her name" when she could only write the first letter of her name by the end of the school year.

At the end of the school year, Kendra scored a concept age of 4-8 and a standard score of 85 on the Bracken Basic Concept Scale, and a standard score of 108 on the Social Skills Rating System. Her self-portrait was much more detailed (see Figure 10.1). She had replaced her physical aggression with verbal expressions such as calling others "stupid" and "ugly" and stating, "I'm telling on you" when she felt wronged. Mrs. Davis was concerned that Kendra could not name or associate colors; however, compared with where she was when she entered the program, it was evident that Kendra had greatly benefited from her pre-kindergarten experiences.

Will

Kendra's classmate Will, a very bright 4-year-old with brown hair and brown eyes, tended to be serious and somewhat shy; he entered the program in October with some emergent literacy skills. Will was a very sensitive child who cried often compared with his peers in pre-kindergarten; however, he was eager to perform tasks and learn new skills. He was very concerned with classroom routines such as who was helper or leader each day, and he volunteered for any job that needed a helper. Will enjoyed making choices in his daily schedule at school; this was verified in his video interview when he said that he most enjoyed playing in "block area, housekeeping, computer, and library areas . . . and doll house" during school.

His Bracken Basic Concept Scale pretest standard score was 94 with a concept age of 4-4 (chronological age 4-9), putting him in the 34th percentile of children his age. Although Will achieved a standard score in the average range (110) on the Social Skills Rating System, his social adjustment was observed to be lower than that of his peers. For example, Mrs. Davis noted that he would cry often for his mother and exhibit high anxiety when his mother left the classroom. Will scored a standard score of 95 on the Bracken post-test with a concept age of 5-0. His Social Skills post-test standard score was 122. His anxiety decreased throughout the year as he appeared more comfortable with the school setting, but Mrs. Davis observed him to be very dependent on his mother when she visited the classroom or accompanied the group on field trips. He acted more immature when his mother was present, but the anxiety of her leaving lessened considerably by the end of the year. It was apparent through observations and test scores that Will's mother worked with him on language, reading, and writing, and read aloud to him at home. When asked about his reading and writing skills, Will said, "I don't know. I can write a little bit. My teacher might say my writing is good."

Will lived with his mother, older siblings, and stepfather in a rural area of the county. He visited his father once each month. Many of his

Figure 10.1. Kendra's October and May self-portraits.

10/30/92

5/30/93

conversations were about his home life and an older sibling in kindergarten. He spoke often about his mother but rarely mentioned his father
or stepfather. Will's mother attended college during his pre-kindergarten year, and Will's responses during the interview seemed to
reflect the idea of the importance of education, perhaps from observing
his own mother as she prepared for school. When asked during the
video interview about whether he thought he might graduate from high
school and college, he matter of factly said, "Yes. Just when you get big
you just do that. You just go to college."

Mrs. Davis believed that Will's greatest benefits from his pre-
kindergarten experience came in the areas of social and emotional experiences with peers and others outside his home environment. She saw
Will become more flexible with changes in their daily routine. At the
beginning of the school year, he didn't understand such aspects of
social interaction as turn taking and schedules; for instance, Will often
demanded to be first in line. By the end of the year, he was more
cooperative with the other children in the classroom.

Ellen

Ellen turned 5 shortly after the school year began; she was one of the
oldest students in the classroom. A seemingly timid blonde, blue-eyed
little girl, Ellen came to pre-kindergarten with listening skills and an
eagerness to learn. She adjusted very well to the pre-kindergarten setting and made many friends among her peers, although she remained
shy around adults. Ellen seemed to enjoy most activities and she
learned easily. Ellen's family background, however, was not encouraging. Her parents dropped out of school before completing the ninth
grade. Her older siblings lacked positive school experiences; one repeated a grade and one was eligible for the learning disabled program.
This family lived in an older, poorly maintained mobile home. Throughout the year the family members were in crisis situations such as unemployment, loss of utilities, and domestic disputes. The family service
coordinator made numerous contacts with this family, connecting them
with appropriate services and counseling agencies. Ellen's parents expressed the desire to better their home situation but had difficulty reach-
ing these goals.

Ellen's work in class reflected her concern about her family. In
questioning Ellen about her 5/30/93 drawing (see Figure 10.2), Mrs.
Davis found that she was very concerned about her mother and the
stability of her home. She had drawn an excellent picture of herself and
her mother, yet her mother's face looked angry, and she had drawn

Figure 10.2. Ellen's May self-portrait: "Mommy was sad and I was unhappy."

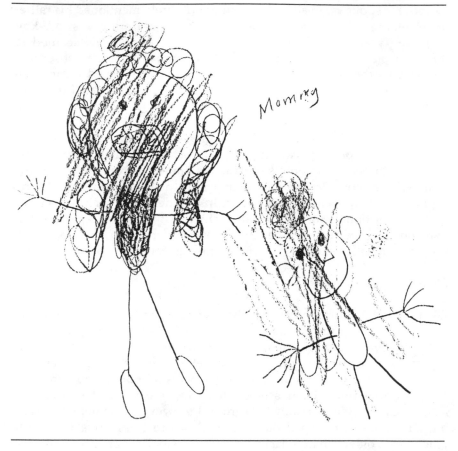

several lines over her mother and herself. When asked to tell about the picture, she explained that her mommy was sad and she (Ellen) was unhappy. Ellen seemed sad and distant during the last month of school and did not return for the summer program, although her mother had registered her. When asked if she thought she would graduate from college, Ellen said, "I might not be going to college. My mama might not put me in college."

Ellen enjoyed free exploration time in the classroom, which involved hands-on activities in various learning centers set up around the room. In her video interview she said, "I liked playing with blocks, making houses, playing with the dollhouse, playing with trucks and playing in centers." Ellen achieved a standard score of 85 on the Bracken pretest with a concept age of 4-5 and a Social Skills Rating System standard score of 97. Ellen's post-test score on the Bracken Developmental Scale was 100, compared with her pretest standard score of 85. Her post-test concept age was 4-10 and her Social Skills Rating System standard score was 124. From information provided by the Bracken Basic Concept Scale, Social Skills Rating System, and teacher observations, Ellen seemed to benefit from the pre-kindergarten program in social and emotional areas. Furthermore, in her interview she made positive comments about her reading and writing skills.

Chad

The final portrait is of Chad, an adorable, very active, blonde with huge hazel-brown eyes and a constant smile. Chad lived with his parents and younger siblings in a rural area of Jackson County. During the school year Chad's family moved from a very inadequate home to another somewhat larger home in better physical condition. Chad's family experienced crisis situations due to unemployment and debt, and utilized the family service coordinator frequently.

Chad's scores on the Bracken Basic Concept Scale were 88 on the pretest and 100 on the post-test, indicating an increase. His Bracken concept age increased from 3-8 to 4-10. Chad's drawings also showed an increase in his development throughout the year (see Figure 10.3). Chad enjoyed working with paper and pencil and used them often when given the opportunity to choose activities during free exploration time. In his video interview, he said that he "liked writing," "liked to color in coloring books," was "good at writing," and that he liked "to write big trucks, houses, boxes, lights, and paintings," thus connecting drawing to writing skills. He mentioned on three occasions in the interview that he liked to write or color. When asked about his reading skills, he said, "I can read real good," and "my teacher will say I'm good at reading"; in actuality, he exhibited few emergent reading behaviors at the end of the school year.

Similar to many other 4-year-olds, Chad's conversations throughout the year were about family members and past experiences. He mentioned his dad's occupation frequently. When asked what job he wanted to do when he was older, he replied, "Building houses." When asked if he needed to go to school to learn this, he answered, "My dad would show me how." There seemed to be a positive relationship between Chad and his father.

Chad's social skills also increased throughout the year as evidenced

Figure 10.3. Chad's October and May self-portraits.

10/30/92   5/30/93

by his movement from 80 on the pretest of the Social Skills Rating System to 120 on the post-test. When discussing his feelings about going to kindergarten, he quickly replied, "Good. I'll like being in school with my friends." This perhaps indicates a positive outlook toward future school-related activities, an outlook that might have been different without his pre-kindergarten experiences.

WHERE THE PATHWAY LEADS: RECOMMENDATIONS

Based on this research study, we intend to address the following areas in future years:

1. The pre-kindergarten program will, and should, be continued. All of the children benefited in a variety of ways. Also, we feel that the findings from this study support the use of developmentally appro-

priate curriculum that allows for self-exploration. Furthermore, a language-rich environment, such as the one in this pre-kindergarten classroom, adds to the early literacy experiences of young learners.

2. We need to keep, date, and file more samples of student work to analyze for future research, especially for possible case study children.

3. We plan to increase interviews of children through the year to access likes, dislikes, feelings, and questions about their pre-kindergarten experiences, and to help us make program and instructional decisions.

4. While we did not collect data to support this recommendation, our interactions with families prompt us to conclude that more parent involvement is needed in classroom activities through scheduled weekly participation. We would like parents to get involved for a time period each week, to come to class and participate in activities alongside children, including art activities, cooking activities, and reading.

State Department officials overseeing the implementation of pre-kindergarten programs statewide were most impressed with this report, which we sent them at the end of the first year. While the numbers from the quantitative instruments point to the success of this pre-kindergarten program's first year, the images of students like Kendra, Will, Ellen, and Chad are what will forever remind us of the need to provide positive learning experiences for all of our students.

ACKNOWLEDGMENT. The authors would like to thank Frances Hensley for her suggestions during the preliminary analysis of the qualitative data and Cliff Gardiner for his assistance with the quantitative data analysis.

CHAPTER 11

"Make Learning Funner, So People Want to Learn": A Longitudinal Study of Students' Perceptions About Schooling

Lolita Brown, Lori Davis, Patty Griffith, Cheryl Poponi, Dorothy Rice, Jane Rogers, Holly Ward, and Jennifer White

In the first 2 years of our involvement in the UGA Educational Initiative, we focused on teacher empowerment and instructional improvement, with particular emphasis on whole language. For us, teacher research was the next logical step in our school's growth and development; we wanted to know what impact the changes we were making had on our students, especially over time. We wanted to develop our own questions and conduct the research rather than turning to outside sources. The larger Benton Research Team met regularly throughout the school year to encourage and support each other. Through these meetings some members of the team discovered that we had similar interests and our research could be combined into a team project. The project became known as "the video study," since we videotaped the interviews.

Although we came from different grades and areas of specialization (see Figure 11.1), we had common concerns. We were interested in examining the perceptions of children about school throughout their school careers. Our research was focused on three major questions.

What are students' perceptions of school and learning? When and how do they change?
What are students' perceptions of themselves as readers and writers?
How do special education students see themselves, and how do their peers view them? What are the perceptions of the special education teacher?

Figure 11.1. Video project participants.

TEAM MEMBERS

Lolita Brown, Chapter 1	Jane Rogers, 1–3 Resource Room
Marilynn Cary, Speech Therapist	Holly Ward, 5th Grade
Lori Davis, Pre-kindergarten	Janet Benton, UGA Consultant
Patty Griffith, 4/5 Resource Room	Jane West, UGA Consultant
Patsy Lentz, Principal	Frances Hensley, UGA Consultant
Cheryl Poponi, 5th Grade	JoBeth Allen, UGA Consultant
Dorothy Rice, 3rd Grade	

This was truly a team project. Members participated in various aspects of question development, student selection, interviewing, transcribing, analyzing, and writing. The authors listed are the people who actually wrote the chapter during the summers of 1993 and 1994, but everyone on the team contributed to the research. We wish to extend our thanks to Julie Parks, UGA graduate assistant, for substituting in our rooms while we interviewed children and for transcribing many of the tapes.

PSEUDONYMS AND GRADE LEVEL (IN 1992–93) OF STUDENTS INTERVIEWED
Pre-kindergarten: Will, Hannah, Ben, Hillary, Carl, Ellen, Kim, Chad, Joe, Kendra
Kindergarten: John, Whitney, Corey, Pebbles, Shaffine
First: Jon, Sid, Mickey, Brenda, Nicky
Second: Carla, Jean, Anna, Todd
Third: Sandra, Paul, Molly, Jenny, Melanie
Fourth: Beth, Kevin, Jake, James; (2nd Year additions) Ryan, Addie
Fifth: Rachel, Brian, Kim, Sam, Ken

RESEARCH DESIGN

In this section we explain our initial research design. It has remained basically the same, with slight modifications in questions, timelines, and data analysis strategies each year, based on reflection about the previous year's effectiveness.

Student Selection

We wanted to make sure that the study included a diverse and broad representation of the student body. Therefore, we asked classroom teachers in grades K–5 to identify students with different academic performance: above average, average, below average, underachiever, and classified special education (excluding speech). We did not define the categories; each teacher constructed her own definitions and identified students accordingly. The only exception to this procedure was special education. All students at Benton who were categorized by their classroom teachers as special education students had been previously identified as learning disabled or behavior disordered and were receiving services from a special education teacher. We selected one student from each category at every grade level (K–5), making a total of 30. Before we made the final selection of students, we also considered who would likely remain in the community throughout their school careers and who would be likely to talk openly in the interview. We also tried to have an equal balance of girls and boys.

An additional 10 children from our pre-kindergarten also joined the study (see Chapter 10). None of these students were classified special education, but some were receiving speech services. All pre-kindergarten students whose parents were interested in being part of the study were included. We secured parental permission for all participating students. The letter explained, in part:

> This year our school is looking at how well we are educating your children. . . . We want to get . . . your children's ideas about school. . . . Over the next few months we may ask to interview . . . your child . . . about their reading, their writing and/or their attitudes about school. . . . Some of us may use this information to teach other teachers about how to help children be successful students. We may write articles or give talks about what we learn. . . . The interviews will be videotaped [each year]. At the end of the study the tape will be yours to keep. . . . We are looking forward to learning more about the students at Benton, how they learn best, and what they think is important about school.

Data Collection

We interviewed the same students every spring. Figure 11.1 provides a reference list of pseudonyms and the grade level of each child the first year. We began in the spring of 1993 (Year 1), interviewed the same students in the spring of 1994 (Year 2), and plan to follow up each year until the original fifth-grade class graduates from high school. We developed an interview guide (Figure 11.2) and in Year 2 learned from Seidman (1991) more about interviewing techniques. Each researcher chose students from one grade level to interview in Year 1 and to follow throughout high school in subsequent years. A substitute teacher covered classes so we could interview students during school hours.

Figure 11.2. Interview guide questions.

1. What is your best memory about learning in school? Think about a time when you were learning something that you really were excited about, or interested in. Tell me about it.
   What is your worst memory about learning in school?
2. When do you feel like you are smart? (Probe: Who makes you feel that way?)
   When do you feel like you are not smart? (Probe: Who makes you feel that way?)
3. What does special ed teacher do? Why do you go to her room? What do the other kids think when you go to her room?
   or
   Why do some kids in your class go to special ed room? What do you think about them when they go to her room?
4. Pretend you are moving to a new school. Ms. _____ is going to call up your new teacher. What do you think she will say about you? (Probes: What will she say about you as a reader? What will she say about you as a writer?)
5. Now pretend you are at your new school. Your new teacher says, "Tell me about yourself. What kind of student are you?"
   a. Tell me about yourself as a reader.
   b. Tell me about yourself as a writer.
6. Your new teacher asks you for some advice. "What should I do to be a really good teacher?" What would you say? (Probes: What would you say about teaching reading? What would you say about teaching writing?)
7. What do you think you will be doing when you are a grown up? (Probes: How do you think you will get to be a _____?) (school training, etc.)
8. How do you feel about going to (the next grade)? (Probes: What things do you think you will do well in (next) grade? What things are you worried about in (next) grade?
9. Do you think you will graduate from high school? Why? Do you think you will graduate from college? Why?

Interviews ranged from 15 to 45 minutes in length. We conducted our interviews on videotape for several reasons. It allowed us to concentrate totally on the interview rather than transcribing. Videotaping the interviews also gave us an accurate and permanent record that could be added to easily each year and enabled us to both hear and see changes in our students over time. This record was valuable and important, not only to us as researchers, but also to parents and students who would receive a copy of it at the end of the study.

Data Analysis

Each of us planned to transcribe the interviews we conducted. We found this to be very time-consuming and eventually hired Mandy

McMichen to do the initial transcriptions, which we later annotated to fill in missing information. During the summer analysis and writing weeks, each researcher got a complete set of the transcriptions, color coded by grade level. We read through each interview, making marginal notes, identifying issues that seemed important, and generating categories. We then took our "cooked" data and individually identified themes relating to our research questions, noting them in columnar form as suggested by Hubbard and Power (1993).

The next step of the analysis was done as a group. We examined the interviews question by question, with each of us reading her own students' responses aloud to the group while we all took notes. We each then wrote a summary of our analysis. Our summaries were shared aloud with the group and discussed until general agreement was reached on the patterns developing within each of the interview questions and their relationship to the research questions. The patterns we identified were further elaborated by small groups of us working on specific research questions. We had two experienced outside researchers read and critique our interpretations of the data.

FINDINGS

We had posed the research question, "When and how do students' perceptions of school and learning change?" Analysis of several questions gave us insights on this question.

Student Perceptions of School

Cheryl and Holly noticed that when the kindergarten and first-grade students came into the classrooms to read, they were very excited about reading and learning to read. Although they may have lacked some of the mechanical skills, they were still confident that they were reading and that their audience would enjoy it. Cheryl and Holly compared the excitement of the younger children with some of their fifth-grade students' lack of enthusiasm during reading time and wondered: When and why did they stop being excited about reading? Was it the same for the other subjects as well? This was the question that brought them to the research project. Upon meeting with the research group, they found that other faculty members had the same concerns.

As the group analyzed the responses to questions concerning best and worst memories about learning in school, we learned what children saw as "fun" and thus enjoyable, and what they saw as "hard" and thus unpleasant.

"I want things funner." Hands-on experiences were very important in making school "fun." In Year 1, students at every grade level talked about best memories in terms of learning actively. In pre-kindergarten and kindergarten, students talked about learning centers (housekeeping, blocks), playing outside, and specific activities, such as making butterflies and participating in the schoolwide Olympics. Beginning in third grade, children talked about learning activities related to units of study. Jenny liked learning about space in third grade because "we got to make neat things," like models of the solar system. James (4)[1] remembered his third-grade field trips, one to the Botanical Gardens, where the students hiked the nature trails, and the other to Zoo Atlanta, where "they had real-like dinosaurs." Sam (5) said social studies was "funner than any other subject—we do projects and learn from them." His favorite was the Civil War unit when they "acted out what it was like then." Rachel (5) seemed to summarize what many of the children expressed by their examples: "I want things funner. When you learn, make it like an activity, an experience or something." Overall, school remains fun if the style of learning continues to stimulate the children's minds and bodies.

Year 2 revealed similar findings, with the exceptions of first and second grades, when the references to classroom experiences focused on pencil and paper activities. For example, Whitney (1) said that a favorite experience was "writing." However, students in kindergarten and grades 3–6 talked about their most memorable experiences in terms of active learning. Addie (4) said that she was excited about learning about another country when "we was looking [information] up and making wind socks and flags."

"I'm excited about being in school." During Years 1 and 2, we saw some patterns in responses from pre-kindergarten and kindergarten, first through third grade, and fourth and fifth grades. There were changes in students' perceptions of school and learning, but not what we expected. The pre-kindergarten and kindergarten students saw school as fun and play. "I like playing with blocks, making houses and playing with trucks," explained Ben (pre-K). Their attitudes were confident and positive about school. Corey (K) said, "I'm excited about being in school." Pebbles (K) stated, "I play games and read, I read all kinds of books."

Students in the first grade often mentioned in their interviews enjoying the general subjects of reading, writing, and math. Brenda (1) said, "Reading. It is fun to read. I've enjoyed it in first grade. It's real fun. When she taught us how to read and write. It's my favorite time." Nicky and Jon (1) thought learning math was their best memory of school because "we do fun things. Tens and ones." Second- and third-grade students named specific topics of study as their most memorable learning experience, including sharks, animals, plants, and counting money. Carla (2) enjoyed learning about teeth: "We learned about how cavities come in your mouth. We made teeth, toothbrushes, and toothpaste."

Fourth- and fifth-grade students continued with content in specific likes (spelling, math, drug awareness, poetry, and presidents) and dislikes (almost all math, although science and reading each got a vote). They also began to emphasize the social aspects of school. Steven (4) remembered disliking square dancing in third grade; his teacher remembers his discomfort dancing with girls. On the positive side, Karen (4) really liked "working in groups [because] people can help you." Rachel (5) said, "Friends are my very best memory."

"I wasn't too good at it." Kids have bad memories of learning experiences that are hard, and of times they felt incompetent. First grader Jon said his worst memory was "reading, because every time you miss a word. If you miss a bunch, then you have to stay in that story." Jon's teacher, who used the basal as well as tradebooks, described him as a below average student, and he had obviously experienced the discomfort of not reading well orally and having to reread in a basal while others advanced to another story. Similarly, Todd (2) said "having to read" was his worst experience when "I don't know some of the words." Paul (4) remembered his difficulty in second grade trying to learn subtracting: "I wasn't too good at it."

Nearly half of the students from first through fifth grade (but none of the younger children) talked about finding some aspect of learning hard as their worst experience. Similarly, West (1993) found children said that work is "hard" when "you're not good at it" or "not used to it." Math was cited most as a worst learning memory. Steven (4) explained, "Doing division in the thousands, adding and subtracting and multiplying all them numbers. We have to do a whole page on it and it takes so long to do one problem." He went on to describe how long it took him to do his homework, "some nights until 10:00." He even had a recommendation; instead of a whole page of math problems, "maybe do at least five problems a day and study it more." Teachers took his recommendation seriously, as we will show in the final section of this chapter.

In addition to asking students about their past and present learning, we asked them to think about their future as learners. We asked them to look forward to the next school year, and we questioned them about their more distant futures.

"I feel good."/"I'm a little nervous." Most of the students from pre-kindergarten to third grade were looking forward to the next school year and feeling optimistic about their futures. As Will (pre-K) enthusiastically declared: "I feel good. . . . I'm ready for kindergarten and I want to go there now." There were, however, young children who were concerned about going to the next grade. For example, first grader Mickey shared his concerns: "I know math is hard in second grade, very hard. I don't know nothing about second grade." As students became older, feelings of anxiety grew. They seemed to be fueled by both what the children did not know and what they had heard through the "grapevine." Karen (4) was a "little nervous" about going to fifth grade:

> 'Cause I don't know anybody. . . . 'Cause there might be new kids and they might not like me. . . . I don't know who is going to be my teacher. I don't know if the work is going to be harder.

Scott (4) worried that "you don't know what you'll have to do" and Beth (4) was anxious because she didn't know "what the teacher is going to be like."

But even when students had information, their anxiety was not necessarily diminished. Sometimes the information added to their anxiety, as illustrated by the comments of two students who were going to middle school. One said:

> I think it will be hard. . . . I looked at my sister's math, it's harder than our class. I don't know what I'll do well in. [I'm worried] about math because I've seen the problems.

Another student worried, "I think people in higher grades will push me around. My sister said they told her at the middle school there was a basement and elevator and I am pretty much afraid of going." There was a definite mythology about schooling, especially the middle school, transmitted from child to child. As Mechling (1986) noted, "The formal school setting becomes the next setting for children's folk cultures" (p. 95).

"I want to be a firegirl." We followed our question about the next school year with questions about future school and career goals. Many of the younger students had definite ideas about future careers and how they would prepare for them. Firemen and "firegirls," police officers, doctors, and nurses often were cited as future occupations by younger students; however, another frequent response was a parental occupation. Their parents, particularly their fathers, served as career role models. As Mickey (1) said when asked what he was going to do when he grew up, "[I'm going to be] a carpenter like my daddy." For some students, apprenticeships were the way that they would prepare for their careers. As 4-year-old Joe said when talking about how he would learn to become a policeman, "real policemen learn you." The mentors or teachers most often mentioned were fathers; students said, "Dad would show me how." "He will teach me—my daddy." Other young students saw school as a part of their preparation. For example, Brenda (1) said that in order for her to become a doctor or nurse she would have to "go to school, a grown-up school, and when I learn how, I can be one."

Older students mentioned a broader but still specific array of future careers. They wanted to be, among other things, a doctor, vet, lawyer, teacher, nurse, builder, mechanic, artist, business owner, police officer, ball player, and writer. A few students wanted to keep their options open, as Ken (5) said, "It's hard to say—gymnastics, policeman. I don't have goals now, could be all kinds of things at different times."

For these older students, the emphasis on training for careers began to shift from apprenticeships to formal schooling. Most of them saw school or college as necessary and they often mentioned going to school. However, Melanie (3) related a past learning experience to her future occupation as a lawyer and thought both practice and school were important.

> Like when you're little, your mom could get you a chair and a table and a hammer and you could practice then. And when you get to be a lawyer, they'll tell you to practice four weeks before you do it. You need more schooling for lawyers because you might have missed something.

Although students mentioned going on to school or college as important in pursuing a career, they weren't always sure of the connections, as Beth's (4) comment illustrates. She "always wanted to be a writer'' when she grows up, and when asked how she would get to be a writer, she replied, "First, you have to go to college or something like that—I don't know." Several students, when they talked about their own plans, also pointed to family members, especially siblings, who were in high school or college. Kim (5) was very proud that her brother had just won a scholarship to college and hoped she would do as well.

The Year 2 data related to careers and preparation for them closely resembled those of Year 1. We continued to note the trends of modeling after fathers as well as goals becoming clearer at successive grade levels. Also, we saw that some children demonstrated some content knowledge about their prospective careers. Ryan (4) talked about what he needed to know to be a soap opera actor.

> They train you to read scripts. And you know how they cut to another scene, well uh, after they do that they stop the camera, and like, you know, how they'll flip to a far away place like on "Full House," they'll flip from a house to the studio up in San Francisco, the studio.

"When you get big, you get in high school." Other aspects of the relationship between the students' futures and school were explored through questions about whether they thought they would complete high school and college and why. Most students, from pre-kindergartners to fifth graders, thought they would complete high school, and many also thought they would graduate from college. When asked why, we frequently heard vague connections between their future and school. However, among those students who did give a rationale for completing school, most mentioned school as critical to future careers. Brenda (1) explained, "If you want to get a job like a policeman, you have to get your diploma and go to college."

For other students, completing school was not necessarily tied to a career but was an expectation that had been communicated to them. Sometimes this expectation was implicit in their comments and other times it was directly stated. Will (pre-K) was very clear: "Yes [I will graduate from high school]. [Why?] Because just when you get big, you get in high school and do that." For Anna (2), who plans to be a doctor, the expectation was more directly communicated: "Sometimes she [my grandmother] says things about college. She says that I need to get a good education." As for Ken (5), his mother had evidently made her expectations for high school graduation very clear: "My mom will make me."

Of the five students who said they did not think they would go to college, three were pre-kindergartners, who might not be able to fathom something that distant. Four-year-old Ellen said, "My mama might not put me in college," and second grader Timothy was more emphatic, "My mama said she'd beat me [if I went to college]." Paul (3) didn't plan to attend college because he knew it was not the best way to prepare for his career goal of being a construction worker or mechanic.

Given the high rate of students who do not graduate from high school in our county, we were encouraged that most of students think they will graduate from high school. Even though responses were positive overall, some children were less emphatic in their statements. While most students gave a clear "yes," others used terms such as "I might," "maybe," "I hope so," and "I want to." One of the reasons we designed this as a longitudinal study was to learn when and why students change their expectations. We will follow this question with particular interest.

Student Perceptions of Themselves as Readers and Writers

Before we began studying and implementing whole language instruction, we taught reading from the basal reader using the workbook, magazine tests, and ability groupings. Very little writing was done; teachers taught language arts skills from an English textbook. Many teachers felt that while our students were learning to read, they were not very excited about reading and read only when they had to. We hoped that attitudes toward reading and writing would improve if we changed our literacy instruction. Results of several studies conducted at the school indicate that many teachers have changed their teaching methods (e.g., West & Rice, 1991), students are reading and writing more, and students and teachers have more positive attitudes about reading and writing (Taxel, 1994). The media specialist has kept records that indicate that our students are reading more (see Chapter 8). Circulation of library books has more than doubled in the past 3 years. The size and use of classroom libraries also have increased dramatically.

As a research team we wanted to gather more specific information about students' perceptions of themselves as readers, writers, and learners. Based on our experience with these children, we believed that in years past they would have described themselves as being readers of a certain level of book in the reading series. We wanted to see if and how this had changed.

One of the strongest findings from analyzing what children said about themselves as readers and writers, and what they thought their teachers would say, was the way children talked about reading and writing in terms of whole texts, just as most of their teachers do. We think anyone reading the majority of these responses would say, "These kids must be in whole language classrooms." In Year 1 most of the children talked about reading in terms of books and writing in terms of stories.

"I try to write good stories." As writers, students used measures including how much they wrote at home and school, how long their stories were, what kinds of stories they wrote (scary stories, fairy tales, autobiographies), and how they shared their writing with children in their own class as well as other classes. They mentioned qualities of neatness and spelling along with imagination and personal experience; Beth (4), for example, said she was a good writer because "I go a lot of places and get information." Children were very positive about writing, and several had helpful insights into their own writing processes. Younger children saw drawing as their writing; as Corey (K) said, "I used to scribble-scrabble, [but] now I draw pretty things." James (4) went into detail when asked what makes a good writer.

> Well, I like writing and I try to write good stories, but some of them just don't turn out the way I want them to. [What happens?] I'll go back and try to figure out what's causing me not to like the story and I'll change it and the story will still sound wrong. I'll go back and change it again, and I'll keep on doing that until I think it gets right.

"I read real thick books." While some students feel that reading and/or writing is hard for them, almost all students had positive feelings about what they could do. As readers, children talked about reading "real thick books," "pronouncing them hard words, real, real long words . . . like 'information' and 'graphic design,'" and most of all, reading "a lot." Many mentioned enjoying reading and some offered favorite books. Pebbles (K) had a good insight into her reading process: "I look at the pictures and then at the words."

Most children were pretty confident about their reading. However, two fifth-grade students said they didn't like to read much; they seem to represent the lack of enthusiasm for reading that prompted Cheryl and Holly to worry about when school stopped being fun for some kids. Ken (5) made his feelings clear with a metaphor: "I can read good if it's interesting. I used to like to read as well as jumping on the trampoline, but I don't jump on the trampoline much anymore." Contrast this with the students in fifth grade who kept asking Holly on the first day of school, "When are we going to get to read?" These responses raise further questions for us about who likes to read, who doesn't, and when that differentiation occurs.

"Sometimes I can, sometimes I can't." Almost all children felt that their teachers viewed them as good readers and writers. When asked specifically what teachers would say about them, Anna (2) suggested, "Anna's been real good in second grade. She knows how to read." Jenny (3) replied, "She'd say I'm a very good writer and I write different kinds of stories." Student responses about themselves usually indicated that they were good readers and writers, even though they might have areas that needed work. For example, Jenny said, "I'm good at writing," even though "I might not know how to spell a word." Corey (K) responded, "As a reader, I can read very good. I can read some books, and I can't read some of the books. Sometimes I can, sometimes I can't." One fourth grader said, "I like writing, but I need help to spell the words." Mickey (1) was worried about his reading and said his teacher would say, "Mickey don't know how to read, he's just learning."

One interesting thing we saw was that the students who were in special education, or identified as below average or underachievers, felt very positive about their abilities; above average and average students made positive statements about their abilities, but also noted specific weaknesses they had. Year 2 data also supported this finding.

"I make bad on my paper."/"I was the best one in my class." Children talked about measurable indicators, especially grades, when they responded to questions about when they feel "smart" and "not smart." Grades became a measuring stick in second grade and continued through fifth, probably because teachers are not required to give letter grades on report cards until second grade. Things that made children feel "not smart" were spelling tests, math papers and tests, and other graded work. As Melanie (3) put it, "[I feel not smart] when I make bad on my paper."

Conversely, children felt smart when they did well on tests and got good grades. Todd (2) remembered, "Last year I had the best ITBS [Iowa Test of Basic Skills] scores. I was the best one in my class." Todd had received an award at the end-of-school honors day for this achievement. These concrete, quantified representations of success were cited by 11 of the 20 second through fifth graders.

Interestingly, the way children talked about themselves shifted around third grade and seemed to be strongly in place by fourth grade.

Younger children talked in terms of what they could do, whereas older children talked in terms of who they were. For example, most kindergarten statements were "I read good," "I can't talk good," and "I'm a real good reader." In contrast, older students said things like "I am smart," "I'm not a trouble maker," and "I'm kind of smart." These more global self-definitions seemed to indicate that students had internalized certain school roles and personas. For many, who they were in school had become who they were, period. With one middle school boy (Year 2), this was especially worrisome, since he saw himself as a troublemaker and said that was what everyone expected of him. He is one we will follow carefully, since this perception had changed from the previous year.

When students were probed as to who made them feel smart, children in the lower grades talked about family members (siblings and parents); however, no fourth or fifth graders mentioned anyone outside of school. Family could make you feel smart, or not so smart, as Timothy (2) felt when he got his math problems wrong at home, or Melanie (3) felt when she brought a paper home that she had not done well on, and "my dad gets mad at me." Children at all grade levels, except pre-kindergarten, talked about their teachers and their friends. Teachers made children feel smart when they told the children directly, as Sid's first-grade teacher did, "You're smart in math." Brenda stated her first-grade teacher "makes me feel smart. She goes over things and goes over things until we know what things is." Sometimes they make you feel that way, as Karen's fourth-grade teacher did, by "help[ing] you learn." There was only one mention of a teacher making someone feel not smart. Todd (2) felt he was not smart in math, especially division: "The teacher says I'm the one that halfway misses it."

Friends also affected whether or not children felt smart. Peers were mentioned on both sides of the question. Corey (K) felt not smart "when my friends won't play with me." Beth (4) felt that way "when somebody hurts my feelings," and Rachel (5) commented on "when people cut me down." Peers influenced Sam's (5) feelings about himself. He pointed out three boys in his class who made him feel smart, and gave an example: "Hank, he likes my projects." Ken felt smart when he helped other people do their math: "It feels good and it's fun."

Beginning in second grade, one child each year said "myself" in response to, "Who makes you feel smart or not smart?" James (4) originally responded that making a 100 on a test made him feel smart, but then he said, "Not really." The interviewer probed, and James confided, "To be who you want to be. To do what you think is right.

. . . *I* make me feel smart. My body tells me what to do. I do what I feel I need to do." These children seemed to be developing a sense of their own ability to determine whether they were doing well and learning. We hope this is connected to the increased emphasis over the past 3 years on students taking greater responsibility for their learning as well as for evaluating themselves.

Student Perceptions of Special Education Students and Teachers

At Benton Elementary, special education students usually have been served in a pullout model. In this model, children leave their regular classrooms for 1–3 hours to receive instruction from special educators in a classroom with other children who have similar learning needs. Jane and Patty, two special education teachers, were concerned about how students at the school viewed the special education teachers, as well as how they viewed their classmates who receive special education services. This concern developed over several years of working with special education students and their parents, who often expressed concern about how the students were viewed by their classmates. Jane and Patty felt that the services they provided were of benefit for their students, but were not sure that the benefits outweighed the separation and labeling issues that their students faced. When they shared their questions with the research team, they found that their colleagues had similar concerns. A series of questions explored how children perceived what special education teachers did within the school, why some of the students received special education services, and what the students thought about their classmates who attended the special programs.

"**Somewhere around in the building. . . .**" When asked, "What does the special education teacher do?" the students described the roles of these teachers in generally positive terms. Some students, particularly the younger ones, offered vague descriptions and understandings. For example, Corey (K) answered, "She takes people to her place and stuff like that. Her place is somewhere around in the building." Sid (1) said, "You [special education teacher] go around and look for people to bring around. You play games and ask them what they do." Some of the students were confused about what happens in the resource room, as demonstrated by Melanie (3), who said:

I want to know what [special education teachers] do. They bring in spelling words. They [special education students] forget them a lot. Then, they have to write them in their [note-book] when we do our spelling. But . . . Christa had the same words as . . . we had [one] week.

It seems that because special education teachers do not follow the traditional teacher model, some children are still unsure as to what the teachers do and even where their rooms are located.

In Year 2, most of the students had an idea of what a special education teacher does and related it in some way to "teaching, helping, and learning." We speculate that may be a result of an increase in the inclusion model of offering special services; most of the special education teachers spent part or all of their time in regular classrooms teamed with the classroom teacher. In their study at South Jackson, Kimbrell-Lee and Wood (see Chapter 3) found that students saw the special education teacher as a "real" teacher when she team taught in their classroom.

Many of the older students gave clearer and fuller descriptions. They described the special education teacher as one who teaches, plays, and assists children with work that they have trouble with. Older students were also aware of other duties, such as Brian's (5) report that "she teaches special education, library work, teaches all subjects and helps in the lunchroom." When the children talked about the teaching role of the special education teachers, they seemed to have a positive view of what the teachers did. James (4) responded, "Mrs. Shank teaches step-by-step, easier stuff so they can catch up with everybody. Some people are slow learners." Students receiving special services for the most part talked about their teachers as helping them learn; for example, Mickey (2) said, "You teach us how to read."

"I think she is getting smarter." We asked why students attended special classes. The younger children in Year 1 often mentioned specific nonacademic activities, such as Shaffine's (K) answer, "They might have to draw a picture and all that and glue stuff in the picture," and Todd's (2) answer, "There is a jungle. [She] lets them play in it." They also answered with more academic answers, like Jenny's (2), "Because they don't know how to do stuff right like reading, writing and math." The third, fourth, and fifth graders' responses suggested a broader and more academic perspective on why students attended special education classes. Kim (5) said that children attended special classes "because they need help with math and sometimes Mrs. Poponi sends them." Although many students described classmates who received special education services as "needing help," only a few students used labels such as "slow learner" to describe their classmates. These answers indicated that the sophistication in understanding why children take part in special education increased as the children got older.

When we asked about students who go to special education classes, many responses focused on students' strengths and achievements. Younger students were again somewhat unclear about what goes on in special education classes, as Corey (K) reported: "I think that they play or something like that. They get a card and they get a sticker and stuff like that." Some students, however, saw their classmates learning more and getting smarter. Brenda (1) observed, "They are learning a lot more than they knew before they went," indicating that she saw a difference in the achievement of her classmates since going to the resource room. When Jenny (3) talked about her classmate Sarah, who goes to special education classes, she observed, "I think she is getting smarter. She can read and stuff." Ashley also commented about James, a student in her room: "Sometimes when we play math games he gets his problems right. I think he's smart. He reads."

In contrast to the strengths and achievements model that one group spoke about, there were incidences in which students described their classmates in terms of their academic struggles or weaknesses. James (4) said:

> I think that they are the people who can't catch up with other people. I think they go there because they can't learn as fast as some people. I was always behind in my math until my mom and dad sat down with me and helped me.

An interesting answer from two of the students centered around a personal view of the students rather than the academic view. For these two students, there appeared to be no distinction between classmates who receive special education services and those who do not. Jenny (3) thought "they are the same as us," and Sam (5) voiced similar sentiments. Although academic differences were noted, the classmates were accepted by Jenny and Sam as being the same as the other students.

As we looked at the data from the labeled students, including two children who were no longer receiving special education services, it was evident that the children viewed special education as a pleasant place to go. As Karen (4) said, "She helps us read and write" and "I'm kinda glad, 'cause I learned how to read." They also talked about what they did as they attended classes. First grader Mickey stated, "I like reading and writing when I come." Even the kindergarten child added, "You play games, read, write, and play."

What about our concern that even if the children were learning in pullout classes, there might be a stigma attached to going? We asked the children who attended special education classes what the other children thought about them when they left the room. Whitney said, "They think I am happy; when she comes to get me I go." Fifth grader Brian expressed mixed feelings: "I needed help in spelling, reading, and language. Others thought it was a retarded class. It's okay." He also saw the pullout as a short-term plan, telling us that "if I do good there, she will put me back in Ms. Poponi's room." The children generally thought that the class helped them, even though they did voice some concerns. They all seemed to believe that "we need help and this is where we get it."

In Year 2 the social aspects of going to special education classes were mentioned more than they were the first year. Meaghann (1) said, "They [classmates] don't like it because they don't get to play with me." Ashley (4) explained that she missed her friend when the friend went to special education class: "It makes me feel sad because sometimes she'll feel lonely, and she says she don't know how to read and write."

The debate on the best way to serve students with diverse needs continues to rage. Researchers have called into question the effectiveness of many pullout programs in terms of instructional time, quality of academic work, and curricular coherence (Allington, 1991). Teacher researchers who have followed children over time have raised issues of lessened engagement and loss of community (Allen, Michalove, & Shockley, 1993). Our reading of the literature and our own observations have led us to implement and assess different delivery models. The information we are gaining about the students' perspectives on special education has been and will continue to be critical in our decisions.

STUDENT RECOMMENDATIONS FOR BEING A "REALLY GOOD TEACHER"

We were interested in hearing the voices of our students telling us what we should do to be "really good teachers." We specifically asked them for advice on teaching reading and writing. We hoped their responses would give us additional insights about how they felt about school and learning. We were not disappointed!

"**Make learning funner.**" Students want learning to be fun, and they enjoy school more when they are actively involved. They point to projects, hands-on activities, field trips, and learning centers as suggestions for teachers. Holly has already taken to heart the advice of Sam (5). He told her he loved the activities in the Civil War unit and wanted to do more projects, so the next year she included more projects and emphasized hands-on learning activities for her fifth graders. James moaned, "We have to do a whole page [of math], and it takes so long to do one problem." He suggested, "Maybe do at least five problems a day, and study it more." Cheryl took his advice and decreased the number of problems she assigned; she also changed her instruction to "study them more." We are, as a research team and as a school, going to listen to Rachel's sound advice: "Make learning funner, so people want to learn."

"**If we be good, she be good.**" Throughout the survey in every grade level, the words "be nice" resounded loud and clear. Paul stated a simple rule: "If we be good to her, she be good to us. If the kids be good, she be good." Affective qualities are important to the children; they simply want us to "be nice." "Don't holler at us," Molly advised, a wish echoed by several children. She continued:

Maybe she should give everyone a chance to be themselves, like if they don't get every math problem right, give them a little bit of time, like if they aren't too good at math or spelling and she starts to yell at them, just give them a little more time.

James (4) thought really good teachers "help me with things I need to be helped with, and whenever she gets real mad not to shout. 'Cause you know some teachers shout when they get real mad."

As teachers we can learn from their advice. Several of us remembered a bad day or two (or maybe more) when we were out of sorts; we know now that our voice and demeanor really affect our students. One teacher has taken the pledge: No More Yelling. Individuals of all ages want the same treatment. We recommend that all teachers and those preparing to teach listen to their "employers." We are teaching for the children, and their suggestions are valuable.

"**I want her to read.**" Children of all ages expressed definite opinions on how to teach reading and writing. "Read us books" and "let us read" were the two things students said most often; not coincidentally, those are two of the most consistent things that happen in classrooms.

Almost every teacher in the school provides time for children to read self-selected books, and the students obviously saw it as a way to foster reading growth, not just as a "free time" activity. Fifth grader Ken even advised what to do after they read: "Let us have literature circles where we all read the same book, have five groups and all do something, a skit or a book report."

Some of us in upper grades were surprised to hear that even fifth graders wanted to be read to regularly. "Read to the class and read with excitement," they told us. Over and over, we saw how important it is to read to the students, and we are more aware than ever how important it is to schedule time every day to read aloud. We read chapter books, picture books, informational books, and poetry, in upper grades and lower, in special education classes and regular classes. One teacher reported that students have given up a recess to listen to the end of a story. Whitney (K) summed up the feelings of students at every grade level when she declared emphatically, "I want her to read!"

"Write stories and stuff." When students were asked about how to teach writing, they offered very specific advice. Many of their suggestions seemed based on the current practices of their teachers. The students expressed an interest in writing workshop where they write "stories and stuff." Practice (regular writing) and editing were important in how they saw themselves succeed. "If it is good enough to publish, if it is good, we publish it and put it up. [Publishing is] when you write pictures and words and publish it. She already published two of mine," Sid said with pride. Students also recommended developing topic lists and modeling. Rachel (5) suggested, "Pick out good books for kids that they would like, make up creative titles, give examples of stories, give guidelines." Sandra (3) suggested:

> She could ask us to read it to us and we could get some ideas. She could put something on the overhead and if she spelled a word wrong, we could help her. Then she could tell us to write it the best way we can. That's the way she could teach writing.

"[Children] need to learn to write when they are small, and when they get bigger they write a lot," suggested Melanie. Beth (4) recognized the importance of the teacher herself being a writer (Graves, 1991), when she said teachers "could write some really good stories."

"Help me with things I need." Encouragement is vital in helping students learn. Karen (4) shared how her teachers helped her: "They helped me learn, they encouraged me a lot, they told me to keep trying and don't give up, don't yell a lot, help me if I need it.'' It seems so simple, but a word of praise and encouragement truly does go a long way. During Year 2, nineteen students mentioned that a good teacher "helps" in some way. Fifteen of those students were in grades K–3. Children, especially in whole language classrooms where collaboration is encouraged, saw help related to types of literacy events (West, 1994); they wanted teachers to help them but also knew that teachers were likely to recommend others in the classroom to help them and would not help during test-like events.

"I want to know what they do." There was a vagueness, especially in Year 1, that seemed to surround special education teachers and the services they provided. The emphatic, "I want to know what they do," voiced by Melanie (3), suggests that this is an area where we can help our students become aware of the roles each of us (children, teachers, administrators, and other staff members) plays in helping each child reach his or her full potential, and thus help satisfy their need for knowledge. We believe that our Year 2 data indicated some changing perceptions. Inclusion may help more students realize that special educators are "real teachers." In addition, class discussions, class interviews with special education teachers, and perhaps individual reports on various school community members could help children understand diverse roles.

"I think they are the same as us."/"Some people are slow learners." Another recommendation relates to the changes that occurred in the way children viewed their peers who received special education services. The changes seemed to go from being very positive to an increased focus on the weaknesses of the children receiving special education services, even though the comments still had a primarily positive tone. While the students were still positive in that they saw their classmates getting help because, as Ken (5) said, "they were slow learners," we have to question whether we really want children to classify certain other children as being the ones who are "slow." Our recommendation is to encourage children to be more reflective and open, acknowledging both the strengths and weaknesses of all of their peers. As teachers, we can foster our students' sense of community by encouraging each of them to be willing to give help and to get help as needed; we're all "a little slow" in some areas. Again, we'd encourage class discussions of the multitude of experiences and abilities we bring to the classroom.

We have completed the first 2 years of a longitudinal study. We read, discussed, categorized, and wrote about what children shared with us in order to learn what they had to teach us, but also to lay a foundation for how they might change. From all the data, other questions have surfaced, and our research team is faced with deciding which questions to pursue. One thing is certain: We have listened to our students' voices and, in some cases, altered our teaching in order to foster success within our learning community.

NOTE

1. Number in parentheses indicates grade level of student when he or she made the statement. See Figure 11.1 for listing of names and grade levels at the beginning of the study.

Action Research:
Where's the Action?

JoBeth Allen

Action is the heart of action research. As Peshkin (1993) wrote, "The proof of research conducted by whatever means resides in the pudding of its outcomes" (p. 23). Peshkin made the argument that qualitative inquiry has many avenues and outcomes, some of which include *description*, which may lead to changes in processes, relationships, settings, and systems; *interpretation*, which may aid in explaining and creating generalizations, developing new concepts, identifying problems, changing behavior, understanding complexity, or developing theory; and *evaluation*, which may affect policies and practices (especially innovations). The studies in this volume represent each of these categories; we are already seeing some of the outcomes Peshkin outlined.

EDUCATIONAL AVENUES AND OUTCOMES

In this section we discuss the action research projects using Peshkin's (1993) framework of description, interpretation, and evaluation, and we reflect on a fourth educational outcome: professional growth.

DESCRIPTION

Lisa Delgado, Mary Jane Hilley, Melvin Bowie, and JoBeth Allen (Chapter 8) said that throughout the study, they made decisions about the media center based on feedback they solicited from teachers. The survey revealed some areas of misunderstanding that they worked with teachers to clarify, areas that they believe will improve relationships. Mary Jane stressed that this kind of research is a continual process: "I really want to continue next year. I need the teachers' perspectives." Lisa agreed, adding she hoped to access more student perspectives; in fact, her second-year study was an examination of how students became independent users of a variety of new technology. Both media specialists also pointed to the importance of the relationship they developed as a result of the cross-school research.

Jan Kimbrell-Lee and Terry Wood (Chapter 3) also saw their relationship as an important part of their collaborative research. Terry pointed out that in analyzing and writing during the summer, "we worked together for 10 hours a day. We really learned what the other one had been thinking all year. Even though we taught together every day, there was no time for *really* getting to know each other." Through analyzing their data, primarily student work, they learned each other's teaching philosophies, goals, and expectations.

Terry also conducted a 2-year project to investigate her students' transition from whole language classrooms to what she assumed were textbook-oriented classrooms in middle school. She learned of specific areas in which her students were (and were not) well prepared. She was also surprised to learn that there are whole language teachers at the middle school; in fact, two of the teachers became so interested in her research that they came to several research team meetings and wrote with Terry! Research team members suggested that Terry share with the middle school teachers her study of students' transition from elementary school. Her description of teaching philosophies and student and parent perceptions has changed her own teaching and perhaps other teachers' processes or, at a minimum, the relationship between fifth- and sixth-grade teachers. Before the study, that relationship was nonexistent.

Interpretation

Interpretation of the pre-K through fifth-grade student interviews reported in Chapter 11 led teachers to some generalizations about what children find important about school. Members of that project team put up an interactive bulletin board, reminding themselves and other teachers of the children's advice, such as: "Make learning funner, so people want to learn," "Read to us," and "Help me with the things I need." Students were invited to show what they thought made learning "funner." Teachers decided that what they learned would be of interest to other teachers in their school and designed an inservice workshop focusing on the teaching/learning implications of each research project.

Researchers from the study described in Chapter 11 said they listened to children in a whole new way and understood them differently; they are modifying their theories about teaching and have already begun changing their behavior. In an interview after the first month of the 1993–94 school year, Cheryl Poponi pointed to specific ways she has changed her teaching as a direct result of her team's research.

1. Active learning: I have more projects. . . . In reading we're going to try to do plays this year. We are painting the wall outside the classroom with scenes from five survival stories. . . . I let them use the computers more for writing—that's to get them excited about publishing. I think that makes it a little bit "funner" for them. I'm going to try to have a field trip with everything that we're doing.

2. Social interaction: I let them work with partners. The only time that they cannot work with partners is when I'm giving a test.

3. Reading aloud: I read to them half an hour every day now. Today it was drizzling a little bit, and I was reading *Hawk's Hill*, and they were saying, "Don't stop. It's raining, we can't go out, so keep reading." It really influenced me when all the kids, every grade level, said they liked their teachers to read to them. I didn't think a fifth grader would like to be read to.

4. Modeling: I'm working on that. I wanted [them to write] these survival stories, but the kids didn't really know what I meant, and it was really my own fault because I didn't model. I'm going to try to lead by example, to write when they write and share my examples with them.

5. Less homework: I have cut down the math problems, and I think I do a better job teaching and explaining about it before they take it home.

6. No yelling: They don't like to be yelled at, so I'm trying this year not to do that too much. It's so hard. It's just really so hard. There are fewer times I need to get on them because we have lots of projects, and they work together, so I expect more talking, and I've really tried to have them make their own choices.

At the end of that year, Cheryl learned that at least one of the changes she made had a real impact. At an IEP meeting for two of her students with learning difficulties, she found that they had exceeded expected gains in math. When the special education teacher asked how they had made so much progress, Cheryl explained, "We did fewer problems, but we worked on them more before we did them."

Learning what students think has made a noticeable difference in the way Cheryl teaches now. Yet Erickson and Shultz note:

> Virtually no research has been done that places student experience at the center of attention. We do not see student interests and their known and unknown fears. . . . If the student is visible at all in a research study he is usually viewed from the perspective of adult educators' interests and ways of seeing, that is, as failing, succeeding, motivated, mastering, unmotivated, responding or having a misconception. Rarely is the perspective of the student herself explored. (Erickson & Shultz, 1992, p. 467)

Evaluation

In a sense, all of the research in our partnership was evaluating the effectiveness of change; as Sirotnik (1988) wrote, "Inquiry for social action is automatically evaluative" (p. 187). Two studies were overt evaluations. When Marilynn and Lori (Chapter 10) told the group about the detailed qualitative and quantitative evaluation of the first year of the pre-kindergarten program, everyone urged them to send the report to the state department, which was sponsoring the program. "They won't have anything nearly this detailed," Mary Leuzinger said. The report has now been passed among several officials in the state department and on to the governor's office. Gwen's (Chapter 6) research was designed as evaluation. She sent her report to the central office as the documentation supporting an official request for a variance in assessment procedures. Not only did they grant the variance, but Mary Leuzinger shared the report with central office personnel from other counties. One county has already come to the school to find out how teachers are evaluating students. "When I pulled out our report to share with them," Gwen recounted, "they said, 'We've already read it!'" Gwen also made an Evaluation Resource Notebook for teachers.

Our work together helped us identify questions, purposes, audiences, and forms of reporting. We had long, thoughtful discussions about who our many stakeholders really were and what forms we could create that addressed their unique needs and interests. Some of the forms we designed were implemented the following year, including the handbook and various presentations (see Figure 2.1). Erickson (1986) notes:

> Reporting to local audiences can be thought of as a process of teaching the findings. . . . Multiple reports of varying length, each designed to address the specific interests of a specific audience, are usually more appropriate [than a single report]. . . . In the local setting oral reports at meetings, and mixing oral and written reporting in workshops, can be effective. (p. 156)

Having identified parents as important stakeholders, teachers at each grade level developed ways of sharing information. In March 1992, the 4 fourth-grade teachers at Benton orchestrated a PTO program to explain whole language instruction. This was an important event in the community; the gymnasium was packed, and many people were dressed up. Each child had a role in presenting aspects of classroom life. Several children did book talks, while others explained that their days were filled with "books, books, books" of great variety, which teachers and children read, wrote about, and talked about; learning to spell words from the books they read—"there are 30 ways we can study them"; writing every day on topics they choose, revising and editing their own work; publishing and sharing with peers—"We do that over and over until our folders are all worn out." One child reported that the 79 children in fourth grade had read 2,060 fiction and 414 nonfiction books since the beginning of the year. One group performed a rap they wrote; another recited an original poem about the Atlanta Braves, which drew hearty applause.

Each speech, poem, story, and song, whether performed by a group or individual, was memorized and delivered with varying degrees of comfort and eloquence, usually straight to beaming family members. Afterward, children led parents, friends, and siblings through carefully arranged displays of commercial and student-authored books, poetry, wall charts, and daily schedules—a real glimpse into four classrooms that were actually quite different from each other but had one thing in common: Children read and wrote extensively. When we asked ourselves, "What do parents want to know?" this highly successful program, and others like it at each grade level, seemed like more effective ways of sharing information than any form of research report.

Professional Growth

In addition to these important outcomes, teachers saw themselves growing as researchers. When Lolita implemented a reading incentive program at Benton, she not only documented the process, she also wrote about it (Brown, 1994). Now other teachers can learn from her thoughtful inquiry. Lisa and Mary Jane initially had felt at a loss about what to do with all the data they had collected about media centers. But together the group designed meaningful ways of analyzing the data. Lisa said, "I can take that process with me into other situations." Sure enough, when Lisa, Mary Jane, Melvin Bowie, and JoBeth met in the summer of 1994 to revise their chapter in this book, Lisa brought with her a completed manuscript describing her research on children's independent use of technology. We provided praise and minimal feedback, and urged her to send it to a media journal, which she promptly did. The published article (and an unexpected payment for it) appeared the following January (Delgado, 1995).

In sharing the video interview project with the whole faculty, Cheryl said, "The research was 'more funner' than I ever thought it could be. . . . Now I can 'highlight' on my own. . . . This is just a really good paper." There were many references to "my research next year." Terry decided to videotape, rather than audiotape, her interviews. Carol will do observational notes differently. Linda planned to restructure her teaching journal. Marilynn and Lori reworded interview questions for the younger children in the longitudinal study.

Teachers learned about research from the inside out. In the middle of presenting their findings the last day of the 1993 summer 2-week session, researchers on the video interview project had everyone take out a piece of paper and write down what they thought made a good teacher. "We're not going to tell you what the kids said until we know what you think," Cheryl explained. The group was thinking like researchers; rather than theorizing about the differences between what children and teachers thought, they decided to ask. Everything was becoming a research question.

Teachers began asking for articles related to their own research because they really wanted to know, not because someone said, "You need to do a lit review." Jan and Terry had been reading articles about inclusion, not, as they said, to learn how to do it, but "to learn how to write an article" about their model of inclusion. Jan had more to say about research writing. "Data analysis is really complex," she noted, "and explaining what we learned [from the analysis] to someone else is even harder." Gwen said that writing "gave me insights on where we got off track" with certain aspects of assessment. Linda found that what helped her the most as a writer were readers; she had six people with different backgrounds and perspectives comment on drafts of her paper, as did many of the other researchers.

Just as important as the people connections were the idea connections. The group, as it constructed its own knowledge base, began making connections among the various studies. Gwen and Linda, at South Jackson, both identified grading as one of the biggest problems of alternative assessment. Holly Ward pointed out that the only time students they interviewed at Benton talked about grades was when they were asked what made them feel smart, or not so smart, in school. Grades rarely entered into the students' responses about being readers and writers, or their memorable learning experiences. Having trouble or working hard at something didn't make them feel "dumb," but grades sometimes did. Grading, a perpetual issue for teachers, is still a problem; but now teachers at both schools have more information about the nature of the problem and the children's perspective.

Jennifer White connected what she learned from a parent survey with what she and her peers (Chapter 11) learned from interviews: The teacher reading to the class was very important. Jennifer's parent responses related that this was what her kindergartners liked best. So there was triangulation, from a large-scale interview study of a whole school to a small-scale survey of one class. Terry Wood, in her ongoing transition-to-middle-school study, interviewed a fifth grader, who said, "I like writing instead of doing work." Dorothy Rice, a teacher from Benton, pointed out how well this fit with the study she had helped Jane West conduct in her third grade, where children defined "fun" and "work" (West, 1992). Lolita Brown, who conducted a survey of all the elementary and middle school teachers in the district about Chapter 1 models and instruction, reported that homeroom teachers found it most helpful when Chapter 1 teachers worked with individuals and small groups within the classroom; this corroborated the benefits Jan and Terry found from the inclusion model they developed (Chapter 3).

Teachers recognized the role research played in their lives. "We seem to have become a more professional group by looking at issues from a research standpoint and not just what we think—although much of what we think is valid," Dorothy Rice reflected. Cheryl agreed:

> It is a positive thing for me to be involved in the research group because you feel more positive about school and going to work and being a professional. Before I would just go to school, just do my job, and leave. And now, . . . I feel like that what I say matters. And the more that I was involved, the more I felt that I could, the more right I had to say something. . . . They might not do what I ask, but at least they're going to listen to me and, you know, take consideration—and have respect.

Administrators also remarked on professional growth. The superintendent was pleased with the acceptance of our research for publication and invited us to make a presentation to the school board. Principals Pam Johns and Patsy Lentz, and curriculum coordinator Mary Leuzinger, were highly supportive of the research teams from the beginning, and Patsy and Mary were involved as researchers. After 2 years of research, Mary said she saw a change from "teacher-as-victim to one who is empowered." In an interview with Jane Rogers, Mary explained:

> Now people talk about their practice, . . . where before it was complaints about what we [central office] were doing to them. When teachers talk about things that are going on in their practice and profession, it is a whole different plane. It is talking about our jobs—learning and teaching.

Being researchers has contributed to this shift. Special education teacher Patty Griffith is planning to use new research she is conducting on inclusion at Benton to talk with the director of special education. Her argument will include data from students and teachers, documentation that says, "Look, this is the way it's been this year, and this is the way we think things would work better next year."

Jane also interviewed the principals about changes they had seen. Pam reported that teachers at South Jackson were more confident in voicing their opinions and concerns, and they now had professional dialogue and discussions throughout the school. Teachers had studied issues such as authentic assessment and used their findings to make decisions. Patsy reported a similar transformation at Benton as a result of all aspects (governance, instruction, research) of their change initiatives.

> I've seen a real evolution in instructional changes, professional development, changes in mind sets, changes in philosophy, changes in self-concept. I think the teachers have definitely assumed greater roles over their classroom and instruction . . . [and] over the school community, just everything: what the report cards look like, how lesson plans are done, what progress reports are implemented, staff development, dealing with parents, making decisions about children. . . . People have confidence in the fact that they can make the right decisions.

At the first Benton Research Team meeting of the 1993–94 school year, five new teachers joined the group; everyone from the previous year returned. Teachers posed tentative questions, proposed exciting new directions, and suggested important modifications to longitudinal studies. In the midst of the dynamic discussion, a visitor from the Georgia State Department of Education came in and was introduced. When the principal (part of the research team) explained what we were doing, the visitor asked, "Is this formal research or action research?" Holly replied instantly, "Both!" There was firm, but of course polite, agreement from every teacher researcher present.

SUPPORTIVE STRUCTURES

> To encourage teacher research, we must first address incentives for teachers, the creation and maintenance of supportive networks, the reform of rigid organizational patterns in schools, and the hierarchical power relationships that characterize most schooling. Likewise, to resolve the problematic relationship between academic research and teacher research, it will be necessary to directly confront controversial issues of voice, power, ownership, status, and role in the broad educational community. (Cochran-Smith & Lytle, 1993, p. 22)

In order to establish communities that support teacher research, Cochran-Smith and Lytle proposed "an analytic framework . . . which can be used to raise questions about current school and university efforts to promote teachers' participation in research." Their proposed framework consists of the ways in which communities "organize time, use talk, construct texts, and interpret the tasks of teaching and schooling" (p. 305). The Kings Bridge Road Research Team is trying to address these issues of restructuring. (The restructuring of time and incentives in the schools pales in comparison to the restructuring of expectations and norms within the academy, but that's another story.)

Time

Teacher researchers need chunks of time to do their research, as well as extended time together to become an effective and reflective group (Cochran-Smith & Lytle, 1993). Grant money[1] has supported teacher research in the ways teachers have requested. The biggest issue teachers identified was time. We hired a certified substitute teacher to be available to teacher researchers, who used this time to interview students, parents, and other teachers; to transcribe videotapes; and to engage in various other aspects of data collection, analysis, and writing. Teachers were paid for their time in the summer, when intensive analysis and writing required 2–3 weeks each year.

Coordination was another time issue. When the Benton Research Team decided it needed a research coordinator at the school, the Coca-Cola grant provided a small stipend. The BRT sought applications from within the group and designed a "Position Announcement" with responsibilities, qualifications, and compensation. Three teachers applied. The team selected Marilynn Cary, based on her previous research experience and her flexibility as a speech teacher. Marilynn arranges meetings, develops an agenda based on group needs, keeps organizational records, and, at the teachers' request, "helps us do what we said we were going to do." Interestingly, South Jackson did not feel the need for a coordinator, perhaps because they are a smaller group; however, Lisa Delgado (media specialist) serves a similar function there.

Many of the teachers have presented their research and shared their practices at conferences, including National Reading Conference, National Council of Teachers of English, the Conference on Teacher Research, Qualitative Research in Education, American Educational Research Association, and the Georgia Children's Literature Conference. The school district has provided for substitutes, registration, and meals, while grant support paid for transportation and lodging. This may become problematic as grant support dwindles and more teachers become interested in presenting, especially at national conferences, which can easily cost $1,000 a person. Time away from children is also a growing concern; even when it is possible to "buy" time, most teachers feel their primary responsibility is to their students as a day-to-day commitment. The larger institutions of schools and districts need to address this issue, perhaps by having "permanent" substitutes who work closely with teachers and classrooms, so that there is continuity of instruction and relationship when teachers fulfill other professional roles, such as presenting.

Grants also have supported university-based graduate students and faculty as needed.[2] According to Erickson (1986), "the university-based researcher can provide valuable distance—assistance to the classroom teacher in making the familiar strange, and interesting" (p. 157). We found our involvement to fit well with the findings of Ward and Tikunoff's 1982 review of collaborative research efforts, as cited in Oakes, Hare, and Sirotnik (1986). They identified four characteristics of genuinely collaborative efforts.

1. University-based and school-based researchers work together on all phases of the educational research effort [see also Allen, Buchanan, Edelsky, & Norton, 1992].

2.   The focus is on "real world" as well as theoretical problems.
3.   Both groups gain in understanding and mutual respect [see also
Carr & Allen, 1989].
4.   The effort addresses both research and development/implementa-
tion issues throughout. (Oakes et al., 1986)

Developing a self-sustaining, institutionalized support for teacher
research is the critical challenge we face in the next 2 years, as grant
support runs out. Fullan and Miles (1992) warned that "schools can
become hotbeds of innovation and reform in the absence of external
support, but they cannot *stay* innovative without the continuing support
of the district and other agencies" (p. 748). How will the schools and
school district sustain the tremendous momentum the researchers in
this volume have built? Will time be allotted to conduct research? Will
the research coordinators at each building be able to continue? Will
there be money for conference presentations, and especially for summer
work?

Researchers on these two teams have a much better idea now what
resources they need to support ongoing inquiry. At the end of the second 2 week summer session, after 3½ hours of reports, reflection, more
questions, and unflagging enthusiasm despite the muggy Georgia afternoon, Holly turned to the UGA Initiative project director: "Joel, we have
two things we need from the grant. First, we all need Powerbooks
[laptop computers]. Second, next summer when we write, let's rent a
house at the beach!"

Talk

"When teachers are working together to construct greater understandings about teaching," Cochran-Smith and Lytle (1992) argued, "their
conversations are recursive, reflecting a fluid, changing view of knowledge" (p. 312). They place into question taken-for-granted "labels,
practices, and processes" of schooling. Conversation in research team
meetings, whether among research partners or the whole group, served
to make us all more reflective and informed about our practice.

Lew Allen, an observer from PSI, asked to sit in on the final day of
the 1993 summer session, when teachers shared what they had learned.
He was a high school teacher for 17 years before coming to the university and worked closely with League schools that were beginning their
own action research projects. Lew remarked afterward:

I have never seen a group of teachers reflecting so deeply on
the questions of *teaching*. They were really dealing with how

children learn, and what they could do that would help them learn. They weren't talking about the issues surrounding that, like class size, but were getting inside how people learn and how can I be the most effective teacher. There was an openness. People were listening to each other. No one was trying to convince anyone of anything, there was no debate, but they were learning from each other; everyone was questioning, wondering. Research seemed to be the tool that led them to this deeply reflective thought. I've seen schools struggle, trying to have conversations like that, and I've never seen such success, but here the research set the climate for it.

Lew went on to compare what he heard with the findings of a research study of what teachers talk about. Susan Rosenholtz (1991) asked teachers about school climates and conversations in *Teachers' Workplace*. In some schools, teachers' conversations focused on simplifying teaching; in these schools there was often a fatalism about the students, the parents, and pedagogy—"nothing we do is really going to make much difference." Teachers still talked about teaching, but they tended to relate incidents and tell stories, rather than discussing issues or planning together. In contrast, other schools talked about the complexities of teaching, and teachers acknowledged the importance of ongoing conversations with colleagues to help solve the problems of how to get better and better. In the less reflective schools, teachers said that it took a year or two to become a good teacher. In the more reflective schools, the teachers said it took a lifetime, and you could not get there by yourself. "The teachers from Jackson County were acknowledging the complexity of teaching," Lew commented. "They weren't looking for quick answers, but were asking questions and conducting research that really led them to a deeper understanding of teaching."

Texts: Connections with the Broader Research Community

Communities that support teacher research create and use a wide variety of texts, both published and unpublished, according to Cochran-Smith and Lytle (1992). The Kings Bridge Road researchers are not alone on the blue highways. More and more teachers are studying their own practice and writing about what they learn. Eleanor Duckworth (1986) argues for teacher research as "the sine qua non" of research in the development of human learning. She makes the analogy of a psychotherapist with a research interest. "She could not possibly learn anything significant about psychodynamics if she were not genuinely engaged in the therapeutic process. It is only because she knows how to do her job as a practitioner that she is in a position to pursue her questions as a researcher'' (p. 487). Similarly, it is those who actively engage in teaching and who work to understand what sense learners are making, who have the biggest contribution to make to educational research.

Cochran-Smith and Lytle (1992) detailed the importance of teacher research for the teaching community in term of benefits, including teachers transforming their own practice, becoming resources to peers, interpreting other research critically, and collaborating with their students as researchers (see Goswami & Stillman, 1987). Atwell (1982), speaking of her experience as a member of a teacher research group, wrote:

> As researchers, we discovered a new pride in being classroom teachers. Our roles and functions in the community of educators have been redefined. We came to see ourselves as professionals, active in and central to the betterment of writing instruction, rather than as peripheral recipients of other's theories, findings, and programs. (p. 86)

Barbara Michalove, veteran teacher and researcher, wrote that the observation and reflection of systematic inquiry leads teachers to an awareness of

> the intricate teaching and learning dance with your students. Researching took me a step further into my students' lives. The more I tune in, the better I become at knowing when to lead, when to follow, or when to play a sedate waltz or a lively rap. And each year I become better at helping them learn, as I learn to listen and hear their inner music. (Allen, Michalove, & Shockley, 1993, p. 33)

Studying change in one's own classroom can lead to further change. Jane Richards, a high school English teacher, said that her research into her writing instruction led to a major insight.

> It came over me that, my god, I'm teaching my literature courses the wrong way. Instead of teaching them the way I think writing courses ought to be taught, I'm still teaching them in the traditional way that I learned in grad school. There's this big gap between my philosophy of teaching writing and what I'm allowing myself to do in the lit class. (Bissex & Bullock, 1987, p. 150)

These examples, all written by teachers, show that teacher research is potentially empowering and transformative. Bissex and Bullock (1987) argue that ''by becoming researchers teachers take control over their classrooms and professional lives in ways that confound the traditional definition of teacher and offer proof that education can reform itself from within" (p. xi). The reports in this volume are from teachers acting on their own knowledge base, expanded by inquiry. Lisa Delgado thinks that this is a permanent change, at least for her. She reported that now her "decisions are based on observations instead of hunches." Erickson and Shultz (1992) make the same point.

> Adept and empathic teachers may make effective guesses about the roles of such matters as attention, trust, and legitimacy in their teaching. They even may be able to make fairly accurate "seat of the pant" judgments about the fit of particular tasks with particular students and about the varieties of student experience in their classrooms. But if this is so, their inferences are for the most part intuitive and transparent to themselves. Hence, their hunches are not available to others with a stake in their teaching—administrators, researchers, parents, and students. Moreover, key aspects of their own understanding are not available to them for critical reflection. Teachers themselves need to know more about varieties of student experience if they are to educate a wide variety of students really well. (p. 471)

It was critical that teachers identified personal areas of interest or concern, articulated their own questions, collected data in a way that was compatible with teaching, analyzed the information within their own frames, and wrote for their own purposes and audiences. Kincheloe (1991) understands teacher inquiry as a "path to empowerment" only if teachers raise their own questions and "formulate questions which expose the conditions which promote social and educational advantage and disadvantage" (p. 39). Many of these projects focused on children teachers worried about, from the pre-kindergarten study (Chapter 10) to the student interview study (Chapter 11) to the special education inclusion model documented by Jan Kimbrell-Lee and Terry Wood (Chapter 3).

If teachers conduct research first and foremost for themselves and their students, that does not mean that other educators should not benefit from their inquiry. Not all teacher texts are meant to be shared, but there is a growing demand for them. In 1986, Erickson wrote, "[Currently,] there is neither time available, nor an institutionalized audience for such reflections. The lack of these opportunities is indicative of the relative powerlessness of the profession outside the walls of the classroom" (p. 157). However, since 1986 the field of publication possibilities has really opened up. Established literacy journals such as *The Reading Teacher*, *Language Arts*, and *The New Advocate* increasingly publish

teacher research, and new journals such as *Teacher Researcher* are devoted solely to the writings of teachers. Organizations such as the National Council of Teachers of English and the National Education Association have established new journals (*Primary Voices* and *Teaching and
Change*, respectively) with the express purpose of creating a forum for
teacher research. There also has been an increase in the number of
books that present teacher research, from collaborative inquiries (Allen,
Michalove, Shockley, 1993; Nicholls & Hazzard, 1993; Shockley, Michalove, & Allen, 1995) to volumes framed and edited by university-based
researchers (Bissex & Bullock, 1987; Cochran-Smith & Lytle, 1993; Gitlin
et al., 1992) to independent teacher research in the tradition of Vivian
Paley (e.g., 1981, 1990).

The broader academic community benefits from increased accessi-
bility to teacher research texts. Teachers add to existing data sources
via teaching journals and other classroom data, reveal seminal issues,
provide rich cases, and contribute to theory generation and revision
(Cochran-Smith & Lytle, 1992). As a teacher educator, I've noticed that
my students find teacher accounts and research more persuasive, more
"real world," than most university-based researcher reports (including
my own).

However, the academy will not reap these benefits if they don't
read teacher research. As Cochran-Smith and Lytle (1993) point out, the
knowledge that teachers generate is often invisible to the academy. The
Handbook of Research on Teaching (Wittrock, 1986), described as "the de-
finitive guide to what we know about teachers, teaching, and the learning process," does not have one chapter written by a teacher, nor is
teacher research cited. "Missing from the handbook are the voices of
the teachers themselves, the questions that teachers ask, and the inter-
pretive frames that teachers use to understand and improve their own
classroom practices" (Cochran-Smith & Lytle, 1993, p. 7).

Tasks of Teaching

Earlier in this chapter we viewed the varied outcomes of action research
on students and teachers using the categories of description, interpretation, evaluation, and professional growth. The greatest impact of our
work has been on the people who live together 9 months a year in that
complex relationship of schooling. Teachers are using the information
they gather, and that others gather and share, to understand their students and improve their teaching. "In teacher research communities,
the task of teachers is not simply to produce research. . . . Rather, the
commitment of teacher researchers is change—in their own classrooms,

school, district, and professional organizations" (Cochran-Smith & Lytle, 1992, p. 318). Having iterated several specific ways South Jackson and Benton teachers have changed as a result of their research, I'll close this section with a widespread sentiment expressed in personal terms by Patty Griffith, commenting on one of the students she interviewed (and on herself).

> He's an LD kid, and when I asked him about being smart, you know, and when did you feel smart, not one time was it at school. It was always when he fixes his granny's light bulb, when he helps his dad fix the VCR. . . . Just that one statement makes me just rethink things that we do in school. . . . Maybe he needs more of the one-on-one than I'm giving him. You know, I need to be more attuned to him. . . . There's just so much you can learn from these kids.

PATHWAYS TO DISCOVERY

Why are we sharing what began as a personal quest to understand ourselves and our students, to evaluate our practices in order to improve them? How can other educators learn from our local experiences? The issue of how such findings generalize to other settings has been addressed by many qualitative researchers, especially those conducting case studies. Glesne and Peshkin (1992) argue that the purpose of qualitative research is contextualization rather than generalizability, and we have tried to provide that context for our readers. We hope readers will make comparisons to their classrooms, schools, teaching, and research, and will determine for themselves whether and how our research illuminates their own experiences. Shulman (1986) argued that "richly described" cases that include critical analysis are for many educators more influential than research findings presented as rules and principles. In *The Reflective Practitioner*, Schön (1983) elaborated the argument by explaining that we can think of cases as "exemplars," ways of thinking about an experience that may be useful to others in similar situations. Educators build a repertoire of cases, which contribute to knowledge through reflection on our own practice in relation to the practices of others.

It is impossible to overstate the growth we all experienced from the first tentative days of thinking about a partnership and the silent, frustrating meetings about whole language teaching, to those 2 weeks in July 1993. Several teachers remarked on the changes. Dorothy, a veteran teacher from Benton who provided insightful comments from the beginning of the partnerships, leaned back after a particularly exciting discussion of the video interview data, and said, "Y'all, can you believe how far we've come in less than 3 years? Our school is really different. We teach differently, and our kids are different." Another member of the group agreed, saying, "Anyone who reads these transcripts could tell immediately that these kids are in whole language classrooms. They talk about books and authors, and they talk about being authors. They like school, and they really see themselves as capable reader and writers."

Teaching communities that are researching communities not only change schools, but also discover how those changes affect learners. They become aware of student perspectives and ideas for change, they evaluate their own effectiveness, and they create new strategies and environments. Blue highways are not just another route to get us to the same destination. They are opportunities to discover places we have never been.

NOTES

1. This project has been supported in part by the University of Georgia Education Initiative, a co-reform effort funded by the Coca-Cola Foundation. In addition, the work of the Kings Bridge Road Research Team was a National Reading Research Center Project of the University of Georgia and the University of Maryland. It was supported under the Educational Research and Development Centers Program (PR/AWARD 117A20007) as administered by the Office of Educational Research and Improvement, U.S. Department of Education.

2. JoBeth advised both research teams, meeting with them, writing summaries, gathering resources, and conducting writing conferences as requested; she also organized summer sessions and was an active participant in one study (Chapter 8). Frances Hensley, who coordinated the many research efforts within the UGA Initiative (the Coca-Cola project), served as a research consultant by helping with data organization and analysis. She became a valued member of the videotape interview project team at Benton and contributed to that report. She and Marilynn Cary conducted and analyzed interviews that contributed to the first two chapters of this book. Jane West, Janet Benton, Terry Warren, Bob Hanley, Liz Black, Mary Carter Whitten, Pamela Dunston, and Ellen Treadway (graduate students) and Donna Alvermann and Joel Taxel (faculty) also supported the research at various times.

References

Allen, J., Buchanan, J., Edelsky, C., & Norton, G. (1992). Teachers as "they" at NRC: An invitation to join the dialogue on the ethics of collaborative and non-collaborative classroom research. In C. K. Kinzer & D. J. Leu (Eds.), *Literacy research, theory and practice.* Forty-first yearbook of the National Reading conference (pp. 357–365). Chicago: National Reading Conference.

Allen, J., Combs, J., Hendricks, M., Nash, P., & Wilson, S. (1988). Studying change: Teachers who become researchers. *Language Arts, 65*(4), 379–387.

Allen, J., Michalove, B., & Shockley, B. (1993). *Engaging children: Community and chaos in the lives of young literacy learners.* Portsmouth, NH: Heinemann.

Allen, L. (Ed.). (1992). *Lessons from the field.* Athens: University of Georgia, College of Education.

Allen, L. (1993). *The role of voice in shared governance: A case study of a primary school.* Unpublished doctoral dissertation. Athens, GA: University of Georgia.

Allen, L., & Glickman, C. (1992). School improvement: The elusive faces of shared governance. *NASSP Bulletin, 76*(542), 80–87.

Allen, L., & Lundsford, B. (1995). *How to renew schools through networking.* Alexandria, VA: Association for Supervision and Curriculum Development.

Allington, R. (1991). Children who find learning to read difficult: School responses to diversity. In E. Hiebert (Ed.), *Literacy for a diverse society* (pp. 237–252). New York: Teachers College Press.

Alvermann, D., & Guthrie, J. (1991, November). *National Reading Research Center: A proposal.* Athens, GA: University of Georgia, and College Park, MD: University of Maryland.

American Association of School Librarians. (1988). *Information power: Guidelines for school library media programs.* Chicago: American Library Association.

Apple, M. (1986). *Teachers and texts.* New York: Routledge & Kegan Paul.

Apple, M. (1993). *Official knowledge: Democratic education in a conservative age.* New York: Routledge.

Areglado, N., & Dill, M. (1992, Spring). A school's journey toward portfolio assessment. *Colorado Reading Council Journal,* pp. 19–21.

Atwell, N. (1982). Class-based writing research: Teachers learn from students. *English Journal, 71,* 84–87.

Atwell, N. (1987). *In the middle.* Portsmouth, NH: Heinemann.

Belanoff, P., & Dickson, M. (Eds). (1991). *Portfolios: Process and product.* Portsmouth, NH: Boynton/Cook.

Benton Elementary School. (1992). *Georgia's initiative for at-risk four-year-old children and their families.* Pilot program application to the Georgia Department of Education Division of Curriculum and Instruction.

Bissex, G., & Bullock, R. (1987). *Seeing for ourselves: Case-study research by teachers of writing*. Portsmouth, NH: Heinemann.

Black, E., & Peters, S. (1991). From resistance to reorganization to results. In J. Taxel (Ed.), *UGA Education Initiative first year progress report*. Athens, GA: University of Georgia, College of Education.

Bracken, B. A. (1984). *Bracken basic concept scale*. New York: Harcourt Brace Jovanovich.

Brown, L. (1994, Spring/Summer). Green thumb literacy. *Georgia Journal of Reading*, pp. 22–27.

Broyard, A. (1983, September 13). Review of *blue highways*. *The New York Times*, section III, p. 20.

Burningham, J. (1978). *Would you rather*. New York: Harper.

Carr, E., & Allen, J. (1989). University/classroom teacher collaboration: Costs, benefits, and mutual respect. In J. Allen & J. Goetz (Eds.), *Qualitative research in education: Substance, methods, experience* (pp. 123–131). Athens, GA: University of Georgia, College of Education.

Chenfeld, M. B. (1987). *Teaching language arts creatively*. San Diego, CA: Harcourt Brace Jovanovich.

Cochran-Smith, M., & Lytle, S. (1992). Communities for teacher research: Fringe or forefront? *American Journal of Education, 100*(3), 298–324.

Cochran-Smith, M., & Lytle, S. (1993). *Inside/outside: Teacher research and knowledge*. New York: Teachers College Press.

Cole, J. (1989). *The magic school bus inside the human body*. New York: Scholastic.

Cooper, M. (1988). Whose culture is it anyway? In A. Lieberman (Ed.), *Building a professional culture in schools* (pp. 45–54). New York: Teachers College Press.

Dahl, R. (1991). *The twits*. New York: Puffin.

Delgado, L. (1995). Elementary students can use CD-ROM independently. *Technology Connection, 1*(6), 9–10.

Duckworth, E. (1986). Teaching as research. *Harvard Educational Review, 56*(4), 481–495.

Dunston, P., & Morrison, L. (1992). Reading assessment and instructional decision making in a whole language classroom. In J. Taxel (Ed.), *UGA Education Initiative second year progress report*. Athens, GA: University of Georgia, College of Education.

Erickson, F. (1986). Qualitative methods in research on teaching. In M. C. Whittrock (Ed.), *Handbook of research on teaching* (3rd ed., pp. 119–161). New York: Macmillan.

Erickson, F., & Shultz, J. (1992). Students' experience of the curriculum. In P. Jackson (Ed.), *Handbook of research on curriculum* (pp. 465–485). New York: Macmillan.

Faust, M., & Kieffer, R. (1993). Portfolio assessment: Reasons, questions, use, and power. *Connections, 29*(4), 30–38.

Fisher, B. (1991). *Joyful learning*. Portsmouth, NH: Heinemann.

Fulghum, R. (1986). *All I really need to know I learned in kindergarten*. New York: Ballantine.

Fullan, M., & Miles, M. (1992). Getting reform right: What works and what doesn't. *Phi Delta Kappan, 73,* 745–752.

Galdone, P. (1974). *Little red riding hood.* New York: McGraw.

Georgia Department of Education Office of Instructional Services. (1992). *Georgia's initiative for at-risk, four-year-old children and their families.* Pilot program guidelines.

Gerstein, M. (1984). *The room.* New York: Harper & Row.

Gerstein, M. (1986). *The seal mother.* New York: Dial.

Gitlin, A., Bringhurst, K., Burns, M., Cooley, V., Myers, B., Price, K., Russell, R., & Tiess, P. (1992). *Teachers' voices for school change.* New York: Teachers College Press.

Glesne, C., & Peshkin, A. (1992). *Becoming qualitative researchers: An introduction.* White Plains, NY: Longman.

Glickman, C. (1992, September). The essence of school renewal: The prose has begun. *Educational Leadership, 50,* 24–27.

Goodlad, J. I. (1990). *Teachers for our nation's schools.* San Francisco: Jossey-Bass.

Goswami, D., & Stillman, P. (1987). *Reclaiming the classroom: Teacher research as an agency for change.* Upper Montclair, NJ: Boynton/Cook.

Grasham, F. M., & Elliot, S. N. (1990). *Social Skills Rating System Questionnaire.* American Guidance Service.

Graves, D. (1991). *Discover your own literacy.* Portsmouth, NH: Heinemann.

Graves, D., & Sunstein, S. (1992). *Portfolio portraits.* Portsmouth, NH: Heinemann.

Greenleaf, C. (1990). Taking charge of curriculum. In N. Atwell (Ed.), *Writing to learn in the intermediate grades* (pp. 149–159). Portsmouth, NH: Heinemann.

Halliday, M. A. K. (1975). *Exploration in the functions of language.* London: Edward Arnold.

Hansen, J. (1993). Synergism of classroom and school libraries. *The New Advocate, 6*(3), 201–211.

Hardy, B. (1977). Narrative as a primary act of mind. In M. Meek, A. Warlow, & G. Barton (Eds), *The cool web: The pattern of children's reading* (pp. 12–23). New York: Atheneum.

Heathcote, D., & Herbert, P. (1985). A drama of learning: Mantle of the expert. *Theory Into Practice, 24,* 173–180.

Henkes, K. (1989). *Julius, the baby of the world.* New York: Greenwillow.

Howe, J. (1984). *The day the teacher went bananas.* New York: Dutton.

Hoyt, L. (1992). Many ways of knowing: Using drama, oral interactions, and the visual arts to enhance reading comprehension. *The Reading Teacher, 45,* 580–584.

Hubbard, R., & Power, B. (1993). *The art of classroom inquiry: A handbook for teacher-researchers.* Portsmouth, NH: Heinemann.

Hughes, S. (1993). The impact of whole language on four elementary school libraries. *Language Arts, 70,* 393–399.

Hunter, M. (1975). *A stranger came ashore.* New York: Harper.

Kieffer, R., & Morrison, L. (1994). Changing portfolio process: One journey toward authentic assessment. *Language Arts, 71,* 411–418.

Kimbrell-Lee, J., & Wood, T. (1994). The inclusive writing workshop. In Teacher-to-Teacher Books, NEA Professional Library's *Toward inclusive classrooms.* Washington, DC: National Education Association.

Kincheloe, J. (1991). *Teachers as researchers: Qualitative inquiry as a path to empowerment.* London: Falmer Press.

Ladwig, J. G. (1991). Is collaborative research exploitative? *Educational Theory, 41*(2), 111–120.

Lamme, L. L., &, Ledbetter, L. (1990). Libraries: The heart of whole language. *Language Arts, 67,* 735–741.

Least Heat Moon, W. (1982). *Blue highways: A journey into America.* New York: Fawcett Crest.

Lieberman, A., & Shiman, D. (1973). The stages of change in elementary school settings. In C. A. Culber & G. J. Hoban (Eds.), *The power to change* (pp. 49–71). New York: McGraw-Hill.

Loertscher, D. V., Ho, M. L., & Bowie, M. M. (1987). Exemplary elementary schools and their library media centers. *School Library Media Quarterly, 15,* 147–153.

McNeil, L. (1988). Contradictions of control. Part 2: Teachers, students, and curriculum. *Phi Delta Kappan, 69*(6), 432–438.

Mechling, J. (1986). Children's folklore. In E. Oring (Ed.), *Folk groups and folklore genres* (pp. 91–120). Logan: Utah State University Press.

Morrow, L. M. (1991). Promoting voluntary reading. In J. Jensen, D. Lapp, J. Flood, & J. Squire (Eds.), *Handbook of research on teaching the English language arts* (pp. 681–690). New York: Macmillan.

Nelson, P. (1988). Drama: Doorway to the past. *Language Arts, 65,* 181–186.

Nicholls, J., & Hazzard, S. (1993). *Education as adventure: Lessons from the second grade.* New York: Teachers College Press.

Oakes, J., Hare, S., & Sirotnik, K. (1986). Collaborative inquiry: A congenial paradigm in a cantankerous world. *Teachers College Record, 87,* 545–562.

Piaget, J. (1950). *The psychology of intelligence.* London: Routledge & Kegan Paul.

Paley, V. (1981). *Wally's stories.* Cambridge, MA: Harvard University Press.

Paley, V. (1990). *The boy who would be a helicopter.* Cambridge, MA: Harvard University Press.

Peshkin, A. (1993). The goodness of qualitative research. *Educational Researcher, 22*(2), 23–29.

Richardson, V. (1994). Conducting research on practice. *Educational Researcher, 23*(5), 5–10.

Rief, L. (1992). *Seeking diversity: Language arts with adolescents.* Portsmouth, NH: Heinemann.

Rosenholtz, S. (1991). *Teachers' workplace.* New York: Teachers College Press.

Rosetti, C. (1992). *Colors.* New York: HarperCollins.

Routman, R. (1988). *Transitions.* Portsmouth, NH: Heinemann.

Rylant, C. (1985). *When the relatives came.* New York: Harper.

Schön, D. (1983). *The reflective practitioner: How professionals think in action.* New York: Basic Books.

Seeger, P. (1986). *Abiyoyo*. New York: Macmillan.

Seidman, I. (1991). *Interviewing as qualitative research*. New York: Teachers College Press.

Shedd, J., & Bacharach, S. (1991). *Tangled hierarchies: Teachers as professionals and the management of schools*. San Francisco: Jossey-Bass.

Shockley, B. (1993). Extending the literate community. *The New Advocate, 6*(1), 11–24.

Shockley, B., Michalove, B., & Allen, J. (1995). *Engaging families*. Portsmouth, NH: Heinemann.

Shulman, L. (1986). Paradigms and research programs in the study of teaching. In M. C. Wittrock (Ed.), *Handbook of research on teaching* (3rd ed., pp. 3–36). New York: Macmillan.

Sirotnik, K. (1988). The meaning and conduct of inquiry in school–university partnerships. In K. Sirotnik & J. Goodlad (Eds.), *School–university partnerships in action* (pp. 169–190). New York: Teachers College Press.

Stanek, L. W. (1993). Whole language: A movement out of sync. *School Library Journal, 39*(3), 110–112.

Steig, W. (1976). *The amazing bone*. New York: Farrar, Straus, Giroux.

Sulzby, E. (1985). Children's emergent reading of favorite storybooks: A developmental study. *Reading Research Quarterly, 20*(4), 458–481.

Taxel, J. (1994). *The University of Georgia Education Initiative: Third year progress report*. Athens, GA: University of Georgia, College of Education.

Tierney, R. J., Carter, M. A., & Desai, L. E. (1991). *Portfolio assessment in the reading-writing classroom*. Norwood, MA: Christopher-Gordon.

Treadway, E., & Bailey, G. (1992). Whole language instruction and teacher development: A descriptive case study. In J. Taxel (Ed.), *UGA Education Initiative second year progress report*. Athens, GA: University of Georgia.

Valencia, S. (1990). A portfolio approach to classroom reading assessment: The whys, whats, and hows. *The Reading Teacher, 43*(4), 338–340.

Van Maanen, J. (1988). *Tales of the field: On writing ethnography*. Chicago: University of Chicago Press.

Verriour, P. (1985). Face to face: Negotiating meaning through drama. *Theory Into Practice, 24*, 181–186.

Vygotsky, L. (1978). *Mind in society: The development of higher psychological processes*. Cambridge, MA: Harvard University Press.

Ward, B., & Tikunoff, W. (1982). *Collaborative research*. (ERIC Document Reproduction Service No. ED 221 531)

West, J. (1992). "Having your way": Children's perceptions of fun and work in literacy learning. In J. Taxel (Ed.), *UGA Education Initiative second year progress report*. Athens, GA: University of Georgia, College of Education.

West, J. (1993, April). "Having your way" and "Being bossed": What children value in literacy learning. Paper presented at the annual meeting of the American Educational Research Association, Atlanta.

West, J. (1994). *Getting help when you need it: The relations among social status, types of literacy events, and third-graders' helping interactions*. Unpublished doctoral dissertation, University of Georgia, Athens.

West, J., & Rice, D. (1991). "And now the day begins": Children's attitudes toward literacy in a changing curriculum. Unpublished manuscript.

Wigginton, E. (1985). *Sometimes a shining moment: The Foxfire experience—twenty years teaching in a high school classroom.* Garden City, NY: Anchor Books.

Wittrock, M. C. (Ed.). (1986). *Handbook of research on teaching* (3rd ed.). New York: Macmillan.

About the Contributors

JoBeth Allen is a professor in Language Education at UGA. She has taught students from preschool through graduate school, and conducts collaborative action research with teachers in whole language classrooms.

Gwen Bailey is the project director for The Publishing Center, which is located at South Jackson Elementary School. During her 6½ years as a kindergarten teacher, she conducted several workshops on portfolio assessment, grant writing, and The Publishing Center.

Janet Benton is an assistant professor at Western Kentucky University, where she teaches courses in teacher education and language arts. Her research interests include issues of cultural diversity in literature and language usage.

Melvin Bowie is an associate professor in the Department of Instructional Technology at UGA. She was a school media specialist for 12 years, and a reference librarian in a public library for 7 years.

Lolita Brown has taught at Benton since 1985; she is a Chapter 1 reading specialist. Graduate studies sparked her to analyze effective reading approaches and to work with the video research group. Her first publication was ''Green Thumb Literacy'' (*Georgia Journal of Reading*, 1994). Lolita holds an educational specialist degree in Early Childhood Education.

Marilynn Cary is a speech language pathologist based at Benton since 1985. She is the research coordinator at Benton. Her research interests include early language development and teachers' involvement in research.

Lori Davis has been a pre-kindergarten teacher at Benton Elementary for the past 2 years. She has an M.S. in Elementary Education and Curriculum and Instruction. She has 5 years experience in early childhood education.

Lisa James Delgado has been the media specialist at South Jackson Elementary for 10 years. She is the research coordinator at South Jackson. Since this project, she has studied student independence with CD-ROM computers and student involvement in decision making throughout the school.

Patty Griffith has been a special education teacher since 1977. She has been teaching in "inclusive" classrooms since 1993. She works with regular classroom teachers to create environments where all students will succeed.

Frances Hensley served as the research coordinator for the UGA Education Initiative. A former classroom teacher, Frances is a member of the public service faculty at The University of Georgia and director of the National Diffusion Network in Georgia. Frances, along with Marilynn Cary, is currently studying teachers' participation in research.

Mary Jane Hilley has been a media specialist at Benton since 1991, and previously was an elementary teacher for 23 years. She was born and raised in the small community of Nicholson in which she now teaches and lives.

Carol Carr Kieffer has been teaching since 1992. Previously, she was a naturalist, working with children, families and educators in several midwestern residential outdoor education centers and with the Indiana State Parks and Reservoirs, where she published a brochure on ferns. Her 1994–95 research involved investigating the effects of a classroom portfolio upon individual student portfolios.

Ronald Kieffer is an assistant professor in Language Education at UGA. He taught grades two, four, and six for 11 years. He conducts collaborative research on portfolio processes, technology applications in the classroom, and collaborative writing among primary grade children.

Jan Kimbrell-Lee has been a special education resource teacher since 1985. She currently teaches fourth and fifth grades at South Jackson Elementary, where her research focuses on including special needs children in the regular classroom. Jan believes all students can learn to read and write if they believe in themselves and their abilities.

Linda Morrison has taught for 14 years, as a learning disabilities resource teacher, third grade teacher, and currently as a second grade teacher. Her research interests focus on portfolio assessment in language arts. She co-authored an article with Ronald Kieffer, published in the October 1994 volume of *Language Arts*.

Cheryl Poponi was a special education teacher for five years. She is currently in her fourth year of teaching in a regular elementary classroom, and her second in an inclusion model. She develops her research questions from needs that arise in the classroom and modifies her instruction based on her discoveries.

Dorothy Rice has taught elementary grades for 16 years. For the past 5 years her classroom has been literature based. She has been a co-researcher on several projects with doctoral students from UGA and believes that action research is a key to improving instruction in the classroom.

Jane Rogers has been a special education teacher for many years. She is also a graduate student working on her doctorate in Language Education at UGA. Her research focus is on children with learning difficulties and literature-based reading and writing programs.

Ruth Rowland has been a fourth-grade teacher in both suburban and rural schools in the midwest and the southeast. She has co-authored a chapter on teaching measurement in *Research Ideas for the Classroom* (NCTM) and an article on reader response in *The New Advocate*. Ruth believes that it is important for students to relate learning experiences to real life activities.

Holly Ward has taught high school and adults; she presently teaches fifth grade. She completed a masters degree in Language Education in UGA in 1995. She believes that writing and reading are truly "lifework"; she has documented ways in which her literature-based reading program made a difference in the lives of her students. Holly's students are also researchers, investigating educational issues of concern to them such as after-school programs.

Jennifer White, formerly a fourth grade teacher, is currently teaching kindergarten. As an active teacher researcher she enjoys investigating home-school connections, and how children learn the alphabet in whole language classrooms. She completed a masters degree in Language Education at UGA in 1995.

Terry Wood is a science, writing, and reading teacher at South Jackson Elementary School. She has taught for 9 years, beginning her career in middle school and teaching fifth grade for the last 5 years. She is currently working on two research projects: One deals with the transitions from elementary to middle school and another focuses on issues of standardized testing.

Index

SUBJECTS